NEW TOWNS

another way to live

NEW
TOWNS

another way to live

Carlos C. Campbell

RESTON PUBLISHING COMPANY, INC.
A Prentice-Hall Company
Reston, Virginia

Library of Congress Cataloging in Publication Data

Campbell, Carlos C

   New towns.

   Includes bibliographical references and index.
   1. New towns—United States. I. Title.
HT167.C33   301.36'3'0973   75-25863
ISBN 0-87909-546-6

© 1976 by
Reston Publishing Company, Inc.
A Prentice-Hall Company
Reston, Virginia 22090

10 9 8 7 6 5 4 3 2 1

Printed in the United States of America.

For Dinos

To Kimberly and Scott
and the others of their generation

Photographs by the author

CONTENTS

FOREWORD   xi

PREFACE   xv

ACKNOWLEDGMENTS   xvii

/ 1 /   INTRODUCTION   1
On America's Bicentennial, 3
The Urban Experience, 3
Urban Growth in the United States, 4
Federal Government Programs, 7
The Quality of Life, 10

/ 2 /   AN OVERVIEW OF NEW TOWNS   15

The New Towns Concept, 17
The Location and Classification of U.S. New Towns, 23
The Rationale for New Towns, 25

/ 3 /   RESTON   29

The Forerunner of the New Town Movement, 31
Some of the People, 39
The Black Experience, 42
Citizen Initiatives, 46
The Lake Anne Nursery School and Kindergarten, 47
The Reston Commuter Bus, 49
The Common Ground, 51
Recreation, 55
Cultural and Performing Arts, 59
Elementary Education, 63
The Social Malaise, 65
Governance, 68
Housing and Development, 73
Housing, 73
On High Rise Buildings, 77
Fellowship House, 81
The Growth Issue, 83

/ 4 /   COLUMBIA   87

Toward the Full Fabric of City, 89
A Profile of the People, 95
The Interfaith Center, 95
The Experience of Racial Interaction, 97
The Women's Center, 103
Grassroots: A Crisis Intervention Center, 104
The Columbia Association, 105
Teen-Agers, 107
A Comprehensive Medical Program, 108
A Broad Range of Educational Services, 109
Early Childhood Education and Day Care, 110
The Challenge of Columbia, 111

/ 5 /   SOUL CITY   117

Not Just Another New Town, 119
McKissick's Philosophy, 120
Dealing with the Feds, 121
People Making a Difference, 126
Pragmatic Politics, 128
The Essence of Cityhood, 128

/ 6 /   PARK FOREST SOUTH   131

An Oasis of Quality in a Desert of Sprawl, 133
A Linear Town Center, 135
Governance, 136
For Some a New World, 137
Governors State University, 138
Hickory School, 139
The Mountain Climber, 140

/ 7 /   JONATHAN   141

The Concept, 143
Social Considerations, 147
The Minnesota Renaissance Fair, 150
Housing, 150
Community Information System, 153
Senator Henry T. McKnight and his Successors, 153

/ 8 /   CEDAR-RIVERSIDE   159

A Bold Experiment, 161
The Neighborhood, 165
Twentieth-Century Reality, 168
Effecting a Housing Mix, 169
Social Planning, 169
Accepting the Burden to Inform, 170
The Arts, 172

/ 9 /   IRVINE   177

The Largest Privately Financed New Town in the World, 179
The Fight to House Moderate Income Families, 184
Urban Planning in Practice, 188
Community Associations, 189
Cultural Shock for Some, 190
Toward Viability, 191

/ 10 /   AN INTERVIEW WITH LUD ASHLEY   193

/ 11 /   AN INTERVIEW WITH ED LOGUE   205

An Overview, 207
The UDC New Towns, 208
Ed Logue, 208
Financial Troubles Set In, 216

/ 12 /   THE DEVELOPERS   219

Robert E. Simon, 221
Jim Rouse, 224
Lewis Manilow, 225
Ray Watson, 227
William H. Magness, 228
Fred Johnson, 230
Gloria Segal, 231

/ 13 /   LEARNING FROM THE EUROPEANS   233

The British Experience, 235
New Towns and Planning in Greater Stockholm, Sweden, 237

/ 14 /   FEDERAL EFFORTS SUPPORTING NEW TOWNS   241

The Federal Government's Role in New Towns, 243
An Assessment of the Federal Government's New Town
     Efforts, 248

/ 15 /   THE CASE FOR NEW TOWNS   255

Governmental Responsiveness, 257
Urban Planning and National Growth Policy, 259
Survival of the Central City, 261
The Human Environment, 262
Economic and Racial Integration, 263
Housing for Low and Moderate Income Families, 263
Community Services, 265
Beyond the Year 2000, 265

EPILOGUE   267

FOOTNOTES   271

INDEX   277

FOREWORD

One balmy August day in the early 1970's I stood with Carlos Campbell in the midst of the stone strewn wreckage of the Acropolis in Athens. Before us lay what was left of the Parthenon and far below, all around us, stretched the ugly modern city of Athens. Carlos and I had just returned from a week-long cruise with the Greek urban philosopher and architect Constantinos Doxiadis. We had sailed around the Aegean Isles with a group of city planners and urban visionaries visiting Patmos, Delphi, Sparta, and the storied sites of the cities of ancient Greece. We were full of ideas and hopes for the future of the city in the modern world as we returned to Athens and climbed the Acropolis. When we reached the top, however, we fell silent. Around us there were only pocked and lifeless ruins, below us only the sprawl of another anti-city. Surrounded by the echo of ancient splendor and the banality of modern mindlessness we both suddenly stopped talking. I am sure the thought that bothered both of us at that time was the same one: is there any hope for the city?

It is a difficult thing to write a good book about the city nowadays. The polis has few friends and many critics. After a decade of high hopes for a new surge of urban creativity we are now experiencing a plunge into despair. One of my colleagues here at Harvard University, Professor Banfield, has written a book on the city which seems to suggest its problems are insoluble. He calls it *The Unheavenly City*. But he is not alone in his discouragement about the possibilities of city life. Middle class people increasingly wish to leave what they think is city life as soon as they have the wherewithal, and move to something they define, often very mistakenly, as "the country". Young people, having experienced little of the nature and spiritual sustenance of a real polis, identify urban living with the cruel caricatures of cities that have arisen in modern America. Therefore, when they get the opportunity, they move as quickly as possible to a rural commune or a wilderness, believing that somehow that is the only other option. After a decade of excitement and hope we seem to have consigned our cities in America to the poor, the sick, and the old—and to the very rich who can hack out for themselves tiny fortresses of privilege within an otherwise teeming pool of misery, crime, and gasoline fumes.

Someone once wrote that "every people gets the government it deserves". One could say the same thing about cities, so it troubles me that there has always been a streak of anti-urbanism in American culture. Not only have intellectuals often sided against the city in the course of American history, but our religious tradition also harbors a kind of anti-urban romanticism. As a theologian I am painfully aware of the extent to which American religious piety has fed a yearning for the idyllic and rustic and has therefore contributed to the distrust and fear of cities which has so marred our national character. For every hymn that says "where cross the crowded ways of life", we have fifty hymns that croon about "I go to the garden alone while the dew is still on the roses". Time after time as a boy I heard it said in church and elsewhere, "God made the country but man made the city". Only as I studied the history of theology and religion as an adult did I begin to notice that this rampant anti-cityism which is so characteristic of American folk piety has no basis in the biblical faith whatever. The career of Jesus drew him to Jerusalem where he died but not without firing a hope in his followers that a "New Jerusalem" would some day arrive. The bible begins in its first pages with a garden but ends in its last pages with a vision of a glorious city where sadness and death have passed away. In its earliest years the Christian movement spread not through the countryside but from Jerusalem to Corinth to Rome and to Alexandria. Its early adherents were the urban poor. Thus, it has been my contention for a number of years now that when the Christians abandon the urban poor they abandon something essential about the Christian message itself. Yet the last two decades has seen the movement of church after church, at least of white churches, out of the cities and into suburban enclaves.

What then do we do about the cities? On the one hand there are those who have lost all hope and simply abandon them. That is obviously no answer at all. On the other hand there are those who feel that simply by doing more of the same we can somehow improve their quality. This latter answer, applying a quantified solution to a problem of quality, will never work either. Lewis Mumford once wrote that "the worst thing that could possibly happen to the future of the world would be a globe entirely covered by a huge city. This would in effect mean," Mumford said, "the disappearance of the city." I think Mumford is right; one essential ingredient of city life is contrast. There must always be a difference between city and country, between rural and urban, if both are to retain their significance. Simply enlarging our present cities along the same lines will lead only to further disasters. We need something else—we need something new.

Here and there around the world, in America and elsewhere, a few people have tried to chart a third course. They have neither abandoned the idea of the city as a good place to live, nor have they stubbornly held on to the present conception of cities as the only one available. These pioneers are the real seekers of the "New Jerusalem". They believe that we need and deserve good cities in which to live, *and* that we need a different *kind* of city than the one which has heretofore been available to us. Some of these pioneers of the New Jerusalem have been content merely to write about their visions of what a city might be. There are hundreds, perhaps thousands, of ideas about what cities could be like. Ideas are not useless and we should be grateful to people who share their ideas even if those ideas sometimes sound visionary and impossible to realize. There is another group of people, however, who have gone beyond the simple articulation of a new vision of the city and have tried to construct actual models of what a new urban way of life would be like—how it would look, how it would feel, how it would taste, how it would actually *be*. Needless to say not all of these new thrusts in urban design have been wholly successful. The people who live in the new cities and new towns are not all deliriously happy about them. Tears and sadness have not been abolished in any New Jerusalem yet known to human kind. Much to the credit of Carlos Campbell, he has not tried to hide the warts and frailties of new cities. Yet even as he describes the problems that have arisen in them one can detect in him a note of hope that remains unwavering. I share that hope in part because I believe we cannot have a future for our race on planet earth unless we somehow invent a new and different kind of city.

All of us are in search of another way to live. No one is quite content with his or her way of life in our confused and drifting society today. Our relationships to our children and our parents seem somehow decimated and confusing, the tension between home and job is often overwhelming, our sense of worthwhile goals and dependable values seems to have become confused. No one suggests that by simply moving to another place we will solve these dilemmas. However, the places we build reflect our hopes and visions, and in turn those places influence and define the way we live. This is a book for people who want to know honestly and accurately what it is like to live in a new town and for those who are seriously looking for another way to live.

Harvey G. Cox

PREFACE

This is a book about a development concept that I feel can favorably improve the quality of life for Americans. This development concept is responsive to many issues that have gained increasing national attention during the second half of the twentieth century. These issues include the growing concern for the environment, the energy crisis, the delivery of community support services, the interaction of people of different racial and economic backgrounds, and governmental responsiveness. This development concept, which will be discussed in the text, is that of *New Towns.*

A number of books concerned with various forms of development in the United States, namely urban and suburban, have correctly been critical. While this book shares some of the criticisms of past development experience, it attempts to discuss New Towns as a constructive alternative to uncontrolled growth or organic development.

In commenting on matters of social concern, I find some difficulty with the limited amount of substantive data available on New Towns. This data limitation results, in part, from the fact that many of the New Towns are not incorporated as separate jurisdictions and consequently fall within the structure of existing cities or counties; and further because most are in the early stages of development. The concentrated research for this book involved visits to about 24 New Town developments. During this process, interviews were conducted with over 500 people including developers, planners, organizational administrators and professional staffers, government officials, volunteers, and residents representing different ages, races, sexes, income levels, and life styles. To a large extent, I have chosen to rely on their observations and judgments as well as my own interpretation of same. In addition to this concentrated research, this book also draws on my involvement with several major international and domestic forums on human settlements, the environment, and the quality of life; government experience; and six years of living in America's first New Town—Reston, Virginia.

Carlos C. Campbell

ACKNOWLEDGMENTS

To the extent to which this book is of value to present and future residents of New Towns, developers, designers, planners, bankers, government officials, environmentalists and others concerned with the quality of life in America, the credit must be shared with those who have contributed toward this book.

I wish to thank the National Endowment for the Arts and Bill Lacey along with the Ford Foundation and Ron Gault for the grant assistance which supported the travel and research for this book.

I also wish to thank the many developers, professional staffers and the hundreds of residents of the New Towns who generously contributed their time for interviews. I particularly wish to thank Jack Guinee, Vice-President of Gulf Oil Real Estate and Development Corporation, and Dick Reese, Vice-President of Planning for the Irvine Company for their technical reviews of the book. Thanks is also due to Robert Dawson and Marcia Fram of the *Reston Times* and Barry Castleman of the *Appleseeds* newspaper for their assistance in research.

I owe a special thanks to the late Constantinos A. Doxiadis for his friendship, encouragement, and particularly for inviting me to the Ninth Delos Symposium which motivated me, in part, to write this book. Three others from "Delos Nine" also must be acknowledged: environmental planner Lawrence Halprin, who provided encouragement; theologian Harvey Cox, who provided the Foreword for this book; and anthropologist Margaret Mead, who provided the Epilogue.

Finally I wish to thank my wife Sammie Marie and our children Kimberly and Scott for their patience and understanding.

/ ON AMERICA'S BICENTENNIAL /

July 4, 1976 marks the two-hundredth year since the founding of this nation. When it was founded, the total population of the United States was slightly less than 3 million people, about as many as presently live in the metropolitan area of the nation's capital, Washington, D.C. Since 1970, the population of the United States has exceeded 203 million, and it continues to grow. Although its population is exceeded by those of the People's Republic of China, India, and the Union of the Soviet Socialist Republics, the United States is the richest nation in the world and has the highest gross national product per capita. In 200 years the basis for our economy has shifted from agriculture, to industry, to service. That is, we now have more jobs in the white collar sector of our economy than in the blue collar sector. Correspondingly, we have undergone a transition from being a predominantly rural nation to being a predominantly urban nation.

Urban Planner Edmund Bacon calls the building of cities "one of man's greatest achievements" and the form of cities "a pitiless indicator of the state of his civilization".[1] If there is any substance to Bacon's assertions, and I believe that there is, we must at this point in our history ask ourselves if the form of our cities and related development is, in fact, the indicator that we want to use to accurately reflect the state of our civilization.

In our short history, it is difficult to point to one city in America that is slum free, that has safe streets, that enjoys quality education and a full range of quality support services. International peace notwithstanding, there is no greater challenge facing America today than that of building its cities—cities that respect the human condition, cities that provide quality services for all of their citizens, and cities that are, in fact, a true indicator of the state of our civilization. This is an imperative for the United States' Century Three.

/ THE URBAN EXPERIENCE /

With most Americans living in urban areas, many of us have experienced the decline in municipal services, the increased journey to work, the traffic jams, the abuse of land, the pollution of air, the increase in noise, the unsightly billboards and overhead utilities, and other conditions that are, at best, adverse.

There has also been the polarization of people in metropolitan areas along the lines of income and race. Added to this is the daily exercise that most of us go through: switching dials, turning knobs, pushing buttons, twisting handles, and reacting to bells, gongs, rings, buzzers, and lights, not knowing the price we are paying for living in an envelope of stress.

City planner Constantinos Doxiadis writes:

> Human settlements are no longer satisfactory for their inhabitants. This is true everywhere in the world, in under-developed as well as developed countries. It holds true both for the way of living of their inhabitants and for the forms we give to shells of the settlements trying to satisfy their needs.[2]

It is incredible that the ascent of twentieth-century technology, which has resulted in the exploration of space, television, and computers, has coincided with the decline of our cities, the abuse of our limited land, and the reduction of people to materialistic slaves who often fail to command respect, particularly when in need of assistance from their fellow man. Alvin Toffler wrote in *Future Shock* that "Great cities are paralyzed by strikes, power failures, riots."[3] The power failures in turn result in elevators, as well as subway trains, coming to a screeching halt. The riots result in loss of life. But even if we manage to cope with these conditions, there is the experience of being "caged" in the rear of a taxi cab, being denied entry on a bus because you do not have the exact change, and, of late, being limited to a few dollars worth of gasoline.

What has often been called a crisis of cities is not a crisis of cities but rather a crisis of adverse human relationships, a crisis of people not respecting each other, a crisis that has manifested itself in the greatly reduced quality of our environment. Be it urban, suburban, or rural, the crisis is there.

/ URBAN GROWTH IN THE UNITED STATES /

The development of cities and related suburbs within the United States has occurred at an incredible pace. Of the approximately 3 million people who lived in this nation when it was founded, less than 3 percent lived in urban areas. As of 1970, nearly 70 percent of the nation's total population lived in urban areas.

During the first quarter of the nineteenth century, turnpikes were built to link cities in the Northeast, steamboats opened the Mississippi River, and the Erie Canal between Albany and Buffalo opened the Great Lakes. By 1860, there were some 43 cities and 300 towns with populations above 5,000. In 1869, the transcontinental railway linked the east and west coasts, and by 1890, the cities of New York, Philadelphia, and Chicago all exceeded one million in population. In the two decades following World War II, some 60 million Americans made their flight to suburbia, and in 1970, the combined suburban population exceeded the combined population for the central cities. Today, there are nearly 250 metropolitan areas with populations above 50,000, the 33 largest of which have populations in excess of one million people. Within and around these metropolitan areas, we now have over 1,000 cities and unincorporated areas with populations above 25,000 people, most of which are unplanned and unable to deal with the dynamics of urban change.

When the 60 or so million people fled the cities in favor of the surrounding suburbs in the two decades following World War II, they left behind housing that was badly deteriorating and neighborhoods that were without adequate municipal services. These neighborhoods soon became home for the poor, many of whom happened to be black, Puerto Rican, or Chicano. The process of "ghettoization"—that is, the isolation of people in specific neighborhoods—that had started long before the turn of the century accelerated at an incredible rate. As a result of the combined processes of suburbanization and urbanization, the metropolitan areas became clearly divided from the suburban areas along the lines of income and race, in the South as well as the North.

Both of these trends were supported by federal development practices. Harvard economist John F. Kain points out that "restrictions on Negro residential choices are among the most powerful forces determining the residential choices of both Negroes and Whites and thereby the spatial structure of U.S. metropolitan areas".[4] In the years following the enactment of the federally sponsored urban renewal program, conditions were further aggravated by the removal of thousands of residents, many of whom were black, from their neighborhoods under the guise of "revitalizing the central city". Further uprooting of blacks and other residents resulted from highway and other public works programs. In the absence of policies and programs to bring about housing opportunities without regard to race, conditions in many of the large central cities became acute by the early 1960s. While some visible projects for housing did emerge, invisible conditions resulted in blacks' experiencing unemployment rates as much as five times those of whites, maternal death rates as much as four times those of whites, infant mortality rates double those of whites, and considerably shorter life expectancies than whites.

In describing the "ghetto," psychologist Kenneth B. Clark wrote in 1965:

> Human beings who are forced to live under ghetto conditions and whose daily experience tells them that almost nowhere in society are they respected and granted the ordinary dignity and courtesy accorded to others will, as a matter of course, begin to doubt their own worth.[5]

Watts, a black enclave in Los Angeles, had become isolated from the economic opportunities in the city's vast metropolitan area. In the summer of 1965, Watts became a household word as it erupted in a major riot which resulted in dozens of blacks losing their lives. Riots around the nation followed. Author Robert Conet's description of the conditions in one section of Los Angeles seemingly brought the prophecy of the Bible into the twentieth century: "The street was a shambles. Half melted metal signs tilted downward like wilted flowers, the top of a palm tree presented a brilliant bloom of flames, from sidewalk to sidewalk the street was a spaghettilike maze of fire hoses. Residents, many of them not unfriendly, were running along the shops, grabbing items here and there as if from an open smorgasbord."[6] It is written in Ezekiel (6:6): "In all your dwelling places the cities shall be laid waste, and high places shall be desolate"; and in Isaiah (24:10-12):

> The city of confusion is broken down; every house is shut up, so that no one can enter; in the streets there is an outcry for wine; all joy has reached its eventide, the mirth of the land is gone; desolation is left in the city and its gates are battered to ruins.

Lyndon Baines Johnson, then President of the United States, in addressing the nation on July 27, 1967, said:

> The only genuine, long-range solution for what has happened lies in an attack—mounted at every level—upon the conditions that breed despair and violence. All of us know what those conditions are: ignorance, discrimination, slums, poverty, disease, not enough jobs. We should attack these conditions—not because we are frightened by conflict, but because we are fired by conscience.[7]

        Johnson subsequently appointed a National Advisory Commission on Civil Disorders that concluded that the nation was moving toward two societies: one white, locating principally in the suburbs; the other black, locating in the central cities.

/ FEDERAL GOVERNMENT PROGRAMS /

Since 1937, a period extending nearly 40 years, the federal government has become increasingly involved in housing and development. The intent of Congress was clearly expressed in the Housing Act of 1937 which stated, in part, that assistance was "for the elimination of unsafe and insanitary housing conditions, for the eradication of slums, for the provision of decent, safe, and sanitary dwellings for families of low income",[8] etc. In the Housing Act of 1949, the Congress affirmed the national goal of "a decent home and a suitable environment for every American family".[9]   In the Demonstration Cities and Metropolitan Development Act of 1966, Congress declared that "improving the quality of urban life is the most critical domestic problem facing the United States" and further that

> The persistence of widespread urban slums and blight, the concentration of persons of low income in older areas, and the unmet needs for additional housing and community facilities and services arising from rapid expansion of our urban population have resulted in a marked deterioration in the quality of the environment and the lives of large numbers of our people while the Nation as a whole prospers.[10]

These loftily worded legislative initiatives, along with others, were translated into a variety of programs.

        In the 10 years preceding and following World War II, Congress created the Federal Housing Administration, which provided mortgage insurance on homes; the Federal Home Loan Bank Board, which chartered and regulated savings and loan associations to finance housing; the Federal National Mortgage Association, which dealt in the secondary or resale mortgage market; and the Veterans Administration, which provided mortgage insurance to eligible servicemen. In addition, Congress created programs for public housing and urban renewal.

        Toward the mid-1950s, federal involvement in development underwent a dramatic increase. In 1954, a program to provide planning assistance to states, metropolitan areas, and cities with populations under 50,000 was enacted. In 1956, the $26 billion interstate highway system was launched. In 1964, an Urban Mass Transportation Act was passed. In 1966, a Demonstration Cities Bill was passed, resulting over the followng six years in almost 150 "model cities" programs designed to provide a full range of economic, social, and physical services to principally "ghetto" areas. In 1968, a small-scale New Towns program was effected. In 1969, "Operation Breakthrough" was initiated, primarily to introduce systems building technology. And by 1970, further legislation was passed to increase the thrust toward New Towns and to develop a national growth policy. It is of significance that in 1964 and 1968 civil rights legislation was enacted to bring about sweeping changes in social practices and in the administration of federal programs and to effect a national policy of equal housing opportunities.

By the late 1960s, the number of federal domestic programs had exceeded 500, with over 70 in the Department of Housing and Urban Development (HUD). These programs or "categorical" grants, as they were called, resulted in countless delays and a seemingly insurmountable amount of "red tape". In an effort to improve federal responsiveness to states and cities, many of the categorical programs were scrapped under the Nixon administration in favor of lump sum payments to states and cities through a "revenue-sharing" program.

The legislative objectives of the Congress, specifically those previously cited in acts of 1937, 1949 and 1966, have not been met. The lack of funds at a level necessary to effect significant results notwithstanding, the administration of development programs to date has left much to be desired.

In 1968, the Report of the National Advisory Commission on Civil Disorders cited the conditions in the cities of Detroit, Michigan; Newark, New Jersey; and New Haven, Connecticut, among others, with respect to housing programs for low income families. These data are for the period before 1967. In Detroit, only 758 housing units were provided for low income families since 1956 or about 2 percent of the total substandard units. This compares to over 10 times as many units being demolished since 1960 for urban renewal. In Newark, some 3760 housing units for low income families were provided since 1959. This represented about 16 percent of the substandard units. Within the same period over 12,000 families were displaced or uprooted as a result of urban renewal, highway construction, and other public programs. In the 15 years following 1952, some 951 housing units were assisted in the city of New Haven, or about 14 percent of the total units that were substandard. Between 1956 and 1967, urban renewal and highway programs caused about 6500 housing units to be demolished.[11]

In 1954, a 33-building public housing complex occupying 57 acres was built in St. Louis, Missouri. This project, Pruitt-Igoe, received praise from the American Institute of Architects and *Architectural Forum* magazine for its design. Few, if any, suspected that this highly acclaimed project would become one of the colossal failures in the annals of public housing and would be demolished before its twentieth anniversary. Those who were concerned with providing a "suitable environment for every American family" failed to deliver even the most basic services for what was a community of about 12,000 people, including some 5000 youngsters. There were only two asphalt playgrounds,

> no schools, no health center, no churches, no cultural facilities, no retail services, no shops, no grocery stores, no restaurants, no bakeries, no barber shops or hairdresser shops, no drug stores, and no taverns.[1 2]

The concentration of the black and the poor without adequate support services is a combination that has a predictable result—chaos. Few outside of HUD realize that Pruitt-Igoe and like projects result from an overemphasis on housing per se, little or no emphasis on necessary community support services and facilities, an insensitivity to social concerns, and an almost absolute lack of program coordination within and among federal agencies. A number of programs such as those for open space and recreation, neighborhood facilities, health services, and commercial development could have been used to support the Pruitt-Igoe project, but this was not the case. If my experience at HUD has any value, it has shown me that officials lack a comprehensive approach toward development. The very programs that HUD was charged with administering were not, for the most part, used to support housing projects. Such programs would include open space and recreation, neighborhood facilities, and comprehensive planning.

It is difficult to describe the overall effect that the lack of a comprehensive approach to development has had on the lives of the millions of residents who live or have lived in public housing projects throughout the United States. In addition to the issue of a "suitable environment", the worth of the government's expenditure of over $90 billion of the taxpayers' money for public housing since 1937 must also be questioned.

The present posture of the federal government's housing efforts is best described by a *Fortune* magazine article published in November 1973: "The federal housing apparatus is the awkward result of forty years of improvising, patching, and rejiggering programs and policies."[1 3]

/ THE QUALITY OF LIFE /

While the term *quality of life* has been used in legislative initiatives and is becoming a subject of increasing concern, it has yet to be precisely defined. A 1972 conference on this subject sponsored by the U.S. Environmental Protection Agency (EPA) refers to the quality of life as "the well being of people—primarily in groups but also as individuals—as well as to the 'well being' of the environment in which these people live".[14] My concern for whatever one wants to interpret the quality of life as being is that the emphasis be placed on the effects of environment on people rather than on the physical aspects of development.

It is paradoxical that while the United States is the world's richest nation, 17 other nations have longer life expectancies and 12 others have lower infant mortality rates. In addition, the rates of suicide, homicide, and alcoholism in the United States are among the highest in the world. Psychoanalyst Erich Fromm wrote in *The Sane Society* that—

> the countries in Europe which are among the most democratic, peaceful and prosperous ones, and the United States, the most prosperous country in the world, show the most severe symptoms of mental disturbance.[15]

In describing the major health problem of the nineteenth century, the tuberculosis epidemic, *World Health* magazine noted that—

> The precipitating causes were the new social conditions generated by the industrial revolution: chaotic expansion of villages into cities; grossly inadequate housing resulting in overcrowding and slums [among other factors including] poor sanitation and medical care.[16]

Of further significance is the extent to which "Sedentary habits, and the stress and strain of modern life" may play a part in heart attacks.[17]

The growing concern for the quality of life, environmental conditions, and human settlements has prompted international attention and has resulted in a number of forums or conferences. Perhaps the most significant of these forums was the 1972 United Nations Conference on the Human Environment held in Stockholm, Sweden.

The UN conference drew some 1200 delegates from more than 110 nations and about 30,000 of the earth's residents who participated in related events. The main issues of the conference centered around the need for environmental protection, population control, worldwide resource distribution, and economic development. On all of these issues, there was conflict between the viewpoints of the developed or industrialized nations and the developing nations. About 78 of the countries represented were developing nations.

Barry Commoner, an environmentalist from the United States, pointed out that "the United States contains about 6 percent of the world's population, but uses 40 to 50 percent of the world's goods".[18] Olaf Palme, Sweden's Prime Minister, stated:

> It is an inescapable fact that each individual in the industrialized countries draws—on the average—30 times more heavily on the limited resources of the earth than his fellow man in the developing countries. . . .[19]

In the Kings Tree Garden, a park near the main conference area, local Stockholm advocacy groups displayed graphics critical of housing and related development in their city. This came as somewhat of a surprise because of the praise that is usually given to Stockholm and its surrounding New Towns by architects and planners from the United States who have visited these areas.

The historic UN conference, which lasted two weeks, resulted in a 26-point declaration which, among other items, cited "the importance of planning human settlements and dealing effectively with urbanization".[20]

In July 1971, a symposium was held in and around Athens, Greece. This, the Delos Symposium, was the ninth in a 10-year annual series initiated in 1972 by the renowned Greek planner, Constantinos Doxiadis. The symposium is actually conducted on board a ship which cruises through the Aegean Sea, stopping at such places as Delphi, Olympia, Gythion, Ios, Santorini, Rhodes, Lindos, Patmos, Mykonos, and Delos. The people brought together to discuss "Shells and Human Settlements" during Delos Nine included physician-scientist Jonas Salk, psychoanalyst Erik Erikson, theologian Harvey Cox, anthropologist Margaret Mead, environmental planner Lawrence Halprin, economist Barbara Ward, city planner Edmund Bacon, and designer-philosopher R. Buckminster Fuller, to name a few of the four dozen or so involved.

While there was a clear concern for the quality of life throughout the world, I found much of the discussion and resulting declaration to be relevant to conditions within the United States. During the course of the week-long discussions, it was pointed out that "People don't need innovation, they need service";[21] and that attention must be given to the problem of overdevelopment, in addition to those of underdevelopment.

The final report covered six areas: the scale of the problem, basic human needs, anti-human construction, policies for human settlements, levels of authority, and the urban tasks.

Under *the scale of the problem,* it was noted that "the provision of shelter for the vast majority of the human race is now a priority only less urgent than the prevention of famine or the elimination of war".[22]

Concerning *basic human needs,* the report called for "protection against such tension-provoking factors as excessive densities and obtrusive noise" and beyond this: "We particularly affirm man's need to be associated in a creative and active way with the building or arranging of his house and immediate surroundings."[23]

On *anti-human construction,* the problems of high rises and monumental buildings were singled out, as well as the city-suburb dichotomy. Of particular note was the contention that "the separation of city and suburb, unless contained by forms of metropolitan decision-making, can starve the inner city's ability to house and employ its people and act as a cultural center", and that "what is lacking is any determination to act on the scale required by the deepening crisis".[24]

Policies for human settlements suggested that government must "take the lead" and "accept, as a fundamental responsibility, a positive and dynamic concept of land use". In addition, the use of high rise buildings was discouraged for family accommodations, and emphasis was placed on preserving the existing housing stock. The basic unit suggested for "satisfying man's immediate biological and cultural needs"[25] was the neighborhood.

With respect to *levels of authority,* the general principle was stated "that broad issues of land use and urban location belong to the highest level of government" and that "decisions about neighborhoods should be in the hands of local groups". Popular participation in local government was cited as a "precondition for lively communities".[26] With increasing emphasis on citizen participation in this country, we ought to take particular note of the statement that popular participation—

> . . .must not become a divisive and exclusive authority, ducking out from the costs of urban society and refusing a human mix of classes, cultures, and races. Participation by the citizen, which is essential to liveliness and freedom of choice in the local community, has to take place within broad public guidelines of equity and equality.[27]

The final part of the Delos report dealt with *urban tasks* and warned that "Nothing is now more vital than a plain and unambiguous commitment to securing decent shelter and community for all the world's peoples."[28]

International conferences and travel experiences help to put problems of development and environment in the United States in a broader perspective. The problems of housing, population growth, and the imbalance between needs and services are far more acute in most of the Third World (Asia, Africa, and South America) nations. Because of the wealth that exists in the United States, it seems to me that we have a special obligation to set the example for the rest of the world insofar as bringing about those conditions that are necessary to provide for a favorable quality of life for all of our citizens is concerned. In this regard, we must assess quality in biological, cultural, physical, and psychological terms—in addition to the economic yardstick. Accordingly, light, air, space, shelter, and the provision of services must be weighed in terms of how and what they contribute to human growth and potential.

AN OVERVIEW OF
NEW TOWNS

/ THE NEW TOWNS CONCEPT /

New Towns, in the contemporary sense, are developments that are planned initially to provide for a broad range of social, economic, and physical activities within a defined area of land and within a predetermined time period. The social activities will normally include educational services from preschool through college, health services, recreational facilities, civic organizations, and religious institutions. The economic will normally include an industrial park, commercial centers, and the like. The physical embraces the provision of roads, utilities, and housing. The housing normally represents a range wide enough to accommodate moderate through upper income categories. Conceptually, all of these activities will exist within an environmentally sound, economically viable, and socially interactive framework. One of the most important aspects of New Town living is the opportunity to participate in governance and to influence decision making during the development process.

Unfortunately, there are no widely accepted limits that tell us precisely at what point a neighborhood becomes a village, a village a town, a town a city, and a city a metropolis.

Using population as a base for conceptualization only, inspection suggests that neighborhoods range up to about 3,000 people, with three to five neighborhoods making up a village. Villages, in turn, might range from 9,000 to about 15,000 or more, with three to five villages making up a town. Towns might range from 45,000 to 75,000 people, with combinations above two towns forming the basis for a city. Cities, following this point of logic, could range from 90,000 to 150,000. Combinations or groupings of cities would then form the basis for a metropolis.

It is recognized that all of these units must go beyond a description of population and relate to function, services, diversity, density, culture, character, age, and so on. Some states use a population of 5,000 as the basis for incorporation of a "city". The Census Bureau gives data for cities with populations of over 25,000, suggesting that level as a "cut-off". Large skyscrapers in New York City house as many as 50,000 people, but these buildings cannot be called cities. The suggested

17

structure and hierarchy of neighborhoods, towns, villages, cities, and then the metropolis are indicated to facilitate thinking in an attempt to understand and properly categorize the New Towns.

It would be incorrect to state that the New Town movement in the United States has resulted exclusively from the "Garden City" advocates, among whom we would find such thinkers as Ebenezer Howard, Sir Patrick Geddes, Fredric Osborn, Lewis Mumford, Clarence Stein, and the late Henry Wright and Catherine Bauer. While a central body of knowledge is lacking as to what city planning and development is all about, the present approach toward New Towns is an eclectic one that draws on ideas of the Garden City advocates, as well as on those espoused by the late French architect Le Corbusier, who represented a much more urban point of view. Current thinking also reflects principles that have evolved out of the history of planning and development as well as real estate marketing practices.

The central ideas behind the New Town concept are those of structuring a definite plan for development over a predetermined time period, balancing the delivery of services with the needs of the resident population, establishing limits for growth, incorporating multiple uses for the land (residential, commercial, industrial, and open space), and developing a largely self-sustaining economic base.

One of the earliest planned cities on record is Miletus, Greece, which was initiated during the fourth century B.C.

During the Middle Ages, over 400 new or "planted" towns were created in England, Wales, and Gascony by the English kings and their subjects. Many of these planted towns grew out of a Parliamentary meeting held in 1297 under King Edward I. The limits for the towns were set by walls or the topography, which was a consideration in site selection. The elements considered necessary for success were social forces, legal title, and geographic potential.[29]

Also developed during this same period, which saw New Towns boom throughout Europe, were 12 towns built by the Dukes of Zahringen in and around Switzerland. These "Zahringer" towns included Offenburg, founded in 1122; Neuenberg, Germany, founded in 1171; and Zurich and Bern, Switzerland, founded in 1171 and 1190 respectively. By the sixteenth century, Bern was the most powerful city state north of the Alps, and in 1848, it became the capital of Switzerland. Today, Bern is the center of a city of nearly 200,000 people. The plan and spatial disposition were regarded as among the key elements for the survival and successul development of the Zahringer towns.

It is also important to note that the Zahringer New Towns were part of a regional plan.[30] The idea of planning the location of New Towns within a regional context continues today in the European experience. This is not the case with respect to the New Towns being developed in the United States.

Town planning in America actually got off to a good start during the seventeenth and eighteenth centuries. The early settlements of Philadelphia, Pennsylvania; Williamsburg, Virginia; Savannah, Georgia; and Annapolis, Maryland, were among those developed initially according to a plan, as were Washington, D.C., and several other cities.

During the nineteenth century, however, the colonial initiatives to plan cities were soon constrained by an anti-urban bias, growing economic competition between cities, and an increase in land speculation.[31] These forces, largely responsible for the early decline of town planning, are very much at work today, in addition to negative social forces and an outdated legal system that effectively mitigates against efforts to plan and develop cities on a rational basis. It is fair to say that the basis for our economy, the free enterprise system, runs counter to the principles necessary to effect rigid land use controls and rational growth, but not the development of New Towns per se.

The early part of the twentieth century saw the emergence of thinking designed to effect a dramatic improvement in the quality of life in cities through the British "Garden City" movement, started by Ebenezer Howard, who in 1902 wrote *Garden Cities of Tomorrow.* Howard defined the Garden City as

> a Town designed for healthy living and industry; of a size that makes possible a full measure of social life, but not larger; surrounded by a rural belt; the whole of the land being in public ownership or held in trust for the community.[32]

Howard's work was the premise for the early British Garden Cities of Letchworth, initiated in 1903 about 35 miles north of London on a site of nearly 4,000 acres, and Welwyn, initiated in 1919 about 25 miles north of London and embracing the same concept. The Garden City movement resulted in New Towns that were located well beyond the urban fringe with principally row houses surrounded by large open spaces and some commercial and industrial land uses.

In the years followng the First World War, the New Town idea unfolded in the United States, resulting in the development of Radburn, New Jersey, in 1929, and the government-sponsored "greenbelt" towns of Greenhills, Ohio; Greendale, Wisconsin; and Greenbelt, Maryland. Following the Second World War, Park Forest, Illinois, was developed, applying some of the Garden City concepts. In all of the preceding cases, the developments remained largely residential in character in that they were unable to attract industry, and consequently could not approach economic self-sufficiency.

The present movement toward New Towns began in 1962 with the development of Reston, Virginia, initiated by Robert E. Simon, for whom the town is named (R-E-S-T-O-[W]-N). Located about 20 miles west of Washington, D.C., near Dulles International Airport in the rolling hills of Virginia, the town has a site of over 7,000 acres and a present population of about 30,000 people. Another development that has had a major influence on the New Town movement is the New Town of Columbia, Maryland, initiated in 1966 by mortgage banker and shopping center developer Jim Rouse. Today, more than 10 years after the start of Simon's bold initiative, there are over 30 New Towns being developed throughout the nation, with as many more in the planning stage.

In addition to New Towns, there is a growing trend toward large-scale developments, particularly *planned unit developments*. Planned unit developments are normally in the area of 300 to 1000 acres. PUDs, as they are more popularly called, usually have a range of residential choices such as multi-family, townhouse, and single-family detached units, combined with open space, recreation facilities, and some commercial facilities. This village scale concept is principally residential in character. In the last decade, PUDs have approached the 2,000 mark and suggest a demand both for amenities and for a departure from the traditional suburb that is entirely residential, often monotonous, without definition, and interrupted only by poorly designed shopping centers and strip development.

Most estimates suggest that New Towns will house only 10 percent of the total population growth expected by the year 2000. However, with an increased awareness of the stress caused by urban living; the necessity to depart from the automobile as a primary means of transportation; the demand for increased recreational activities, accelerated by experience with a four-day work week; the demand for a more efficient and higher level of health, educational, and other municipal services; and the need to establish new life styles and social patterns, New Towns could very well become the norm for development rather than the exception. Within the development process of New Towns, the opportunity for citizen involvement through a variety of organizational and political arrangements has given a new and perhaps a more powerful voice to those wishing to shape the character of their community.

The development of sites for New Towns starting from raw

open land has provided an opportunity for all of the design and engineering professions to demonstrate their combined talents without being subjected to the constraints of limited space and crowding that are found in many of the larger cities. Consequently, the New Town movement has given new life to urban design and in many cases has resulted in the design of award-winning buildings and plazas.

The neighborhood is used considerably throughout the development of New Towns as the basic residential unit within which residential units are grouped or "clustered" together with an increased amount of open space resulting for common use. The village, representing several neighborhoods, is a major focal point of activity within New Towns. Village centers usually have as many as 30 shops representing a variety of services such as drug stores, supermarkets, barber shops, appliance shops, clothing stores, and the like. Many of the New Towns also contain regional shopping centers that include as many as 150 stores and, in some cases, one or more major department stores.

Many of the New Towns separate automobile and pedestrian traffic through a network of footpaths that bypass roads with underpasses and foot bridges. In addition to these design features, there is a concerted effort to limit the removal of trees and other forms of natural growth in the New Towns.

The governance of New Towns varies considerably. Some are incorporated cities, others exist within urban or rural counties, and others have become annexed by or are a part of an existing jurisdiction.

Population projections for the New Towns range from as low as 17,000 to well above 400,000. For the most part, however, they fall in the range of 50,000 to 100,000 people on sites ranging from a few hundred to well over 50,000 acres, with most in the area of about 5000 to 10,000 acres. Of particular significance is the fact that goals are set by the developer to guide the growth of the New Town in its economic, environmental, and social aspects.

The racial integration that has resulted in the New Towns has been evident in both housing and the development of small business. This aspect of New Towns is particularly important because throughout the development of housing in America, blacks have been, for the most part, concentrated in separate neighborhoods. This has been the case both in the large cities, many of which now have black or near black majorities, and in rural areas, where black families still live on property handed down from slave owners. A combination of financial, real estate, government, and other institutional practices, along with the capricious use of zoning and racist attitudes, has polarized life in metropolitan areas along the lines of race. In contrast to this, the New Town of Reston, located in the cradle of slavery, the state of Virginia, has a black population of about 10 percent, and Columbia, Maryland, located in a county that voted for George Wallace in 1968, has a black population of nearly 20 percent. It must be recognized, however, that the resulting racial mix in New Towns is contingent upon existing population characteristics in the region, in addition to other factors such as financial situation, the range of housing choices available, social attitudes toward fair housing practices, and advertising practices.

Aside from reflecting a new respect for people, the citizens of the New Towns are building their own institutions and setting about to control their destiny. The anonymity that once existed in the urban high rises and sprawling suburbs is giving way to involvement, interaction, and a thrust toward community.

Although it is difficult to be precise in defining a New Town, it is important to note that most of the developers have established periods for development normally in the area of 20 years. This distinction is important because the terms *New Town* and *New Community* are used by some companies that are principally engaged in the sale of land to individuals for "investment" purposes. They are not dealing in the full fabric of building a Town. While size and population are important insofar as bringing about a critical mass is concerned, the balance between population and services provided is by far a more important aspect of New Town development.

Until 1968, when the Interstate Land Sales Full Disclosure Act was passed, the federal government was, for all practical purposes, uninvolved in the regulation of land sales. The legislation that was enacted was brought on by an onslaught of people being "taken" by a host of sales gimmicks and the proverbial "suede shoe" routine. In an attempt to assist prospective purchasers, HUD ran a very successful media campaign with television advertisements that said, "Before you buy in Rainbow City, make sure there *is* a Rainbow City." A report released in 1973 on "The Use of Land," sponsored by the Rockefeller Brothers Fund, dealt with the subdivision of rural land largely for recreational purposes, and noted that "In 1971 an estimated 625,000 recreational lots were sold by over 10,000 subdividers."[33] The same report stated that "For the nation as a whole, at least six recreational lots were sold in 1971 for each second home constructed", and that

In California, between 50,000 and 100,000 acres of rural land were subdivided annually in the late 1960s and early 1970s by recreational lot sellers. By 1971, however, houses had been built on only 3 percent of the lots sold in the previous decade.[34]

/ THE LOCATION AND CLASSIFICATION OF U.S. NEW TOWNS /

Of 29 New Towns well into development, including 16 backed by the U.S. government, all but two are located in or near metropolitan areas in 15 states, California having the most. Southern California, with the New Towns of Westlake, Valencia, Irvine, Mission Viejo, Laguna Niguel, Rancho California, Rancho Bernardo, and Rancho San Diego, represents the most intense area of this type of development. These eight New Towns alone represent a planned population of nearly one million people and are all within an hour or so of the Pacific Ocean.

Another area of intense New Town development is metropolitan Washington, D.C., where within a radius of about 30 miles the New Towns of Reston, Virginia; Columbia, Maryland; St. Charles, Maryland; and Fort Lincoln (Washington, D.C.) are all located.

New York and Texas also contain a large number of New Towns. New York State, under the Urban Development Corporation, is developing the New Towns of Audubon, near Buffalo; Radisson, near Syracuse; and Roosevelt Island, in New York City. In addition, there are two New Towns being assisted by the federal government, Riverton and Gananda, both near Rochester, bringing New York's total to five. In Texas, there are the New Towns of Flower Mound, located near the New Dallas-Ft. Worth Intercontinental Jetport; San Antonio Ranch, near San Antonio; and The Woodlands and Clearlake, both near Houston.

In the Midwest, there are the New Towns of Park Forest South, near Chicago; Jonathan, near Minneapolis; and Cedar-Riverside, near downtown Minneapolis. The New Town of Soul City, North Carolina, located in a rural area, is an entrepreneural effort by a black businessman.

Conceptually, New Towns might be classified as being *satellite,* located on the edges of metropolitan areas and somewhat dependent upon an existing economic base; *free standing,* designed as largely self-sustaining and located in rural areas; and *in-town,* located within an existing city.

The satellite concept represents the majority of those in development. While most of these are attempting to balance their profile with commercial, industrial, and residential activities, it is unrealistic to think that any New Town can exist entirely as an entity unto itself. If over the long run—that is, after development is complete—half the population can enjoy living and working in the same New Town, I would consider it successful.

Rurally located New Towns are often called free standing. This again suggests that the town is self-sustaining, and this again is incorrect. New Towns located in rural areas must serve the region that they are located within and recognize that anything less will be strongly to their disadvantage. Because of the lack of realistic regional planning and development policies, and because of the diversity provided by urban areas, rurally located New Towns represent a unique challenge. It is quite likely, however, that the increasing demand for recreational activities, the advances in communications technology, and the reduced quality of life in most metropolitan areas will cause a reversal of the present urbanization trend. Such a reversal, however, is not likely to occur in a rapid fashion without a firm national growth policy.

Because of the negative character of large sections of most of the central cities in the United States, especially where the metropolitan areas are in excess of one million people, the New-Town-in-Town has special significance. It is this concept that offers the greatest promise for social responsiveness. It is also here where the greatest difficulty may be encountered by public and private officials in trying to deal with citizens who still remember the false promises made under the guise of "urban renewal" and the painful neighborhood destruction and "relocation" that followed.

There are two New-Town-in-Town projects presently in development, Cedar-Riverside in Minneapolis and Roosevelt Island in New York City. A third, Fort Lincoln in Washington, D.C., is in limbo. The Fort Lincoln project was first announced in 1967 by President Lyndon Johnson. Since that time the proposed site of 342 acres, which is largely open and planned for some 16,000 people, has been caught up in a "shell game" involving the quasi-federal District of Columbia Redevelopment Land Agency, the government of the District of Columbia (namely, the City Council and the Mayor's office), HUD, and the White House. The relationship between the private development company Building Systems International and the Redevelopment Land Agency that is administratively responsible for the site appears to have been strained. Building Systems International has been associated with the project since about 1970 when in conjunction with Westinghouse it was responsible for doing a feasibility study on the proposed New Town. Westinghouse pulled out of the project around 1972, and BSI remained as the developer. Following a public review of plans in 1972, demands were made for jobs and equity participation. These demands were met with what appeared to be favorable consideration, and a number of programs and policies were announced. The area that apparently has become an issue is that of equity participation—that is, the ownership of stock and how much by whom, as it relates to the local community and the development corporation.

On February 21, 1975, John Gunther, chairman of the Washington, D.C., Redevelopment Land Agency, made public a telegram from Building Systems International indicating that the developer for the proposed Fort Lincoln New Town was withdrawing from the project. The telegram stated, in part—

> Despite an extraordinary amount of mutual effort by BSI and the RLA to find practicable solutions to the very difficult and complicated problems in the development of Fort Lincoln, it has not been possible to work out arrangements satisfactory to all parties. Because of this situation, BSI has determined that the best interests of Fort Lincoln would be served by its withdrawal as the developer.[35]

The future of the proposed Fort Lincoln New Town has probably never been bleaker in the eight years since it was first brought to public attention by the late President Lyndon B. Johnson. The uncertainty of Fort Lincoln's future is a blow not only to the people of the District of Columbia but also to the residents of central cities throughout the nation. Given what has happened in the Fort Lincoln experience, private developers might unfortunately be scared off from undertaking the development of New Towns in the large central cities where they may be needed the most.

/ THE RATIONALE FOR NEW TOWNS /

For many of the residents, New Town living represents an escape from what some may call the "rat race" or the "squirrel cage"—the back-and-forth, rush-rush, pattern that millions of people find themselves being subjected to who live in the suburbs and work in the central city. For others, it represents a bold and seemingly pioneering step toward a new way of life. For those who are fortunate enough to live and work in the same development, New Town living can represent freedom from the automobile. For others still, a New Town can be a chance to get away from the rigid pressures of small town living without being subjected to the anonymity and stress that can be a part of central city living. In addition to the provision of a full range of services in response to the needs of residents, New Towns through community associations provide citizens with an opportunity to affect decision making related to the development process.

In considering New Towns, it is essential that some thought be given to the issues of loneliness or personal isolation, loss of community, and the total needs of people both individually and collectively. Vance

Packard in *A Nation of Strangers* writes: "Personal isolation is becoming a major social fact of our time."[36] Erich Fromm in *The Sane Society* raises the question:

> Could it be that the middle-class life of prosperity, while satisfying our material needs leaves us with a feeling of intense boredom, and that suicide and alcoholism are pathological ways of escape from this boredom?[37]

Ralph Keys in *We The Lonely People* writes: "Loss of community. That seems to cover the feeling, the feeling unknown, but when we try to pin it down, the term is elusive."[38] Indeed, these are extremely important issues, and because of their being identifiable and perhaps of a manageable size, New Towns may serve as a vehicle to define more precisely what our nonmaterial needs really are.

In September 1971, Eleanore Carruth wrote in *Fortune* magazine: "The new town movement is about to come of age in America. Powerful forces—public and private, natural and directed—are converging into a thrust toward large, planned communities all over the U.S."[39] *Architectural Record* in December 1973 stated of contemporary New Towns: "Nowhere else can one take a long hard look at an overall design for living, the delivery of human services, and the expansion of opportunities for all."[40] Architectural Critic Wolf Von Eckardt writes in *A Place To Live* that "New Towns have special significance for the United States", and that "They offer the only workable answer so far to counteract the disruptive effect of unlimited automobility and megalopolis."[41]

In her visit to Reston, anthropoligist Margaret Mead heralded New Towns "for the chance to try new things" and pointed out that people can often accept many things in a new setting that they could not in an old situation. Of particular interest to her was the mixing of income levels and the evidence of racial integration. While she felt that New Towns were perhaps ahead of the rest of the country insofar as accommodating different life styles is concerned, she felt that the inclusion of three generations of people would be necessary for New Towns to become viable.

In making the case for "*another way to live*", seven New Towns have been selected for review in the following chapters. The items discussed include the concept and character of the New Town, the observations of some of the residents, racial integration, social issues, citizen-initiated programs, governance, community services, housing and development, and planning. Since these New Towns are in varying stages of development, the above items are not necessarily discussed for each community.

New Towns are not ideal havens for urban escapists. Those who come to New Towns in search of utopia will probably be the first to be disappointed. The transition to New Town living from a previous environment could be painful for some. There are adjustment problems. The behavioral implications centering around the transition between the old and the new environments need to be researched and well publicized.

One of the most complex and perhaps most sensitive issues is that of socio-economic integration. Since the implications are strong between housing and income level, I feel that particular care must be taken by developers, citizens, and public officials to avoid a repeat of the past practice of building houses that are identifiable by their residents' income levels. Where possible, this must be avoided in favor of programs such as rent supplements that allow lower economic groups to live in residential units without their economic status being exposed.

While it is important to provide the poor with a full range of community services, caution must be exercised not to subject them to the pressures from those who desire to climb the economic ladder and enjoy a life style that is commensurate with their level of achievement. This might be brought about by allowing the lower end of the economic spectrum to be absorbed more within the middle income range, rather than leaning toward the higher economic echelons.

The integration of races across economic boundaries is probably the most difficult socio-economic change to bring about. The oportunities that exist for personal interaction through recreation, education, employment, and citizen participation may very well achieve more in the long run than the sheer exercise of public authority which, while necessary to effect an initial transition, can quickly reach a point of diminishing returns.

The New Towns concept represents the best approach to date for those who wish to experience a greater degree of social and economic diversity than that which exists in most communities in this nation. In addition, this concept has the best potential of any development scheme to date for alleviating the polarization that exists along the lines of income and race in this nation's metropolitan areas.

/ THE FORERUNNER OF THE NEW TOWN MOVEMENT /

Nancy and Paul are a young couple who moved to Reston in 1971 from northern New Jersey. Nancy says:

When we first came to the Washington area, we looked around the suburban areas. All we saw were apartment buildings just there on a plot of land. There was no place for the kids to play except little dirty playgrounds, and a lot of traffic. I was so depressed. I cried for three days when we drove through there. I just thought that if this was where we would have to live, in some apartment complex, just on a plot of land, I would go crazy, and Paul said, 'Just for kicks let's go out and take a look at Reston because I've heard so much about it.' Well, the minute we drove through, we just fell in love with it. The way everything fits into the land, the way the roads curve, everything was just so beautiful no matter where you went. Everything is really pretty.

After about a year of living in an apartment, Nancy and Paul purchased a home in Reston. The experience of Nancy and Paul is typical of many who have chosen to make Reston their home. Reston is the first New Town to be built in America since the Second World War. In contrast to the unplanned villages, towns, and cities that exist within and on the fringes of the metropolitan areas of the United States, Reston is a comprehensively planned, environmentally appealing, socially inter-active community of about 26,000 people (as of the spring of 1975).[42]

Conceived and initiated by developer Robert E. Simon in 1962, Reston is the forerunner of the New Town movement currently under way in the United States. Ten years after starting his first New Town venture, developer Simon reflected:

> Reston was an early, serious experiment in urban planning undertaken on a city-wide scale and an attempt to discover what should be done to create a quality environment. A lot of what I see going on today was part of Reston thinking back in the 1960's.[43]

The "Reston thinking" involved the development of a New Town for which Simon set forth seven goals:

1 / That the widest choice of opportunities be made available for the full use of leisure time. This means that the New Town should provide a wide range of recreational and cultural facilities, as well as an environment for privacy.

2 / That it be possible for anyone to remain in a single neighborhood throughout his life, uprooting being neither inevitable nor always desirable. By providing the fullest range of housing styles and prices—from high rise efficiencies to six-bedroom townhouses and detached houses—housing needs can be met at a variety of income levels and at different stages of family life. This kind of mixture permits residents to remain rooted in the community—if they so choose—as their particular housing needs change. As a by-product, this also results in the heterogeneity that spells a lively and varied community.

3 / That the importance and dignity of each individual be the focal point for all planning, taking precedence over large-scale concepts.

4 / That people be able to live and work in the same community.

5 / That commercial, cultural, and recreational facilities be made available to the residents from the outset of the development—not years later.

6 / That beauty—structural and natural—is a necessity of the good life and should be fostered.

7 / That Reston be a financial success.

The seven goals have been or are in the process of being met. In the physical sense, recreational opportunities exist through already completed facilities: seven swimming pools, eighteen tennis courts, and an 18-hole championship golf course. There is also a private golf and country club that has an 18-hole championship golf course, an indoor Olympic-sized swimming pool, and tennis courts. In addition, there are three lakes, over 25 miles of walkways, a riding stable, six pedestrian underpasses and one overpass, bridge paths, garden plots, tot lots, and play areas. The key to providing opportunities for a broad range of income groups is housing for low and moderate income families. As of the fall of 1973, Reston had more than 1000 units of housing for low and moderate income families. Over 127 business firms and associations representing almost 5500 jobs have located in Reston. Included are the 2500 jobs provided by the $50 million headquarters complex of the U.S. Geological Survey which was occupied during the latter part of 1973. In 1972, under the management of Gulf-Reston, Inc., Reston became the only New Town in America to operate in the black.

The physical design of Reston is nothing short of spectacular. The site of some 7,000 acres consists of rolling hills with an abundance of trees, in addition to three large lakes and a number of ponds. The footpaths are linked throughout the New Town by interesting and well-designed bridges and overpasses, continuing the separation of pedestrians and automobiles.

Within this environmentally appealing envelope, some of the nation's leading architects—Clothiel Woodward Smith, William Conklin, James Rossant, Charles Goodman, and Louis Sauer—have designed an interesting selection of residential units. These include townhouses, garden apartments, high rises, and single-family detached homes. Many of the residents enjoy views of one of the two golf courses, Lake Anne, or the trees.

Architecture has been given a new life in Reston. If there is an architecture of stimulation, it is here. Not that it does not exist elsewhere—it is just that in Reston there is such abundance, as part of a

total concept, visable and uncluttered, transcending its presence to the people.

To date, there are three villages under development and an international center. Eventually there will be five villages and a town center. Lake Anne is by far the most attractive and exciting of the present village centers. The sculptures on and around the plaza are magnets to the young and perhaps an inspiration to everyone else.

Physical achievements notwithstanding, the real essence of the Reston experience is the interaction of a broad cross section of talented and concerned people who have come together to make the New Town a reality. It is this aspect—the efforts of the people—that warrants attention.

Reston is, however, not a utopia; it is a New Town that is reaching toward being a community. This community consists of company presidents, elected officials, professionals, government employees, laborers, senior citizens, teen-agers, blacks, whites, and a wealth of foreign nationals. With over 11 members of the Washington Redskins football team living here during the season, Reston is probably the best represented New Town in professional football.

To be fully appreciated, Reston and other developing New

Towns must be contrasted with the dying central cities and the sprawling suburbs that, at best, offer sterility. In a quest for the good life, Reston is a beginning. But it is only a beginning because even here there are problems. Reston has managed to come to grips with most of what troubles it, but not without experiencing the painful agony that is often necessary to bring forth an awakening. This agony has been experienced by some of the merchants and many of the other citizens of Reston. It was certainly experienced by Robert E. Simon who was forced out the year following the official dedication for financial reasons. It has been experienced by the current developer, who has had to live with less than cooperative county, state, and federal governments. The continuance of Reston as a viable New Town has been brought into question more than once with heated debate between the citizens and the developer, between the developer and the county, and, I expect, between the developer and the financial partners, although I am not privileged to that information. In an atmosphere of questionable certainty, the drama of Reston unfolds. It somehow has gathered a momentum over the years to stay on track, to

cope with economic difficulties resulting from county wide growth controls imposed in 1973, and to build America's first New Town.

/ SOME OF THE PEOPLE /

Judy is a 26-year-old government employee who makes about $13,000 a year. When she first moved to Washington, D.C., from San Francisco, she lived in a high rise in the center of the city near 14th Street and Rhode Island Avenue, and her friends told her she was "crazy". After 14 months she moved to another high rise farther from the city's center near Belmont Road and Connecticut Avenue where she stayed for only a few months. After a girl on the floor above her was murdered, she moved to Arlington, Virginia, where she soon found her 12-story high rise oppressive. The halls were dark, the grounds were not landscaped, and the people were unfriendly. She paid $190 a month for a one-bedroom apartment described as "old and small". On the advice of a friend, Judy moved to Reston. In contrast to her previous residences, she finds the environment secure and is well pleased with what she is getting in her $215-a-month one-bedroom ground-floor apartment. She says she loves the view from her bedroom where the golf course and trees can be seen, and has begun riding her bicycle and walking along the pathways.

Frank is an executive who works in downtown Washington, D.C. Along with his wife and family, he has lived in Reston since 1970. They moved to Reston in 1970 from Minneapolis after hearing about it from friends.

My main reason for moving to Reston was because of the children and because Reston appeared to be the least prejudiced of all the communities in the metropolitan Washington area, including Maryland. And also because of the school system. We would have chosen to live in Washington, D.C., had it not been for the school system. Having lived here for four years, I think it's sort of antiseptic in a way. . . .it's nice for small children. . .not necessarily for teen-agers. . .they need a lot more than just swimming, tennis, and sitting around at the coffee house. My wife feels that Reston is too isolated and would much prefer to be in the city where things are happening.

Frank feels that the New Towns have not dealt with the needs of housewives. He thinks that New Towns are really planned from a male chauvinist point of view:

It's great for the man who drives to the city every day and
is involved in the hustle of urban life. . .and then comes home
on the weekend to get away from it all.

Lauri is typical of some of the young singles who rejected the
traditional suburban complexes in favor of the New Towns. Unlike Judy,
who ended up in Reston after a series of negative experiences, Lauri was
immediately attracted to Reston because of the abundant open spaces
which reminded her of her native California. An airline stewardess, she
appreciates the Reston location which is only seven minutes from Dulles
International Airport, her base.

In addition to the open spaces and the walkways, I like
the proximity of having tennis courts and a swimming pool
within a few minutes walking distance of where I live. Also,
having met people here from all over the country, I feel that I
have broadened my social interests considerably.

Adrian and Barbara, an interracial couple in their early
thirties, moved from Southwest Washington, D.C., to Reston with their
two young daughters in 1971 and remained for a year before moving to
Cambridge, Massachusetts. They left Washington, D.C., because of the

school district and were initially attracted to Reston by the California-style architecture of the townhouse they subsequently bought. They had never experienced suburban living and expected to find a sense of community. In reflecting on their Reston experience, they have expressed several misgivings.

> It didn't take long to find out what it was about. We were burdened with several layers of government which we felt were not necessary. We lived among 37 attached houses which was called a cluster. The cluster association bought the street and made it private. They also planted trees in our yard and didn't tell us anything about it. We didn't want the trees. There was a terrible imposition into our life.

They did, however, enjoy the commuter bus, the swimming pools, and the footpaths. Barbara considers the experience of having lived in Reston invaluable and admits that they had a tendency to get turned on to visual things. She feels that her family was disintegrating in Reston and that they were mortgaged over their heads.

Sandy and Steve moved to Reston from Poughkeepsie, New York, in 1970 and find that their experience to date represents "an urban feeling without the hassle of living in the city". During the summer, they spend most of their weekends at the neighborhood pool. Before moving to Reston, they spent well over an hour driving each way to get to recreational facilities. Sandy feels that the Reston environment is "more spontaneous and liberal". Both Sandy and Steve grew up in a predominantly Jewish neighborhood and enjoy both their children and themselves being involved with a broad cross section of people.

Darlene moved to Reston from an 11-story high rise because of the open spaces and heavily wooded environment. She feels free to get out and roam around and jog. "Where I lived before, people would give you a funny look if you walked around or jogged."

Tom is 33 and lives with his wife and four children in the federally assisted apartment complex, Cedar-Ridge. He was born and reared only about five miles away in the black enclave of Oak Grove. The former Air Force veteran is employed at nearby Dulles International Airport and views Reston as a necessity. His reasons for moving to the New Town centered around the availability of housing at a price that he could afford and the quality of the schools. He still maintains his social contacts in Oak Grove. Ultimately he wants to build his own home on about five acres, raise his own vegetables, and become as self-sufficient as possible.

Mary is a 15-year-old who has lived in Reston since 1970:

The first year I enjoyed it a lot more than I have the last two because things were new. Reston seems sort of artificial now, like it is a nice place to go but it is not like the city. . . .it really gets boring after a while.

Moira is a professional urban planner turned housewife and community volunteer who has lived in Reston since 1972 with her real estate salesman husband. Both are in their early thirties with a two-year-old. He was able to give up his government job which paid about $16,000 a year to take a position as a commissioned salesman—something he has wanted to do for most of his adult life. His wife says he was able to do this because—

Reston is wide open. We only have one car, and I am just three blocks from the Village Center where I shop. Reston is an ego trip. . . .we were not only able but encouraged to participate in this community.

Moira is a member of the communications committee of the Hunters Woods Village Council and feels that the Council has been pretty effective in promoting interaction and increasing services to people.

As an urban planner, I feel that by applying my planning skills at the community, I have done more good for more people since I have been here than I did in all the years of being employed professionally.

/ THE BLACK EXPERIENCE /

Since its inception, Reston has been a place where people could rent or buy a home without regard to race, creed, or ethnic origin. And as of the summer of 1974, over 2,000 blacks could call Reston home. Where there is an economic cross section ranging from those who live in federally assisted housing to those with homes well above $100,000, the great majority of the black families are those of professionals who have enjoyed substantial success. There are high-level government executives, doctors, dentists, attorneys, corporate managers, professional athletes, airline ticket agents, real estate sales personnel, school teachers, principals, engineers, technicians, and construction workers. Overall, the black population is about 9 percent of the total Reston population.

According to Jane Wilhelm, former director of community relations for Reston under Robert Simon:

Of the first 500 people that moved into Reston, only about 2 percent had to be "educated" on living among blacks. In 1966 a white family from the Deep South said they didn't mind living in an integrated community but objected to living next door to a black family which they found out after they had moved in. The developer persuaded them to stay.

Wilhelm also indicated that following the first home owners association election, a white board member resigned rather than sit in conference with a black person who was elected. In contrast to the isolated incidents of bigotry, Wilhelm pointed out that "A large number of white families moved into Reston simply because it *was* an integrated community."

By the early 1970s, and after several increasingly visable Black Arts Festivals, the black population in Reston moved to its present level of about 9 percent. Except for Cedar-Ridge, which its manager estimated at being about 30 percent black, this population is dispersed well throughout the community. I find that many middle class blacks are more "middle class" than middle class whites. I expect that they are where whites were about 20 years ago with respect to those values that lead to the single-family detached homes, the wall-to-wall carpeting, the showcase living rooms, the custom-made drapes (professionally hung, of course), the station wagon, the riding lessons, the kids in private schools, and the membership in the country club. A management consultant in his mid-thirties stated:

I am not going to apologize for being middle class. I tell people about this place and they don't believe it. I'm happy. When I was coming up, Negroes didn't have a place like this to live. I feel as much a part of this place as any white person. It never dawns on me that there are people who don't want me here. In other neighborhoods I was keenly aware that white people questioned my being there. Blacks in Reston are bourgeoise. There is a superficiality about being black in Reston. There is a brother down the street and his lawn is the best on the block.

The involvement of blacks in Reston and in Fairfax County appears to be issue-oriented rather than "involvement for involvement's sake". When problems arise in the schools or at the child care centers, this will normally bring a response from several blacks. When there was an issue involving testing for sickle cell anemia or the trait, over a hundred people turned out to get information and to take action. A prominent physician and Reston resident, Dr. "Pee Wee" Marshall provided very significant leadership along with Mrs. Mona Blake, a member of the Fairfax County Board of Education, and channeled the energies of the group so that the matter was resolved favorably. In addition to Blake, other blacks such as Robert Secundy, a member of the Fairfax County Civil Service Commission, hold positions of leadership in the county and in the New Town.

Several blacks are engaged in their own businesses in Reston, and another sits on the Board of Directors of a savings and loan association located in the New Town. One of the entrepreneurs is Meredythe Holmes, president of the Reston Employment Service. She began her activities by assisting the Common Ground Foundation, a Reston-based nonprofit community service organization, with job placement; then she set up a business housed in her home and subsequently moved to a posh location in the offices of the town's International Center. With three full-time counsellors, two part-time counsellors, and a secretary, the Reston Employment Service has served such clients as the General Electric Corporation, the General Research Corporation, the MITRE Corporation, Polaroid, and Xerox. After starting with just a few thousand dollars of family savings, Holmes expects to gross about $100,000 in 1974. This multi-talented entrepreneur, dancer, choreographer, and musician was voted the most likely to succeed when she graduated from high school in Camden, New Jersey.

While she says that she "was not exposed to racism the way a lot of my contemporaries were (the schools were predominantly white)",

Holmes established her employment business in part because she "wanted to be sure that blacks had a piece of the employment action here in Reston. I am interested in making this a success. . .just as I am interested in being a successful wife and mother. But that is not enough." She adds: "I am interested in the business world. . .for me this is almost the ultimate test for the total person. . .managing your own business."

It is probably difficult for whites to fully understand the pressures that blacks are subjected to in assimilating into a predominantly white environment. When we attain that rung on the economic ladder that makes us middle class, we frequently have the choice of living in an all-black or a predominantly white environment. The latter choice for the most part is one where the patterns are more like 98 percent white, and one where black children may have the most difficult circumstances with which to cope. Reston is a rare instance where the racial mix is close to the national average and one that allows blacks to enjoy some real visibility in a predominantly white environment. For many blacks, the experience of living among whites is entirely new and one that may cause some psychological discomfort.

My assessment of the Reston experience is that we have learned to relax and that few, if any, are about to apologize for being middle class. In 1969 and 1970, a time when there were few blacks in Reston, all-black house parties were quite common, and this was a time when they could "let their hair down". Except for rare occasions, the all-black parties have given way to those that are well integrated with whites. The outlet has shifted, at least for the men, to Sunday morning. On Sunday morning a predominantly black group of about 30 men assembles ostensibly to play basketball. In reality, this turns out as a re-enactment of many of those childhood experiences indigenous to the black ghetto: agitating, signifying, and instigating. One Sunday, a brother showed up with a cap pulled tightly over his head and proceeded to play ball. His hat came off and revealed that his hair was heavily greased, at which time he became the center of attraction. After about 10 minutes of pointing, laughing, and shouting, the game continued. The following week, the same player showed up without the cap and with his hair in an "Afro" style. The Sunday morning crowd includes doctors, lawyers, government executives, professional athletes, high school students, and the like. While sports can represent an outlet for all who participate, there is something unique about this Sunday morning experience.

I consider the black-white experience in Reston to be highly positive. I would be hard-pressed to cite another community in the entire United States where there is as much harmony between the races on such a scale. This happened before there was a National Fair Housing Act, which didn't pass until 1968. What has unfolded in Reston resulted from Robert Simon's decision to make Reston open from the outset. From that point on, the people knew precisely what they were getting into, and they, along with the present management, have carried Simon's initiative through. The developer's role and his leadership are critical. The growth of Reston has been consistently balanced with housing for low and moderate income families. There has been, and I expect there will continue to be, pressure exerted on the developer, the federal government, and the county government from forces within and outside of Reston to continue the housing provisions for low and moderate income families. This pressure comes from people who care—people who know that Reston must show that people of different races and economic stations can live together in relative harmony.

The attitudes toward race in Reston represent a dramatic departure in a state where interracial marriage was prohibited by law until the late 1960s. The decision of the Supreme Court of the United States that favorably supported interracial marriage was based on a couple living in the state of Virginia. The fair housing section of the Civil Rights Act of 1968 also drew on the experiences of housing discrimination in Virginia which occurred during the mid-1960s. Today, Reston, as a New Town, embodies the freedom that has resulted from these judicial and legislative acts, but, moreover, the citizens have provided through their attitudes an exceptional atmosphere for racial and other forms of freedom to be enjoyed. This does not mean that all of the interracial couples, the black couples, and the couples living together have found the "promised land"; they have not. It does mean, however, that the community has gone beyond the physical structuring of environment and the high delivery of social and recreational services, and is dealing with the delicate issue of freedom.

/ CITIZEN INITIATIVES /

In the process of developing a New Town, the developer can acquire the land, ensure that provisions are made for roads and utilities, build houses and other physical structures, and arrange for the provision of schools and other community support facilities. It is almost impossible for any developer to provide the full range of services that meet the needs of citizens in a timely manner. Consequently, there is much that the citizens can do to support the development of a New Town and, accordingly, determine the character of the community. The citizens of Reston have, from the beinning of the New Town, put forth a considerable effort in terms of initiatives that were not part of a master plan and that today stand as clear examples of what can be done. Such examples are the

Lake Anne Nursery School and Kindergarten, the Reston Commuter Bus, the Common Ground Foundation, recreational activities, and cultural and performing Arts.

/ THE LAKE ANNE NURSERY SCHOOL AND KINDERGARTEN /

In 1965, there were no public kindergartens in Fairfax County, Virginia, where Reston is located. The idea of establishing a kindergarten was essentially that of developer Robert E. Simon; he wanted the Lake Anne Nursery School and Kindergarten (LANK) to serve as a model. LANK was structured as a nonprofit corporation with a 15-member Board of Directors drawn from the community. The school was located in the Village Center in a specially designed space above the supermarket. Subsidized by a developer who regarded LANK as a community facility, LANK's initial lease called for a $2,400 annual payment. Until it moved into its present facility, LANK accommodated about 100 students from the community or from the families of people who worked in Reston.

Shortly after the management and control had shifted to Gulf-Reston, Inc., the LANK lease came up for renewal. The new developer indicated that commercial rates would be charged. (This decision was made, in part, in order to open up the way for additional day care facilities from other sponsors. In other words, a continuance of the LANK subsidy would have been inequitable with respect to other day care operations. The developer was also concerned with the selection process for the 100 students enrolled in LANK.) This rate increase was to be phased upward to $4,400 annually during the 1969-1970 period, then to $8,000 during 1970-1971, and finally to about $10,000 annually. This increase created a crisis, and in February 1969, about 250 people from the community met and through their representatives decided to negotiate an alternative with the developer.

The LANK Board of Directors, under the leadership of architect Christopher Raphael, concluded that they were left with essentially three alternatives: to increase the tuition; to stay with the present situation; or to construct a new facility. Raphael persuaded his fellow Board members to expand the enrollment to 200 as a basis for planning for a new facility and led the move to acquire a site. The developer agreed to make a two-and-one-half-acre parcel available for only $10,000 (which reflected the raw costs) and subsequently agreed to "interest only" payments for two years. The next move was to design a facility and raise enough money to get bank financing.

A local architect whose children used the facility donated his time for the space planning and was hired, on a deferred payment basis, to come up with working drawings and renderings. One of the Board members, an attorney, donated his time to design the financing package with the assistance of another Board member, an economist with one of the nation's leading consulting firms. This high-priced talent effectively put together a $150,000 development package on a volunteer basis.

During the period of September to November 1971, $50,000 was raised through the sale of bonds. Each member of the Board put up $1,000 which amounted to $15,000, about 100 parents provided a total of $12,000, the Reston Home Owners Association purchased $10,000 worth of bonds, and the balance came from "friends of LANK in the community". The terms were set for retirement over periods of 5, 10, 15, and 20 years at rates varying from 5 to 11 percent. In December 1971, the Potomac Bank and Trust Company, a local savings and loan association, was approached for financing. Ground was broken for the new facility in May 1972, and construction was complete in October 1972. While the building construction was professional, parents did all of the painting and outside site work. With the new enrollment of 200 students, tuition covered about 80 percent of the school's operating costs in the first, and probably the most expensive, year. LANK was also rededicated as the Robert E. Simon Early Learning Center.

According to Dorothy Bearman, LANK's dynamic director from its opening in 1965 until early 1973, this was the second nursery school in the United States with both an open space plan and an open education philosophy. In addition to the director, there are normally 12 head teachers, 8 assistant teachers, 4 teachers' aides, and a number of volunteers. In the fall of 1972, two students from Antioch College in Yellow Springs, Ohio, worked on the staff. The tuition costs from $200 to $600 for a nine-month school year; students may attend two, three, or five days a week, depending on their age. Normally 10 scholarships are provided on the basis of need, and interest-free loans are made available to parents requiring this type of support.

The LANK experience is an excellent example of citizens, on their own initiative, successfully solving a problem through "self-help". The significant aspect of this is that the people were interested in solving the problem, they had the talent or skills necessary to effect a workable solution, they made themselves available without charge, and they were able to provide or otherwise obtain the financial resources necessary to make their ideas a reality.

I point this out because the conditions that normally exist in low and moderate income neighborhoods tend to mitigate against self-help efforts. Even where the problems are recognized, it is difficult to get enough interest stimulated in community issues. In addition, the talent required is rarely located within the community, and when it is, I expect that it is difficult to obtain on a nonfee basis. Even if all the other components are brought to bear on a problem, the identification and collection of money pose the toughest of problems.

/ THE RESTON COMMUTER BUS /

The most widely acclaimed volunteer effort in Reston is the Reston commuter bus. About 50 buses each day transport almost 2000 passengers between the New Town and downtown Washington, D.C. There are even two buses that provide express service to National Airport. This effort costs about $400,000 annually and is handled almost exclusively by volunteers. Starting in 1968 with one bus, the system had grown to 51 buses by 1973. The cost is only $1.50 each way when a book of 10 tickets is purchased and $1.75 for a single ticket. Reston's senior citizens ride for only $.25. The overhead expenses for the entire operation amounted to slightly more than $16,000 in fiscal year 1972, which is about 4.1 percent of the total expenses.

Once again the management reflects high-priced community-minded volunteer talent. The president of the Reston commuter bus nonprofit corporation is a television news producer with the American Broadcasting Company. The vice-president is a labor lawyer who was formerly with the National Labor Relations Board. The treasurer is a certified public accountant with one of the "big six" accounting firms, and the secretary is a Lieutenant Commander in the U.S. Navy. And if this is

not enough, the planning officer is with the U.S. Department of Transportation.

RCB president William Knowles says:

What we've done here is develop a concept of express commuter bus service that represents the type of transportation from the suburbs that can work. The country isn't ready for mass rail transit in many of the areas where it is necessary. The RCB concept proves that express town-to-central-business-district service is viable. We hope that someday this will be commonplace throughout the entire country.

The idea man behind the original commuter bus service in 1968 was Karl Ingerbritsen, then chairman of the Reston Community Association's Transportation Committee. Ingerbritsen, one of Reston's most active citizens, feels that energy and pollution problems can be substantially alleviated if people are willing to change some of their wasteful habits. Military service in Korea had given him first-hand contact with thousands of people existing off of America's waste, and he found it "an emotionally upsetting experience to return to the United States to find so many of us carefully drowning in our wealth". The source of the bus idea, says Ingerbritsen, was the DeCamp bus service that ran between suburban New Jersey and downtown New York City in the mid-1940s.

In the summer of 1973, a major breakthrough was achieved when the Dulles access road, which bisects Reston and connects the Capital Beltway to Dulles International Airport, was opened for the use of the commuter buses. This effort involved the developer of Reston—Gulf-Reston, Inc., which paid about $300,000 for the access ramps; the Federal Aviation Administration, which changed its policy of limiting the four-lane divided highway to airport-only traffic; and several other federal, state, and local agencies. Two of the prime movers in minimizing many of the delays that occurred were John E. Hirten, a special assistant to the Secretary of the U.S. Department of Transportation, and Martha Pennino, a member of the Fairfax County Board of Supervisors representing the district in which Reston is located. The personal efforts of elected and appointed officials must not be taken lightly. Such acts not only save money, but more importantly allow for needed services to be delivered in a timely manner.

Rider surveys have indicated that 21 percent of the RCB users have reduced the number of automobiles in their households because of the bus service. The survey also indicates that almost 44 percent of the riders would not have moved to Reston if the bus service did not exist and that only 17.7 percent did not have an automobile available for the trip to work. Of those who use the bus service, about two-thirds work for the federal government, with the balance being employed by the private sector.

In addition to being quicker, cheaper, and less polluting and less energy absorbing than the automobile on a per user basis, the Reston bus is also a social experience. One of the fun things about riding the bus is that there are always new people to meet and always someone who is anxious to debate the issues—a more than frequent passtime in the Washington, D.C. area.

/ THE COMMON GROUND /

The Common Ground is the name of both a coffee shop and a nonprofit foundation that acts as an umbrella agency for a variety of community services. Located in the Lake Anne Village Center, the coffee shop was initiated in early 1969 by the vicar of Reston's Episcopal congregation, Embry Rucker.

The coffee shop is normally open from 8:00 A.M. to 5:00 P.M., and again from 8:00 P.M. to 10:00 P.M., Monday through Friday, and 8:00 A.M. to 5:00 P.M. on Saturdays. Except for one person, it is run entirely by volunteers. These volunteers usually number 70 or 75 people a week. Weekdays most volunteers are women, while during the evenings and on weekends, several men may be found serving food and drink.

Embry Rucker finds that "people are delighted to volunteer to work behind the counter". The one salaried person is the kitchen manager of the Common Ground Coffee House, Mary Alice Glenn, under whose direction the food is prepared.

The Common Ground is where people from all over the New Town can get together. In addition to the coffee house, the Common Ground provides a mini-bus that travels a fixed route through the New Town during the day. The volunteers who drive the bus include people like retired foreign service officer James Grady, who gladly takes a turn

at the wheel once a week. Gas and service are provided free by the local Gulf station. Many of the local merchants have bought advertising space on the exterior of the bus which helps defray cost to the Common Ground Foundation.

Another service sponsored by the Common Ground is the Open Air Market every weekend on the plaza at the Lake Anne Village Center. Artists, craftsmen, photographers, musicians, and merchants exhibit each Saturday, weather permitting, while hundreds of people look over their wares. The most exciting thing about the open air market is that it promotes interaction among the people and makes good use of the exterior space. A similar experience can be found in Rome, Italy, where people shop almost daily for fresh fruit and vegetables in and around plazas or just stand around and talk.

The Common Ground Foundation also runs a child care center, an employment referral service for young people, a sitter referral service, a welcoming service, a counselling referral service, a community center, and a newspaper collection service for recycling purposes.

Embry Rucker, rector of the Episcopal congregation, is the director of the Common Ground Foundation and sees himself principally as an "enabler". Through what the Common Ground is doing, he has closed the gulf that exists between so many churches and their communities. He has made the church part of the community and the community part of the church. When it comes to people, Embry is one of the main individuals they turn to in a time of need. Because of his willingness to listen and the nature of his work, Embry has dealt with many of the "gut" problems that beset people within the New Town. Suicides, alcoholism, nervous breakdowns, teen-age runaways, divorce, separation—many of the things that seem out of character with the form of the New Town—are daily experiences for Embry Rucker. Some people like him, others love him, still others worship him, and a few dislike him—but most respect him. When people need someone and there is no one they can turn to, they call Embry. When teen-agers need a place to crash, they call Embry. When a woman is upset because her husband leaves her, she calls Embry. When the elderly get lonely, they call Embry. When you haven't been to church in a long time and you want someone to marry you or to bury a friend, you ask Embry. This happens because Embry Rucker sees the "congregation as an action, not a roster". And he carries this out by dealing with people and their needs. In his words, "the church is always behind society and we must become a part of the community". His strongest position is on church buildings: "There should never be another church built. . . .we should be in the people business, not the building business." He feels that religious groups that put up buildings bleed off money from the community and reduce pressure for viable facilities that people need such as a large multi-faceted community center.

Rucker feels that it is important for people to do things for themselves and for government. The full significance of what Embry and the Common Ground are about unfolds on Sunday mornings. He stands before several hundred people in the Community Center; a black man plays the piano; a visiting black gospel choir sings; teen-agers, elderly, blacks, whites, the very well-off, and the poor drink from the same cup and break bread from the same loaf. A banner on the wall shows a human figure in stripes of black, yellow, red, and white with a caption reading: "He's your brother. Love Him."

/ RECREATION /

As Reston has grown during the period from 1969 to 1974, few things have been as visible as the involvement of adults and children in a variety of recreational activities such as tennis, swimming, golf, bicycling, boating, horseback riding, and jogging.

Depending on the season, a number of pick-up games take place in ice hockey, football, basketball, and volleyball. Volleyball is somewhat of an exception to the seasonal changes: Each Sunday morning regulars meet—rain, shine, or snow—and play their weekly game.

With respect to organized activities, the Reston Youth Athletic Association, a nonprofit corporation, sponsors seven programs: baseball, football, swimming, basketball, soccer, golf, and girls' football. This association is entirely staffed by volunteers, and in 1973 it sponsored activities for over 3000 youths—with a budget of about $40,000. Soccer seems to be the most popular sport, involving about 750 youths, boys and girls, between the ages of 6 and 16. Parents spend countless hours coaching and carpooling to get their children out for the games, usually held on Sundays during the fall.

Coach Houston Park, after leading his soccer team "The Rascals" to an unbeaten and untied season in 1973, reached into his own

pocket and purchased trophies for all of the "champions" on his team. Although some of the parents have been known to get carried away yelling from the sidelines, an additional benefit from the activity is that people get to meet other people.

In contrast to the Reston experience, in reflecting on my childhood in Harlem, at the age of five I saw a young girl, who was playing in the streets in front of my house, killed by an automobile. During my teens, I became proficient in "stickball", a game unfamiliar to most suburban children, and had also built a scooter from a wooden box, a two-by-four, and a roller skate. The only time I went swimming was during the summer, and then I only learned to wade in the water. My high school wasn't able to support a football team, in terms of either space or money. Living in Reston, both of our children, Scott and Kimberly, have learned to swim, and both have played soccer, my son earning one of the trophies from Houston Park's team.

What is most remarkable about the recreation program in Reston is that the parents take the initiative to organize, supervise, and coach. Very few people talk about the positive aspects of children's getting together and competing against each other at an early age. This

process is one of many that help to build and mold a strong community spirit. Individually, sports can give a person a greater appreciation for his body and mind, and eventually the spirit that holds the two together.

/ CULTURAL AND PERFORMING ARTS /

Reston has attracted hundreds of architects, urban planners, photographers, potters, weavers, artists, craftsmen, dancers, and performers; yet in 10 years, the New Town has not yet become an environment in which the arts can truly be said to flourish. Part of this may be attributable to not being able to "compete" with the culturally rich nation's capital, which is home for the John F. Kennedy Center for the Performing Arts, the Arena Stage, the Wolf Trap Farm Park for the Performing Arts, and a whole host of art galleries and museums. Other factors that may be responsible for the cultural limbo in Reston are the lack of organization among the few groups that exist and the lack of a facility in which theatrical and similar performances can take place.

Of the less than 10 formal cultural groups that exist, one of the most active is the Reston Players. One of the earliest groups to form, the Players were organized when Reston had less than 500 families. They had to raise about $5000 for their first performance and managed to sell

2000 tickets through the efforts of some 400 families who invited ticket holders to dinner as an incentive to come to Reston and attend the performance. The original developer, Robert Simon, felt that theatrical groups should start up in each village.

The Reston Players usually give six performances a year in almost as many different places within the New Town. "A Sleep of Prisoners" was performed in the Baptist church. In the fall of 1973, "Coriolanus" was put on outdoors at the Hunters Woods Village Center in what is normally a skating rink in the winter and a wading pool in the summer. The versatile players have also performed on a makeshift stage in an open field and in the Lake Anne Community Center where the audience can see the actors and actresses change offstage.

The Reston Performing Arts Workshop is sponsored by the Reston Home Owners Association and gives about two performances a year. In 1973, they put on the "Mikado" with children and "Save the People" mainly with teen-agers.

The Reston Chorale includes about 50 people who are interested in classical singing. They normally put on four or five performances each year.

Each spring there is an annual celebration of the New Town's birthday. This "Founder's Day" festival usually attracts speakers, performers, craftsmen, and artists from the greater Washington area. The festival weekend is one of the most exciting of the year, and in the evenings there are usually dances on the plaza at the Lake Anne Village Center and private parties.

Since 1969, Reston has had a Black Arts Festival each fall which has provided the New Town with culturally rich experiences based on the heritage of many of the New Town's residents who descend from Africa. Having lived in the New Town during the period of each Black Arts Festival, I have observed some changes in its direction over the years. When the festival was first put on in 1969, I expect that there was a desire to make a constructive, yet definitive, statement about being in the New Town that was, at the time, about 96 percent white.

There was a fashion show, a dance, some exhibits of African art, and wide participation from blacks and whites within Reston. The festival really didn't draw until the second or third year. As the festival began to grow each year, more people, especially blacks, came from Washington, D.C., and the statement changed from what I feel was one of harmony and concern to one of arrogance, charity, anxiety, and apology for living in the white man's world. The whites have, over the years, become both less involved in the actual workings of the festival

and visibly absent from the audience. The attitude has shifted from active acceptance to passive tolerance.

During the day while the festival is in progress, many of the participants can be seen in colorful African dress. African dance troupes perform to the beat of the bongo drums. Bean pies are sold from Washington's Shabazz Bakery. Others make available a variety of tasty dishes that come under the general heading of "soul food". A variety of exhibits on black history and achievement is displayed, and prominent writers and lecturers are invited to speak and share their views. Many of the local churches invite black ministers to perform services during the weekend of the Black Arts Festival.

During the last several years, the Black Arts Festival has contributed its proceeds to the Howard University Mississippi Project and to AFRICARE, an organization that assisted the drought-ridden countries in Africa.

/ ELEMENTARY EDUCATION /

Reston has four elementary schools, the oldest of which is Lake Anne with an enrollment of almost 600 children.

I discussed education at the elementary school level with Mrs. Marge Thompson who has been principal of the Lake Anne Elementary School for over four years. This discussion centered around parental involvement, children's knowledge of the parents' roles, the impact of separation and divorce, children's values, awareness of the New Town experience, race, the principal's role, foreign students, planning, and preschool.

The parents of Reston, according to Mrs. Thompson, "are willing to spend time in the school, and we have access to their rich backgrounds". Many of the parents act as teachers aides on a volunteer basis and serve as resources to help the teaching teams. The school maintains a file on the skills and experiences of parents who can be called upon to participate when needed.

In discussions with children about what their parents did, she found that they were able to give labels such as "doctor", "lawyer", etc., but had little working knowledge about what their parents actually did. According to the principal, Lake Anne children, ages 5 through 12:

> . . .value time, that is freedom. . .time to pursue what they want to do. They tend to value money and what it will buy. They tend to question honesty and truth. Many of our children, however, have what might be called a pretty traditional set of values. That is, honesty is honesty, and truth is truth—it is always truth and it is always honesty. They always know what to do in a given setting. Others either

reflect the ambivalence of the value system of the home, or their parents are allowing them to develop their own value system.

Within the social studies area, the school has developed a program on "The Making of a Restonian". This program is designed to give the students an awareness and appreciation of the unique experience of living in a New Town. The program deals with community resources, responsibility to neighbors, leadership, conservation, and the like. Some of the students who have moved to Reston from other parts of the country have made statements such as "I really didn't know about how important it was for me to conserve a bush or a tree", or "I really didn't realize that what I throw down as paper is my responsibility", or "I didn't know that there might be a place in which I could live my entire life out if I wished to and have plenty of things to keep me going."

Of the nearly 600 children in Lake Anne Elementary School, Mrs. Thompson estimates that between 10 and 12 percent are black. She points out that there are some racial problems such as name calling.

> You have a certain amount of unwillingness to bring feelings out on the part of white children. For example, they think that somehow it will be better if we don't talk about that kind of thing.

Racial problems are normally dealt with on an individual, case-by-case basis unless they occur in front of the entire classroom. On the issue of racial balance, Mrs. Thompson emphasizes the importance of housing:

> It seems to me that the New Town that offers low income housing, middle income housing, upper income housing. . . many different alternatives for housing, may be the real key.

Mrs. Thompson sees her major responsibility as—

> . . .creating an environment in which all children are accepted and are made to feel comfortable, regardless of their race, religion, or whatever."

and she places emphasis on learning rather than on teaching per se.

During her four years as principal, Mrs. Thompson has encountered about 10 foreign students who did not speak English. To assist them in learning English, the school located students at the high school level who were fluent in the language or who were natives of the country of the child needing help.

Marge Thompson feels that educators who are going to teach in New Towns ought to be an integral part of the planning process. She would like to see planning for education given at least the consideration that planning for open space, recreation, and other areas is given.

As a result of the Lake Anne Nursery and Kindergarten and other preschools, a considerable number of enrollees into the Lake Anne Elementary School, which some young children call "the big school," have already been introduced to the formal learning experience. Because of this, the programs at the elementary school for the five- and six-year-olds are much more accelerated than in other schools in the county. Mrs. Thompson attributes this to the quality of the preschool education in the New Town.

My wife has spent two years teaching in the Lake Anne Elementary School, was president of the Co-op Nursery School, and was also on the Board of Directors of the Reston Children's Center. She feels that the pressure from parents was considerable because they wanted the best for their children and pushed for innovative techniques. She also notes that the regular Parent Teacher Association meetings have been replaced with a "mini-concept" whereby the parents and teachers meet in small groups so that they can plan topics that are relevant to the needs of the children. In addition, she has been a member of the Fairfax County Human Relations staff for two years and was engaged in their efforts to "humanize the entire county school system".

/ THE SOCIAL MALAISE /

In its attempt to depart from the banality of life, Reston like other communities throughout the country has had its problems. While such problems as drugs, burglaries, divorce, and even homicide may not seem out of place in most communities, they do, in fact, receive an inordinate amount of attention in this New Town. It would be incorrect, however, for anyone to draw conclusions about these problem areas without hard statistics which are not presently forthcoming; nevertheless, it is important that we recognize that the problems do exist and that New Towns are by no means utopian.

The most publicized case of criminal activity in Reston's 10-year history was the murder of a 17-year-old girl which occurred on June 4, 1972. The victim, Gwen Ames, was the daughter of one of the community's most prominent families. Her family had moved to the New

Town in August 1965 when the population was less than 200. Her father worked with the developer, and her mother became active in community affairs. The murder took place during the weekend of the annual spring festival. In contrast to the gaiety that had surrounded the weekend, this tragic event served as a sobering reminder of man's inhumanity to man.

The murder of Gwen Ames was initially thought to have been drug related because of the teen-ager's previous experience. This was subsequently disproven. In the following week, the grief-stricken parents found themselves the recipients of hundreds of letters from people they didn't even know. One such person wrote from her hospital bed after giving birth to her third child: "We don't know your family or Gwen, but she is very real to us and her death has taught us a great deal; I hope knowing this might relieve some of the grief you feel in losing a child, especially such a brave one as Gwen." The funeral drew over 500 people. In elegizing his only child, Ardee Ames said of his daughter: ". . . .at this time last year she was deep in drugs and she had pulled herself out. We saw her getting better and these last few months have just been an absolute joy to her mother and me in terms of the progress she was making. And that's what makes it especially painful. . . . To all of the young people here today, and you are the hope of the future, I just ask you to think of Gwen from time to time, and help her death add a little more meaning and purpose to your own lives."

Following their daughter's death, the Ames had considered moving but decided to remain in Reston. This decision was affected, in part, by the manner in which many members of the community had responded following their tragic experience. In reflecting on this about a year later, Ardee said, "What the community did for us from the moment and to this day was unbelievable." As a reminder of the tragic event, a yellow poster hangs in a glass booth advertising a reward of $2500 for information leading to the arrest of Gwen Ames' murderer—who remains at large.

In 1971, a 14-year-old Reston resident died of a reported drug overdose while in Florida. The trauma resulting from the funeral held in Reston spread throughout the community. The minister presiding at the funeral of the teen-age girl said he couldn't accept this. During the same year, a major drug-related arrest involving over three dozen people occurred in Reston. These and perhaps a few other incidents began to give visibility to drugs as a serious problem in this New Town. The plaza area at the Lake Anne Village Center was, according to a long-time Reston resident, the only place in Northern Virginia where teen-agers could gather without being bothered by police or local merchants. It was the plaza where drugs were reportedly passed around right in the open.

The person who was then director of the Community Center, which was located on the plaza, said of the 1971 era: "I would sit in this office and see kids out at the coffee house table bringing the dope out. It would consist of pills, mainly pills." The 1972 period was one of increased police activity which appeared to result in a decrease of drug-related offenses. Statistically, data on drug offenses are not broken down by area within the county; consequently, it is difficult to determine how Reston measures up against the county and the metropolitan area.

Divorce is another one of those difficult-to-assess social maladies that has considerable visibility in Reston. In the early 1970s, two former ministers discontinued their religious duties on a full-time basis and became counsellors. One such former minister, Palmer Hartl, says, "I think there is something about this place that magnifies personal problems because it puts a burden on the family as a primary unit." Because of its outwardly appearing utopian character, some suggest that Reston attracts people with problems who somehow feel that the solution to such problems lies within the community instead of within themselves. A factor that may give increased visibility to divorce is the existence of nonsexist leasing and mortgage practices in the New Town. Unlike many communities, a woman—single, widowed, divorced or whatever—can rent or purchase a home on the strength of her own income. Consequently, women who find themselves divorced do not have to leave the community.

The experience of one couple follows to show the effect that Reston had on their relationship. Mr. and Mrs. Jones (aliases) moved to Reston from a conservative Midwestern suburb in 1971. Mrs. Jones didn't realize until after she had lived in Reston for almost a year how much she had adapted to the conservative environment of her former neighborhood. When the Joneses moved to Reston, they wanted to avoid bringing up their four children in a "gilded ghetto" and deliberately sought this place out because of the advertised social and economic diversity. Their family income was about $60,000 a year; the husband was a corporate executive with an advanced degree, and the wife had completed three years of college. Mrs. Jones, in her early thirties, feels that she has always been more liberal than her husband:

> With him being very active and successful in the business community, the differences between us didn't so much surface as intensify after living in Reston. He became more conservative and I became more radical. As our income went up, his political thinking, his areas of involvement, and the types of contributions he made changed. He stopped giving

money to **Biafra** and the **NAACP** Legal Defense Fund and started giving money to Harvard and establishment organizations.

Three years after moving to Reston, the Joneses separated.

I feel that living here had a lot to do with my getting separated, although my husband would say it was mainly the feminist movement. Living in a town where it is possible to live in accordance with the things that I believe in and not having to concern myself with fitting into a closed environment, the growth that might have taken place in about 15 years took place in just a couple of years. This is a very rich environment for me. It has enabled me to find out what interests me and what matters to me. In our case, I found out that what interests me and what matters to me is extraordinarily different from what matters to my husband.

Mrs. Jones feels that Reston is wide open in terms of developing personal talents:

I discovered that all of those organizational skills that made me hot stuff with the PTA made me hot stuff in other areas. I began to find a great deal of pleasure in all of the things that I could do outside the home. My husband, who had always encouraged me to express myself when there wasn't any outlet for it, became quite threatened because he felt that because I was finding myself I would leave. I think he felt that by keeping me in a dependent position where all my joys came through the family and in the home, he would keep me there indefinitely. Reston is wonderful. If you want to go out and do something and you are willing to start small, you can do pretty much what you damn please.

After Mrs. Jones became separated, she noticed a drop in the usual invitations that were extended for dinner parties and surmised that her girlfriends' husbands became threatened because they felt their wives might become envious of her freedom.

/ GOVERNANCE /

In *Politics*, Greek philosopher Aristotle draws several distinctions between citizens and slaves. One such distinction implies that citizens are those who can participate in government whereas slaves cannot. The real strength of Reston, insofar as staying power is concerned, is the participation of the citizens in the process of government.

Reston is not an incorporated city and does not have self-government. Reston comes under the jurisdiction of the Fairfax County, Virginia, government and is represented on the nine-member Board of Supervisors by the supervisor from Centreville District of which it is a part. Within the boundaries of Reston, which is technically a 7400-acre "residential planned community", there are a number of associations, councils, and organizations that play a part in the day-to-day management and in decision-making affairs of the New Town. These consist of the Reston Home Owners Association; the Reston Community Association; the three Village Councils representing Lake Anne, Hunters Woods, and Tall Oaks; and some cluster associations, which presently number 31 and are still increasing.

Fairfax County was created in 1742 and presently has an area of 406 square miles, with a 1973 population in excess of 560,000. Between 1960 and 1970, the county population grew by more than 74 percent, compared to about 13 percent for the nation and about 39 percent for the Washington metropolitan area during the same period. The rapid rate of growth in Fairfax County has been a major factor affecting the development of the New Town and has been the cause of numerous confrontations between the developer and the Board of Supervisors and other governmental jurisdictions.

From my observations, only a few of the Board members seem to fully understand and appreciate the New Town concept. However, the Centreville supervisor, Martha Pennino, has been particularly supportive of Reston and has exercised extremely effective leadership on numerous occasions.

In April 1973, a management study financed by Gulf-Reston, Inc., indicated that Reston contributed a surplus of $1.5 million in revenues over expenditures to Fairfax County for fiscal year 1972. In 1982, when the New Town is completed, this surplus will exceed $16 million. A graph showing the relationship between expenditures and revenues during fiscal year 1972 through fiscal year 1982 is shown on the next page. [44]

Decision makers at the county and state levels have not kept pace with the development of Reston. There are serious deficiencies in the provision of schools, social services, community facilities, water and sewer facilities, and road construction. By comparison, the New Town of Columbia, Maryland, is ahead in many of these areas. It is particularly significant that Reston, under the present form of government, will never

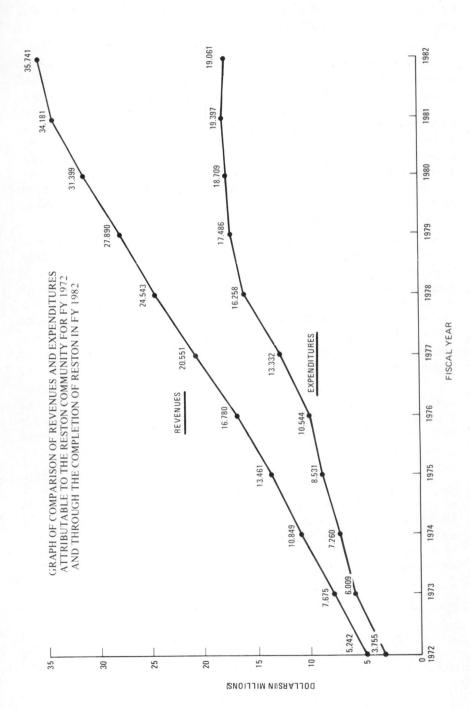

GRAPH OF COMPARISON OF REVENUES AND EXPENDITURES
ATTRIBUTABLE TO THE RESTON COMMUNITY FOR FY 1972
AND THROUGH THE COMPLETION OF RESTON IN FY 1982

REVENUES

EXPENDITURES

FISCAL YEAR

DOLLARS(IN MILLIONS)

be a controlling force in the county. The 1973 population is only about 3 percent of the county, and even when Reston is completed in 1982, it will probably represent less than 10 percent of the total county population.

Within Reston is the Reston Home Owners Association, "a nonprofit corporation created to operate and maintain parks, parking areas, open spaces, paths, and other facilities". "RHOA", as it is more popularly called, is governed by a nine-member board, of which three members are elected residents and the remaining six are developer-appointed. Each home owner is assessed $60 annually in dues. The developer also pays a comparable assessment for each apartment unit and recorded lot. As the percentage of privately owned units increases in relation to developer-owned ones, the three-to-six ratio is expected to shift accordingly.

The Reston Community Association is an independent organization, organized in 1967 to "promote Reston's growth as a New Town within the framework of county government, and to help foster a community spirit."[45] RCA has no formal staff and is an all-volunteer association. It has operated on an ad hoc issue-oriented, crisis basis since its inception and has been a watchdog, advisor, agitator, and advocate in its dealings with the developer, the county, and its citizens. Unlike some associations of its kind, RCA has been astute enough to address the problems of development both within and around the New Town. One of its most active members is a 37-year-old physicist, Dr. John Dockery, who sees RCA's purpose as "keeping the spirit of the Master Plan operative". Dockery, chairman of the RCA zoning committee, feels that the "organization may be defunct because it is falling below critical mass". During the period of 1968 to 1973, RCA had either taken the lead in or been a party to efforts expended to ensure the provision of housing for low and moderate income families, to effect integrated advertising, and to question the location and/or construction of four different high rise complexes and other initiatives that have affected the growth of the New Town.

Each of the three existing villages in Reston has a council governed by elected officers. One of the most active councils is the one representing Hunters Woods. The Hunters Woods Council is further broken down into 14 area and 150 block representatives. In the past, elected members of the various councils have acted in an advisory capacity to the Reston Home Owners Association, but this relationship has changed and the Councils are now acting more autonomously.

The third level of "government" within the New Town, and perhaps the most active, is that of the cluster association. As of 1975 there were some 33 clusters in Reston and by the time the New Town is completed, there will be more than 50 of these associations. The cluster associations have elected representatives who govern, publish newsletters periodically, hold meetings, and raise funds by assessing home owners anywhere from $100 to $220 a year in dues. The thrust of the cluster associations is toward the maintenance of the common areas, the enforcement of covenants, and those issues that are peculiar to each area represented. Some of the cluster associations have used their funds to build additional tot lots, construct overhead lights along walkways, repair faulty construction of common parking areas, assign curb parking spaces to residents, put up "private property" types of signs, and the like. One resident of five years devoted a considerable amount of her time to the study of cluster life in a New Town and also exercised some very effective leadership in bringing the clusters together to discuss and share common experiences. From her experience and studies, Rita Berman feels that—

> The developer has an inherent responsibility to ensure that buyers of townhouses understand that they are buying into a concept and not merely purchasing a row house with a small piece of land.

The "concept" is essentially an entirely different life style that requires a high degree of participation in management and decision making relating to a variety of maintenance, social, and recreational activities within each area defined as a cluster.

In looking at the number of organizations that are involved with the internal affairs of Reston and, to a large extent, with those matters that affect the development around Reston, the question must be raised as to whether or not these organizations are structured to operate effectively. It seems to me that there may be too much activity at the cluster level and not enough at the RHOA level. It also seems that with RHOA, RCA, the village councils, and the cluster associations existing as they do, much of what needs to be done in providing social and cultural services falls through the cracks. The activities of RHOA appear to reflect a narrowly construed interpretation of their charter to deal principally with the maintenance of the common lands and the provision and maintenance of recreational facilities. Little, if any, emphasis is given to those areas that cover the broad reach of social services, such as teen centers and related programs, the provision of day care for toddlers, counselling, and other services that address the health and general well-being of the residents. There are also the larger questions of how representative RHOA is of those who do not own homes and whether the organization is the appropriate vehicle to represent the collective interests of the citizens. In speaking on the area of tenant representation, RHOA Executive Director Thomas Burgess says:

> . . .they feel an exclusion or a coldness, of being left out. Whether it is there by intent or not, they feel that RHOA is a distant institution which really does not provide anything for them.

On getting into the broader area of dealing with social problems, Burgess says RHOA "doesn't have the will; we don't have the policy that says we are going to get involved".

RHOA has, however, from time to time supported such groups as the Common Ground that are more active in this area. The efforts that are necessary in the area of social programs test the very foundation of the New Town's movement and cannot simply be left to the whim of loosely structured or narrowly functioning organizations. This is an area of weakness that must be corrected within the structure of a permanent citizen-controlled body.

In Reston, as well as in other communities throughout the nation, citizens have come to realize that they have an immense "negative power", which means that they can often delay and sometimes stop projects. By the same token, citizens can also accelerate the process of decision making. Underlying the development of Reston, and a growing trend nationally in New Towns, is the participation of citizens in the decision making process.

/ HOUSING AND DEVELOPMENT /

The development of Reston has brought many successes, the most noteworthy of which is the provision of a broad range of housing and community facilities. Of particular significance is the housing provided for low and moderate income families which includes the elderly. In spite of success in this area, the developer has had to wrestle with citizen groups from time to time over the issue of building high rises and with the county government on the growth issue. If there is an obstacle to be reckoned with, it is that of controlling growth in the county and the way in which the county government chooses to deal with Reston's development in this context.

/ HOUSING /

The socio-economic profile of any New Town will be largely influenced by the housing opportunities that exist. Reston's developers have sought to

Table 1

ESTIMATED RESIDENTIAL UNITS TO BE CONSTRUCTED
IN THE DEVELOPMENT OF RESTON
New Residential Units Occupied as of January 1 of Each Year*

fiscal year	single-family	garden court	townhouse	garden apartment	high rise apartment	cumulative total	new total
Through
1968	416	0	358	330	61	1,165	1,165
1969	87	0	81	64	0	1,397	232
1970	217	0	188	363	0	2,165	768
1971	260	2	246	476	69	3,218	1,053
1972	208	38	387	836	69	4,756	1,538
1973	137	65	599	1,144	100	6,801	2,045
1974	148	70	708	658	282	8,667	1,866
1975	266	97	685	363	308	10,386	1,719
1976	280	158	604	655	500	12,583	2,197
1977	225	200	461	922	960	15,351	2,768
1978	250	200	388	791	870	17,850	2,499
1979	225	215	400	619	700	20,009	2,159
1980	135	143	325	934	715	22,261	2,252
1981	35	27	125	946	750	24,144	1,883
1982	0	0	0	300	450	24,894	750
TOTAL	2,889	1,215	5,555	9,401	5,834		24,894

*Average estimates were used when a range of future projections had been made.

provide a broad range of opportunities and, through a variety of schemes, have enabled a good proportion of moderate income families to enjoy the benefits of New Town living. In 1973, the developers issued a report that contained the estimated residential units to be constructed in the development of the New Town. Table 1 indicates these units from those completed through 1968 to the development completion date of 1982. To appreciate the results achieved to date with respect to housing assisted by the federal government in Reston, the posture of the county must be brought into perspective.

According to Gene Schneider, acting director of the Fairfax County Housing Authority, as of early 1974, Fairfax County had about 3600 assisted units, of which 20 percent are located in Reston. This disproportion is indicative of the resistance that developers and county officials are subjected to when trying to provide increased opportunities for moderate income families throughout the county.

In 1971 the Board of Supervisors favorably considered an ordinance to establish a 15 percent "set aside" for housing low and moderate income families in planned developments throughout the county. This initiative was subsequently struck down by the courts. Schneider says the resistance is based on both race and class. Further, he describes the intensity of resistance as least for the elderly, moderate for constructed rent supplement units, and strong for constructed public housing and moderate income ownership units, the latter two of which do not exist in the county.

It is easy to debate the issue of providing housing for the poor in the abstract. It is another matter entirely to debate this issue in an emotionally charged hearing room or to discuss it with a group of suburbanites who candidly admit that "we moved out here to get away from those people" or "they will crowd the schools. . . ."

Within Reston, there has been virtually no resistance because most of the people who move in "know what they are getting into", according to the manager of one of the real estate offices. In point of fact, Shirly Chambers, resident manager of the 198-unit Cedar-Ridge complex, the first federally assisted housing to be built in Reston, admits that there is some friction among some of the residents. This friction appears to be between those who are upwardly mobile—that is, those who are residing in Cedar-Ridge temporarily and who will soon move on to being home owners or into market rate rental units—and those who are relatively fixed in their economic position and who, as a result, will remain indefinitely. Chambers describes the typical resident of Cedar-Ridge as being "in his late twenties, married, and with three children", and notes that there are practically no vacancies with only a

few units opening up each month, except for June. After Cedar-Ridge, most residents seek ownership either in Reston or elsewhere in the county. The complex is about 30 percent black, almost triple the percentage of the black population of the New Town in its entirety.

After her experience with the Cedar-Ridge complex, Chambers does not support the idea of concentrated housing for low and moderate income families, and advocates dispersed housing throughout the community, preferably through assistance provided by rent supplements.

A bonus for those who reside in government-assisted housing in Reston is that they can enjoy most of the services provided for the residents who live in market rate rental and purchase units. As of 1973, the developer had provided nearly a million dollars in cash contributions and rent subsidies toward numerous community facilities and organizations which include the following:

Marina	$ 20,800
Community Center	$ 30,000
Nature Center	$ 75,000
Music Center	$182,000
Community Preschools	$ 42,000
Day Care Center	$ 46,000

Lake Anne Hall	$141,000
Reston Foundation	$ 75,000
Transportation Study	$ 15,000
Georgetown Community	
Health Program	$ 79,000
South Golf Course	$150,000

The extent to which these and other services affect the residents is best brought out by the low eviction rate and the number of apartment dwellers who subsequently buy homes in the New Town. Bill Johnson, property manager for Gulf-Reston, Inc., points out:

> Our eviction rate throughout all of Reston is less than one percent, and the vacancy rate is only about five percent. About 45 percent of the people who live in apartments eventually end up buying homes in Reston. The people literally use the apartments as a 'look see' into the whole community. More services are extended to apartment dwellers in Reston than anywhere else. . .and in some respects, the people get spoiled.

/ ON HIGH RISE BUILDINGS /

The construction of high rise buildings for residential use has become a subject of increasing debate in Reston. On January 3, 1974, the Reston Community Association (RCA) held a public meeting to hear a presentation from a developer of a proposed high rise complex of four 14-story buildings of 170 units each on a 22-acre site near the Hunters Woods Village Center. In attendance were about 45 people, including the RCA's Board of Directors. The reception accorded the developer was, at best, hostile, and one member of the audience drew an enthusiastic "here. . . here" when he shouted to the developer: "You people are upping the density and creating an irreversible process." The chairman of the RCA Planning and Zoning Committee seemed to be carrying his own torch against the proposed complex, and his comments did not allow for a substantive debate in an atmosphere of rationality. The expressed concerns regarding the proposal were that the resulting density would be higher than calculated; the complex would subject the existing amenities, described as marginal, to an additional load; the crowding in schools would be increased; and the access from the high rise complex to the Village Center would require crossing a street (Glade Drive) that does not have a pedestrian underpass or overpass.

The Hunters Woods high rise proposal is only one of a series of

projects under scrutiny in Reston. Three of these projects are in the Village of Lake Anne: a proposed high rise of 150 residential units is in court; another complex of three towers representing 620 units is awaiting acceptance of its development plan by the county Board of Supervisors; and another two buildings representing 276 units await county approval of land use design. In addition, two high rise buildings for the elderly—one of 200 units in the Tall Oaks Village Center and the other of 224 units in the Hunters Woods Village Center—are in process. These latter two have not been the subject of controversy within the community but have been snafued by federal and county government difficulties.

The issue of building high rises both within and outside New Towns has long been the subject of debate and concern of city planners, architects, sociologists, civic activists, and the like. In 1922, the late French architect Le Corbusier, in his *Plan for a Contemporary City*, envisioned a city of three million inhabitants living in vertical communes of 1500-2000 residents each. Corbusier, or more familiarly, "Corbu", has exerted a major influence in the architecture and planning of many European developments, especially in France, Germany, and Sweden. Corbu's arguments for the high rise dwelling units were that they saved costly urban land, gave everybody a favorable orientation, enabled all of the residents to benefit from the grouping of common services, and promoted the use of open space. Corbu viewed sun, space, and vegetation as key components to town planning. He felt these components satisfied man's natural needs and that they were being denied by modern life. Perhaps most representative of Corbu's thinking is his Unit of Habitation in Marseille. Known also as the "Marseille Block", the high rise residential unit included a roof-top swimming pool and elevated play areas for children. Within his concepts of the Vertical City, Corbu advocated high-level interior streets with a wide range of common services such as kindergartens, gymnasiums, shops, and theatres.

Le Corbusier's philosophical counterpart is Greek city planner Constantinos A. Doxiadis, who decries the construction of high rise buildings as "the gravest" of architectural crimes. According to him:

> Such buildings work against Nature by spoiling the scale of the landscape. The most successful cities of the past have been the ones where man and his constructions were in certain balance with nature (ancient Athens, Florence, etc.).
>
> The high rise buildings work against Man himself, especially against children who lose their direct contact with Nature. Even in cases where the contact is maintained it is subject to parental control. As a result, the children suffer and so do the parents;
>
> These buildings work against Society because they do not help the units of social importance—the family, the extended family, the neighborhood, etc.—to function as naturally and normally as before;
>
> The high rise building works against Networks since they increase the density, overload the roads, make servicing with water more difficult and expensive and, what is more important, create vertical Networks;
>
> The conclusion is that high rise buildings work against all other four elements of human settlements and this is true also from the economic point of view (the city is overloaded with people and costs), from the social and political points of view (the few—the owners of this land—benefit against the interests of the many), and from the technological and cultural-aesthetic points of view. [46]

The issues centering around the development of high rises are quite subjective and cannot readily be argued in terms of Aristotelian dichotomous logic. However, there is merit, considering high rise development within the context of New Towns and the realities of urbanization.

The density of Reston is about 11 people per acre overall, with high rise units permitting up to 60 people per net acre. The "Garden City" advocates who essentially gave rise to the modern New Town movement suggested a gross density of about 13 people per acre. The New Towns of England, for the most part, have gross densities in the order of 10 and 15 people per acre. The New Towns in Sweden, Finland, and France boast substantially higher densities, with Tapiola, Finland, registering about 25 people per acre. In addition to having increased densities, the Swedish New Towns are about 90 percent multi-family units. For example, Vallingby, a New Town in the Stockholm area, is 92 percent multi-family, with 8 percent of the units being single-family detached. Overall, 10 percent of Vallingby's residents live in the single-family units, 70 percent live in low-rise multi-family units, and the remaining 20 percent live in high rises.

On the issue of height per se, it is difficult to draw firm conclusions with regard to behavioral implications. The assertions by Doxiadis might gain some philosophical support from many of the "Garden City" advocates. The late architect Frank Lloyd Wright wrote:

> The skyscraper of today is only the prostitute semblance of the architecture it professes to be. The heavy brick and stone that falsely represents walls is, by the very setback laws, unnaturally forced onto the interior steel stilts to be carried down by them through twenty, fifty, or more stories to the ground. The picture is improved, but the picturesque element in it all is false work built over a hollow box. These new tops are shams, too—box balloons. The usual service of the doctor-of-appearances has here again been rendered to modern society.[47]

A report on "Social Insights to Guide the Design of Housing for Low Income Families", presented at the National Housing Policy Forum of the National Association of Housing and Redevelopment Officials in Washington, D.C., in February 1967 by Dr. William Michelson, stated that "it is generally agreed that upper floors of high rise apartments are no place for families with children".[48]

Dr. Stanislav V. Kasl of Yale University noted in a report on "Effects of Residential Environment on Health and Behavior" that a study undertaken in Germany showed that there were more neurotic complaints from women and children living in flats. (This can be interpreted as apartments, as opposed to single-family dwellings.)[49]

Because of the scattering of experiments and limited research with respect to behavioral implications peculiar to height, it is almost impossible to establish a firm cause-and-effect relationship on the consequences of high rise living.

In addition to height per se, the factors of density, space, location, services provided, noise, color schemes, comfort, vegetation (plants), and light, as well as the individual human characteristics of income, age, education, and cultural background, must be effectively weighed in determining the actual relationship between man and his immediate residential environment.

Density per se must not become the sole determinant in making decisions on high rises, and caution must be exercised in attempting to transfer living experiences from one city to the next, much less between countries. What is perhaps most significant is to consider the quality of life provided for residents resulting from the built environment and the delivery of services. In the case of Reston, high rise residential units must be considered as a valid quid pro quo for the open space provided throughout the New Town, without which the development would not be economically feasible.

/ FELLOWSHIP HOUSE /

Fellowship House is a federally assisted high rise that houses about 160 senior citizens in the New Town of Reston. The complex, which opened in May 1971, is located within a few minutes walking time of the Lake Anne Village Center and is under the direction of its founder, Dr. Scherzer. Scherzer is a retired Lutheran minister with over 40 years in the ministry behind him.

Residents, who have to be at least 62 years of age with an income below $5,600 a year, or $7,200 a couple, come from throughout the United States. About 95 percent have families within the area, and being near their children is the principal motivation for their wanting to live in Fellowship House. According to Dr. Scherzer:

> It never works out for the parents to live with the children because the life styles are so different. I think it is helpful and supportive for them to live with their own peers—I know it doesn't make sense sociologically, but the old people can't cope with tension or competition. They just can't keep up with the active life of younger people. They support each other magnificently.

Regular newsletters are provided to all tenants to keep them advised on how to deal with emergencies. The experiences that have been gained to date have provided the residents with an atmosphere of security because of their success in dealing with various crises that have arisen.

Recreational activities are coordinated by the Fellowship Reston Senior Citizens Club. These activities include bus excursions and trips to concerts and plays. Each Thursday the county library bookmobile stops by Fellowship House for about an hour.

Some of the residents work as volunteers, others work as teachers aides, and some work in the shops around the plaza in the Lake Anne Village Center. A great number are employed by the Common Ground Sitter Referral Service.

Ethnic groups, other than whites, have ranged from 10 to about 30 percent since the opening. One black couple from Washington, D.C., after signing up to move, changed their minds because they didn't want to leave their church and friends.

By the end of 1972, the number of turnovers amounted to only 24, most of which were for medical reasons. Fellowship House has been virtually 100 percent occupied since its opening and has almost 1000 inquiries a year for space. Dr. Scherzer indicated that he has never had to ask anyone to pay their rent and has not had to spend one dollar on vandalism.

In spite of the fact that there is a high demand for Fellowship House and that there is good management internally, HUD cut the original proposal for 240 units back to 140 units because they felt the total number of units could not be marketed successfully.

The German-born Scherzer came to the United States in 1920 and was inspired to plan the Fellowship project because of the negative treatment he felt the elderly were often subject to. He says, "I want to be with people—I want to help people in some small way." In dealing with the elderly, Scherzer feels that management must value and respect human beings for what they are, that they must love human beings, and that they must play the role of the enabler rather than that of the manager.

The next housing facilities for the elderly will be incorporated within the Village Centers of Tall Oaks and Hunters Woods. This follows a practice that exists in many of the European New Towns such as Skarholmen, Sweden.

While many of the residents whom I have talked with say that they like the experience of living in Fellowship House, I interpret this to mean that they like the convenience more than anything else. The concentration and isolation of the elderly may not be the best alternative.

It might be better if we could absorb all of the elderly into the housing throughout the New Town.

/ THE GROWTH ISSUE /

On December 30, 1970, the Congress of the United States enacted the Urban Growth and New Community Development Act. In so doing, it recognized new communities as "an alternative to disorderly urban growth". Although Reston is not a federally assisted New Town under the legislation, its development, perhaps more than any other New Town's, represents the spirit of the Urban Growth and New Community Development Act. Ironically, almost since the passage of the Act, the New Town of Reston has been caught up in the politics and dynamic forces of the growth issue. During the period from 1960 to 1970, the nation as a whole grew by 13.3 percent. During the same period, the Washington, D.C.-Maryland-Virginia standard metropolitan statistical area grew by 37.8 percent. Fairfax County during this period grew by a phenomenal 74.1 percent, making it one of the fastest-growing counties in the entire country.

During the fall elections in 1970, the issue of growth was a major subject of debate for those seeking office as members of the county's Board of Supervisors. Several candidates were elected apparently because of their advocating a policy of "no-growth". By the fall of 1972, the growth-conscious Board of Supervisors determined that the capacity of the sewage treatment facilities had been reached in view of the number of taps outstanding (reportedly many builders anticipated the restrictions and purchased enough taps for over 10,000 units throughout the county). This action by the Board precluded the construction of further building without a sewer tap but not the re-zoning of land. The normal process within the county involves the following steps: zoning approval, preliminary subdivision plan approval, site plan approval, purchase of sewer tap, purchase and issuance of building permit. The county, in effect, used the sewer taps as a means to deal with growth in the absence of any other "time sensitive" controls. During the previous April the County Attorney had indicated that there were essentially three options: to effect a moratorium until new plans were drawn to deal with zoning and site planning, to use environmental impact statements, or to make development contingent on the provision of adequate public facilities.

The effect of the growth pressure on the costs of housing in the county was dramatic. The median cost for a house increased from $18,700 in 1960 to $35,400 by 1970 and to $52,500 in June 1974. The vacancy rates for the county were 1.8 percent for home owner units and 2.4 percent for renter units.

In April 1973, the developers of Reston issued a report that showed that the New Town returned $1.5 million in taxes to the county above what it received in services for 1972. The chief executive officer of Gulf-Reston, Inc., cited three needs affecting the future growth of Reston: schools, roads, and a sewage treatment facility. The developers also publicly indicated that they were considering the construction of a sewage treatment plant that would cost between $10 and $15 million and cited 2500 units a year as being necessary to carry the overhead for Reston.

On September 10, 1973, the issue of Reston's future came to a head when the Board of Supervisors had to consider a zoning decision for some 650 acres representing Reston's fourth Village Center, Twin Lakes, and housing for almost 8000 people. Supervisor Martha Pennino, within whose district Reston is included and who has been a constant and vigorous supporter of the New Town, spoke persuasively in favor of approval. She told the Board about a meeting she had attended in Reston on August 28. About 250 people attended, and one black man said, "I had a dream and I found it in Reston." Martha Pennino said also, "If Reston has done anything, it has developed a community."

Another supervisor, Rufus Phillips, who earlier headed the county's Land Use Planning and Control Task Force, expressed concern for meeting the needs of the people of Reston without hurting the people outside of Reston.

Supervisor Jack Herrity stated that "the credibility of government and the ability of people to rely on its decisions" was an issue that had not been addressed, and reaffirmed his support of the 1962 decision approving the residential planned community zoning for the New Town. After some further debate, the Board of Supervisors voted 8-1 in favor of Reston's zoning request. The negative vote was cast by a "head in the sand" no-growth advocate.

A *Washington Post* editorial on September 14, 1973 applauded the decision and noted that "The Fairfax supervisors have brought the New Town dream a decisive step closer to reality."[50]

As the forerunner of New Towns in the United States, Reston has, in the words of Dick Bonar, its planner since 1972, "no parallel especially when you consider environmental quality, socio-economic mix and the interaction between the residents". The strength of Reston lies in having both a committed developer who has combined fiscal reality with social responsiveness and concerned citizens who, through their initiatives, are providing programs and participating in organizational efforts to shape the character of the community. The weakness of Reston lies with the county government. If the New Town fails to meet its economic and social objectives, it will probably be because the county was unable to work out a manageable solution insofar as their being able to support Reston's development is concerned (granting of building permits; providing sewer services, schools, and community facilities in a *timely* manner) while controlling growth in the county as a whole.

/ TOWARD THE FULL FABRIC OF CITY /

In 1968, rural Howard County, Maryland, voted for George Wallace for President of the United States. In 1973, within this same county, is the nation's fastest-growing and most racially integrated New Town, Columbia. Seven years after its initiation in 1967 by Jim Rouse, one of the country's leading mortgage bankers and shopping center developers, Columbia's population passed 30,000 and is rapidly moving toward a 1984 objective of 110,000 people.

Perhaps the most highly serviced living environment in the entire world, Columbia represents a rare example of approaching what Rouse calls "the full fabric of city". This New Town is unfolding in a scientifically and comprehensively planned manner to address the physical, environmental, economic, governmental, and social aspects of developing a New Town.

In initiating the New Town, developer Rouse set forth four goals:

Columbia would provide the best environment for the growth of people; Columbia would be a complete and balanced community, providing a broad range of opportunities for housing and employment, including major institutional, recreational, and cultural facilities; Columbia's plan would respect the land, providing major areas of permanent open space, lakes, parks, and scenery. Trees, streams, valleys and other natural amenities would be preserved, enhanced, and cultivated to the maximum extent possible; and by building a good environment rather than a poor one, the undertaking would be profitable for the company.

It is not unusual for a developer to pay more than a million dollars to plan a New Town. This normally involves allocations for engineering, landscape architecture, design, economic modeling, and legal considerations. What is unusual is for a developer to spend several hundred thousand dollars for social planning, as Jim Rouse did. According to his top planner, Mort Hoppenfeld, "the social planning has paid off".

Columbia is located in the fast-growing Baltimore-Washington corridor about 45 minutes by car from Washington, D.C., and about 30 minutes from Baltimore. Columbia, since its inception in 1967, has consistently contributed more in taxes to the government of Howard County than it has required for services. Internally, Columbia is governed by what, in my opinion, is the most effective community organization within any of the U.S. New Towns, the Columbia Association.

Conceptually, Columbia consists of seven Villages, each of which will have a population between 10,000 and 15,000; a downtown that will have a population between 5000 and 10,000; commercial and industrial sectors absorbing over 2000 acres; and 3000 acres of parks and open space including several lakes—all within the total space of 15,000 acres. Each of the Villages will consist of three or four neighborhoods, each served by its own center. Neighborhood centers include an elementary school, a community meeting room, a swimming pool, parks or a playground, and, in some cases, a convenience store.

By the end of 1973, Columbia completed most of the development for three Village centers, and a fourth was well under way. If there is such a thing as a "hat trick" in New Town development (aside from being able to assemble large parcels of land), then Jim Rouse pulled it off in getting the General Electric Company to locate its $250 million

appliance assembly and warehouse facility on an 1100-acre site adjacent to the New Town. According to Tom Wolff, head of the Columbia Industrial Development operation at the time, Jim Rouse got word of "some guys [from General Electric] riding around looking for a possible assembly plant site". Rouse reportedly called the president of General Electric, got the president of Connecticut General Life Insurance Company (Rouse's financial partner) to call him, and succeeded in getting several General Electric representatives to visit Columbia to "take a look". Rouse reportedly was also able to get permission for the Penn Central Railroad Company to use the Baltimore and Ohio railroad tracks that pass by Columbia. Wolff pointed out that this was "something that had not been done since World War II". The General Electric complex will ultimately provide 10,000 jobs or nearly 20 percent of the Columbia employment base.

Within the rest of the industrial and commercial area, Columbia is expected to have about 800 businesses and industries providing some 60,000 jobs. The focal point within Columbia is the downtown, which has as its center a year-round environmentally-

controlled shopping center referred to as "The Mall". Already in operation are two major department stores and over 100 retail shops. Additions to The Mall will include three more department stores and will provide a total of more than two million square feet of retail space. The design of the multi-level Mall is particularly attractive, with indoor fountains and sculptures around which people often congregate.

Also within the downtown area is Lake Kittamaqundi. The approach to the lake is one of the most scenic sights in all of Columbia, thanks to a well-designed plaza, which includes a fountain around which are spiralling steps and the "People Tree" sculpture, the symbol of Columbia.

Dave Luecke, pastor of St. John's Lutheran congregation in the New Town, says,

> If you compare Columbia to your image of utopia, it will be a big disappointment. If you compare it to the suburbs west of Baltimore, it is a pretty good place in which to live.

Columbia is not utopia. Columbia is a place for people—and as the people came, so did the problems. As has been the case with Reston,

when problems surface in the New Town, they tend to become highly visible. What is significant is that most of these problems are being dealt with by newly created institutions, Village Councils, ad hoc groups, and individuals. The people are not rolling over and playing dead. They are going about the business of constructively dealing with the problems of youth, women, drugs, and race.

The planning and leadership efforts of Rouse resulted in the Interfaith Center, representing a collective ecumenical effort of some 11 religious denominations; the Columbia Association; and a comprehensive health program. All of these institutions provide social services to the community. More importantly, however, those such as Grassroots, Inc. (a crisis intervention center) and the Women's Center have come into being to meet specific needs that may not have been anticipated.

In form, Columbia is new, attractive, and representative of some of the nation's best efforts in planning and design. In substance, it is becoming increasingly responsive to problems that beset most communities of its size.

/ A PROFILE OF THE PEOPLE /

According to the Columbia Association, the people of Columbia are young, with over two-thirds of the adults being under 35 years of age and 86 percent under 45. Nearly 75 percent of the women and about 90 percent of the men have been to college. Married persons comprise 70 percent of the New Town's population, with the single (13 percent) and the divorced or widowed (10 percent) making up the balance. The size of the average family is about 3.5 persons, with the median family income being about $17,000.

The people who move to Columbia come from all over the United States and, in some cases, from around the world. The main attractive force appears to be the desire for both a new environment and a new quality of life.

In Columbia, as in Reston and other New Towns, the "values" of the New Town tend toward accepting all races, participating in community activities, and promoting the concept of community. The strongest traits that I have sensed about Columbia are a desire to make the concept of the New Town work and a positive attitude about solving differences that may arise.

/ THE INTERFAITH CENTER /

On September 20, 1970, a $1.1 million Interfaith Center was dedicated in Columbia. Within this modern complex, services are held by Catholics,

Protestants, and Jews. The center also provides space for community activities.

Within the New Town, the Columbia Cooperative Ministry, organized in 1966 "is providing new vistas of ecumenical understanding and cooperation in the practice of the faiths".[51] Involved within this ecumenical effort are the American Baptist Church, the American Lutheran Church, the Disciples of Christ, the Episcopal Church, the Lutheran Church of America, the Lutheran Church–Missouri Synod, the Presbyterian Church, U.S., the United Church of Christ, the United Methodist Church, the United Presbyterian Church, U.S.A., and the Church of God (Anderson, Indiana).

In February 1973, I attended services at St. John's Baptist Church which were held at the Interfaith Center. The congregation consisted of about 150 blacks and 1 white. The Rev. Walter Long

preached and recited frequently the prophecy of Isaiah. A choir of about 10 sang "O Happy Day" and "Wade in the Water". For me this was an unusual treat, having attended Baptist services regularly in my youth. For the members of the congregation it may very well represent the successful transfer of a religious experience that could have been left behind in the central city.

In the private office of Rev. Long is a small sign that seems to be in place in Columbia. It is a quotation from the forty-third chapter of Isaiah which reads: "Behold I will do a new thing." Although his congregation is almost entirely black, Rev. Long says he wants St. John's "to become an inclusive church—to cross socio-economic as well as ethnic lines". This native of Independence, Kansas, is a pastor of some 34 years and previously had churches in Coffeyville and Topeka, Kansas. Reverend Long asserts that Columbia is "a microcosm of America with great potential". He also feels that leadership and input from the black community are essential if Columbia is to fulfill its goals as a New Town.

The Reverend Dr. David Luecke has been pastor of St. John's Lutheran Church in Columbia for over three years. "It is great to be a pastor here; I wouldn't want to be anywhere else." Reverend Luecke feels that the community is family-oriented and a good place for children. He further states that "New Towns offer less resistance to change" and that "women are re-defining their roles; men are threatened; children are asserting their personhood". According to Luecke, about 13 percent of Columbia's residents are involved with the institutional church, compared to a national average of about 30 percent.

/ THE EXPERIENCE OF RACIAL INTERACTION /

The population of Columbia is about 18 percent black, the highest of any New Town within the United States. Developer Rouse has stated:

> We yearn for Columbia to become a place where there is a festival of race and ethnicity, where being proud to be black isn't just an activist word or phrase—but a social condition of pride and humor and gaiety.[52]

In moving toward this end, Columbia has provided opportunities for blacks in two critical areas: in the business sector and in housing for low and moderate income families. As entrepreneurs, blacks operate and own 13 businesses, which are located in The Mall, the Village Centers, and the industrial park. This is again a high among New Towns. In the area of housing, there are over a thousand units for low and moderate income families, and in some instances, the black population within a complex will approach 40 percent, according to an executive with the Columbia Association.

From an institutional standpoint, no New Town is as active as Columbia in transferring organizations that were once peculiar to the ethnic enclaves throughout the nation. Columbia has institutional representation from the Urban League, the National Association for the Advancement of Colored People, the National Council of Negro Women, and two black sororities. In spite of these organizations and a black population that, according to newspaper publisher Zeke Orlinsky, "has a higher income level than whites in Columbia", Columbia has not been without racial problems. Orlinsky further asserts that "this is not really an integrated community".

Columbia Association President Padraic Kennedy says the New Town is "reflective of a 1960 liberalism" and that it is "basically not a pluralistic community". Kennedy calls Columbia a "white middle-class community" and states that "we have to work toward making Columbia a pluralistic society".

Theresa Stewart, a black staff member of Friendship Exchange, a community service organization in the New Town, says, "There is no instance where blacks have shaped decisions; we react but do not orchestrate."

Mel Blanheim is the director of security for the Howard Research and Development Company, developers of the New Town. Blanheim, himself black, criticizes the teen centers, a frequent location of trouble between the races:

> . . .they are the worst I have ever seen. They are set up only as hangouts. There is no thrust toward activities. [The Columbia Association did, in the early part of 1973, establish programs for teenagers with directors at each of the three active centers.]

Blanheim added that—

> . . .everything in this city is based on the middle-class white kid. Anything that is done for black kids will have to be done by black people. This is called the Next America, but it was built by people from the Old America.

Blanheim feels that whites are the biggest troublemakers, particularly during the summer, and ironically points out that "people call the police whenever they see a group of three or five blacks together, especially during the summer".

Al Washington, manager of employee relations for the Rouse Company, says, "I see a real problem in blacks not knowing who they are when they come to Columbia. For instance, we seem to think that we have made it—that this is really where it is". Dr. Luecke indicated that "by and large black people of Columbia don't mix with the blacks of Howard County, and the middle class blacks here are probably more uptight about poor people moving in than whites". He also indicated that he was "told by blacks that people move here black, and gradually lose their sense of consciousness and solidarity".

Reverend Long of the predominantly black Baptist congregation feels that much of the present racial situation is an overreaction. Long says that "tension can result from a white calling a black 'boy' or 'nigger'; interracial dating; and the choice of music played in the teen centers". On the subject of interracial dating, he especially noted that black women seem to get uptight over black men dating white women. It has been pointed out that in more than one instance, black girls have attacked white girls who have been seen dating black men. Reverend Long feels that the polarization in Columbia is along the lines of both race and class.

Bill Ross, a Columbia resident since 1968, noted that The Birches, an area of Columbia where the houses range from about $40,000 to $100,000, has about a 25 percent black occupancy—and that the area is popularly referred to as the "Gold Coast".

Bob Taylor, a native of Augusta, Georgia, is the director of the teen centers. A former halfback with the New York Jets and a graduate of Maryland State, Taylor has gained the respect of black and white teen-agers alike because of his ability to maintain a firm grasp on the centers' activities and the participants involved. Having worked three years for the District of Columbia's Department of Recreation, Taylor finds his present position more challenging. There has been a noticeable drop in friction between the races since Taylor has taken over. Bob's way

with the teen-agers is both physical and mental. I made the rounds with him and several other staff members of the Columbia Association one evening. I noticed that the crowd at the Oakland Mills Center, listening and dancing to the music of a local rock group, was almost entirely white. At Slayton House, which is under Taylor's direction, the crowd was almost entirely black. The Slayton House scene was somewhat different from that at Oakland Mills where the music was fast and loud and the crowd was quite talkative, with no outside activity. Slayton House's medium-sized auditorium was filled with teen-agers. A rock band on stage played music that was slow and funky. There was little chatter on the scarcely lit dance floor as the dancers held each other tightly and moved only enough to acknowledge the presence of the rhythmic sounds. Outside the dance area about three dozen or so "brothers and sisters" waited to get in. The two Centers reflected two distinct experiences.

Columbia has had over a dozen black-owned businesses start up at various locations in The Mall, the Village Centers, or the industrial park. All but a few of these have succeeded in staying in business. While the major credit is due to the individual entrepreneurs, it must be shared with Dan Russell, the director of the Rouse Company's Small Business

Development Office, as well as with developer Rouse. All but four of the black-owned businesses were "recruited" by Russell's office. Russell, a product of public housing in nearby Washington, D.C., and a graduate of American University, underscores the importance of the leadership provided by Rouse in support of his office:

In any corporation or institution, the leadership must come from the top. Once the true feelings of the man at the top are known, things happen. . . .I personally think that he [Rouse] is a very sincere cat. . . .he is into it because he takes time to look at the business. . . .he is fantastic because he is a very astute businessman and because he is very human.

One of the most popular shops in The Mall was the Hill and Reed Haberdashery. Inside one could find the latest in men's fashions, a complete array of furnishings and a decor that is in tune with the "age of transience".

The proprietors, Harvey Hill and Donald Reed, are the best of what comes from the expression of "young, gifted, and black". Behind their mod clothes and stylish Afros is the experience of combat in Vietnam: Both are former Green Beret Captains, and between them they have three Bronze Stars, a Silver Star, two Army Commendation Medals, four Vietnam Crosses of Gallantry, a Purple Heart, and two sets of paratrooper wings. Having survived the rigors of an early childhood in "the ghetto" and the war in Southeast Asia, the two applied many of the lessons learned to develop their business.

They started their business in 1971 with a loan from the Small

Business Administration and expected to break even in 1974. Harvey Hill says of the developer: "He was very helpful in assisting us in getting started", and adds that "I am sure we have more grief than white businessmen; people either think they can rip us off or that we are trying to rip them off." Hill and Reed have not limited their talents to sales. They provided the fashions for the film "Super Fly".

About a year after our initial meeting, I met Harvey Hill at Bixby's Restaurant in downtown Washington, D.C. I asked how business was and he told me that "Hill and Reed closed its doors in December of 1973."

Diane Gayle is the attractive and intelligent proprietor of a women's clothing store in the Columbia Mall which bears her name. After some very tough negotiations with the Rouse Company and some financial hurdles, Gayle opened her business in November 1972. A graduate of Emerson College, the former school teacher is glad she made the move to Columbia from a previous location in downtown Washington, D.C. She expects her business to turn the corner around 1975.

Rowlette's Barber Shop has been located in Columbia in the Village Center of Harper's Choice since 1971 and services a mixed clientele of blacks and whites, male and female. Mr. Rowlette, the proprietor, moved his business to the New Town from downtown

Baltimore where he had been in business for about 12 years. He has not experienced any problems in Columbia.

Other black-owned businesses in Columbia are The Riverboat, a fast food stand; Corby's Cleaners; Wiggen's Home Improvement Company; Rob Harper's Dry Cleaners; The Shelf Shop Furniture Store; Richard's Liquor Bowl; Cordoba's Beauty Salon; Rice's Durclean Carpet Cleaners; the Trade Passport Corporation (discount buying); and Toy Emagineering, a toy manufacturing firm located in the industrial park.

/ THE WOMEN'S CENTER /

According to one of its organizers, the purpose of the Women's Center at Columbia is "to help women to become aware of their own resources". Meetings are held twice weekly in the Interfaith Center complex. On Tuesday between 9:30 A.M. and 11:15 A.M., lectures are given on a variety of subjects of interest to women, and on Thursday, during the same time period, the women undergo an "experience" session and discuss common interests. These discussions might include educational objectives, returning to work after raising children or before, marital problems, and so on. About 30 women normally turn out for these sessions.

The Women's Center is an all-volunteer effort which a local reporter—a woman, I might add—called "a halfway house for shell-shocked housewives".

A 1972 survey indicated that 75 percent of the women in Columbia have been to college, that 40 percent are college graduates, and that 20 percent have had some graduate work. Of the men 90 percent have been to college, with 70 percent graduating and 40 percent having done some graduate work. This survey suggests that the New Town of Columbia has an abundant resource in its highly educated women.

In terms of the Women's Center, the number of women participating appears to make up less than 1 percent of the adult female population of the New Town. Rather than remaining a loosely structured "volunteer" effort, the Columbia Women's Center might enjoy greater success if it were to formally organize to provide opportunities for women to express their views politically; to collect and dispense resources for educational purposes; to express themselves creatively; to deal with problems of sexism in communications, especially television programming; to address the issues of employment and advancement; and perhaps to conduct workshops to "sensitize" men to their plight. I find in Columbia a parallel between sexism and racism that suggests that the barriers to both will have to be fought long and hard.

/ GRASSROOTS: A CRISIS INTERVENTION CENTER /

The flyer advertising the services of this crisis intervention center reads : "HOTLINE 730-DRUG OPEN 24 HOURS". It further states that: "We are a group of young people, ages 17-27, who are trained to deal with personal crises of all kinds—suicides, drug overdoses, bad trips, runaways, and medical emergencies."

Grassroots operates in a small office provided by the developer of the New Town in the Wilde Lake Village Center. During some months, Grassroots, operated by 7 paraprofessionals and some 15 volunteers, gets as many as 1500 calls from residents of Columbia and the surrounding area of Howard County. In the fall of 1972 "the police department officially arranged to call upon Grassroots in cases where county mental health emergencies occur after hours. Situations such as suicide attempts, drug overdoses or simply cases of emotional distress might warrant the assistance of the crisis center".[53]

The paraprofessional I interviewed at Grassroots expressed alarm about the problems of drugs, alcoholism, sex, and racial tension. He also pointed out that Grassroots, while located in Columbia, functions countywide and is not limited to the boundaries of the New Town. The thinly funded organization received a contract in November 1972 from Howard County for about $18,000 to provide counselling and drug abuse emergency services. From what I could gather, although very effective as an intervention center, Grassroots has been unable to obtain widely based community financial support, and thus it operates on a shoestring. In more than one instance, staff members have saved a person from succeeding with a suicide attempt. Grassroots is a reality born of the necessity to deal with the anguish of the human condition, contrasting sharply with the often described utopian backdrop.

/ THE COLUMBIA ASSOCIATION /

"CA", as it is more popularly known, provides the most comprehensive range of services of any of the New Town community-oriented "governance" organizations I have studied. CA was incorporated on December 10, 1965, about 18 months before the first residents moved

into the New Town. It provides the type of services that are not extended by either the county or the developer. The responsibilities of CA cover the building, operating, and maintenance of parks, community services, and recreational activities.

CA President Padraic Kennedy, a former Peace Corps official, says CA staff is—

> . . .committed to assisting the new city's residents to define their own programs, so that the organization effectively services their needs and is responsive to their aspirations. This is CA's central goal. This is our overriding purpose.[54]

The association operates under an eight-member Board of Directors that is controlled by the developer. In 1977, control of the Board will shift from the developer's appointees to those elected by the citizens. By 1981, all of the terms of the developer-appointed Board members will expire. Within CA are three operating divisions that functionally cover the areas of commercial operations, physical planning, and human services.

CA is financed through funds provided from assessments and fees collected from commercial operations. According to CA Vice-President Roger Ralph, the organization is expecting an operating income of nearly $4.0 million in fiscal 1974. In January 1973, $15 million worth of CA bonds were sold to nine major financial institutions. These bonds are scheduled for retirement on December 1, 2002, and are secured by the assessment income.

The CA-operated mini-bus covers a fixed route for 35 cents with one hour between trips. There is also a call-a-ride service that costs 50 cents. Service for the elderly and for children under 11 is provided at a lower rate.

One of the most innovative concepts to be employed by CA is the "package plan" for recreational services. Under this concept, a family can enjoy the use of the swim center, tennis club, ice rink, athletic club, neighborhood pools, and mini-bus for a flat fee of $200 a year. The services can also be enjoyed by families of people who work in Columbia but do not reside there; in the case of someone neither working nor living in Columbia, the package can be purchased for $400 a year. Under an "earn-a-membership" program, in the case of a Columbia resident, the package plan can be obtained by working 100 hours for CA in support of its operations. This scheme was put together by Paul Duncan, 31, vice-president for commercial operations who, like his boss, Padraic Kennedy, was formerly with the Peace Corps.

The success of the Columbia Association is due to the leadership provided by Kennedy, the quality of the professional staff, and the open manner in which business matters are conducted. Executive meetings are open to the public, and regular press conferences are held, as are open house sessions. In addition, advice is sought from a number of committees made up of highly skilled resident professionals who volunteer their time to community affairs.

This is not to say that there are no confrontations. From time to time, the association finds itself in the middle of a debate involving the development of the community, and it can provide a forum for heated exchange. What is good is that CA is a visible organization to which people can turn in order to have their grievances dealt with.

/ TEEN-AGERS /

Columbia, like its New Town neighbor, Reston, has had some difficulty in meeting the needs of the teen-age population. In addition to the problem of drugs (which may not be out of proportion for a like sampling of teen-agers of similar socio-economic profile), Columbia has also been beset with some friction between the races.

Of the three existing teen centers, two have become virtually all black. This split resulted from differences that surfaces over musical preferences and from problems that arose around dating choices. The frustration that is apparent is best expressed by newspaper publisher Zeke Orlinsky, who says of the teen-age problem, "No one knows how to handle it."

In November 1972, the Columbia Association conducted a survey of 416 teen-agers in an effort to bring about increased responsiveness to this age group from their own and other organizations. Some of the major findings were that 53 percent of Columbia teens do not belong to any clubs or organizations, 56 percent of the teens rate sports as their favorite leisure-time activity; 60 percent say they would like to volunteer their time to help others, 79 percent use neighborhood pools and 52 percent use the ice rink at least once a week, 62 percent never use the village teen centers, 80 percent indicate that cost is never a factor affecting their participation in activities, 40 percent report they are interested in counselling on employment and college, and 66 percent indicate that they have been employed during the summer.[55]

With respect to the teens who do not use the teen centers, 30 percent indicate "that there is nothing going on there that interests them"; 26 percent say that they don't use the centers because their friends don't go there, and 9 percent give racial tension as the reason for their not attending.[56]

One of the most significant findings from the survey is that 80 percent of those surveyed "felt there was limited opportunity for them to do things they liked during the school year".[57] Considering that there are, according to the Columbia Association, some 100 organizations currently operating in Howard County that provide programs and services for teen-agers, CA feels the adequacy of these services must be questioned.

The Columbia Association's response to this part of the survey stated: "perhaps not enough attention has been paid to age, sex, and race differences in developing programs for teens".[58] It was noted that blacks had a greater interest in social dances than whites, that men had a greater preference in meeting friends than women, and that the interests in sports was higher in younger teens than in older ones.

/ A COMPREHENSIVE MEDICAL PROGRAM /

The establishment of a comprehensive, prepaid medical program in Columbia has attracted national attention and is designed "to improve and maintain the good health of its members, and reduce the need for lengthy hospital care through a program of preventive medicine".[59]

The Columbia plan became operational on October 1, 1969 and functions out of the modern, octagon-shaped, 75,000-square-foot Columbia Medical Center. This center includes 60 beds, ambulatory clinics, an emergency department, a radiology department, a laboratory, a pharmacy, surgery facilities, delivery suites, and supporting services.

The staff consists of specialists in internal medicine, pediatrics, psychiatry, obstetrics / gynecology, and general surgery on a full-time basis, and child psychiatry, ophthamology, optometry, neurology, orthopedics, otorhinolaryngology, radiology, and urology on a part-time basis.

The Columbia medical program is one of the first cases in the entire country in which a university hospital and a medical school have joined with an insurance company to provide comprehensive health care. Although rates vary depending on the size of the group covered, benefits, and other factors, the Connecticut General Life Insurance Company's plan for Columbia residents costs approximately $21 a month for an individual, $39 a month for a family of two, and $68 a month for a family of three or more.

The present facility will be expanded during the next 10 years to provide for 180 beds and a total of some 200,000 square feet. Within this modern complex, which has a brightly colored interior, there are facilities to allow for cable television to be connected when the New Town acquires this capability.

/ A BROAD RANGE OF EDUCATIONAL SERVICES /

The New Town of Columbia, with its population of about 30,000, has a broad range of educational services. Starting with the preschool and day care level and going through the college level, the opportunity exists for many residents to realize much of their potential in the academic area.

Within the public school system, there are nine elementary, three middle, and two high schools. The number of public schools in Columbia might be contrasted with the number in Reston, Virginia, which coincidentally has a similar population of about 30,000. Reston has only four elementary schools, no middle schools, and no high schools. This means that some Reston students must be bused to elementary schools in Great Falls and others to the high school in Herndon.

Columbia also has four institutions of higher education: Howard County Community College, Antioch Human Ecology Center, Dag Hammarskjöld College, and Loyola College.

/ EARLY CHILDHOOD EDUCATION AND DAY CARE /

In visiting the Swedish New Towns of Vallingby, Farsta, and Skarholmen, I was struck by the presence of the day care facilities throughout. From what I could gather, the women in Sweden have a far greater opportunity than their American counterparts to participate in and enjoy the full educational and employment opportunities that their society offers.

Within this country, the provision of facilities and programs for day care and early childhood education is a serious problem. Only during the Second World War was an appreciable number of day care facilities operational within the United States. In Reston, the provision of day care facilities was essentially left up to the dynamics of the marketplace. In Columbia, the Columbia Association has exercised some very effective leadership in developing programs and facilities in this area, and it reacts to the advice of an Early Childhood Education Board. This eight-member board was set up at the direction of the developer, Jim Rouse. Within Columbia, the Columbia Association administers a variety of programs that include day care, half-day care, hourly care, before and after school care, and a nursery school.

In addition to the Columbia Association efforts, there are six cooperative nursery school programs operating throughout Columbia, a Montessori Children's House for preschool-age children, and the Roslyn Rise Day Care Center for children of parents who are working or attending school.

Donelda Stayton holds a Ph.D. in child psychology, is the mother of two children aged one and seven, and is a member of the Early Childhood Education Board in Columbia.

I think that it is essential that we have a quality day care situation for mothers who are going to work. We should assess the demand for services; I think we have a social obligation to provide quality day care. I do not believe that day care centers will induce women to work. We have to take moral and ethical judgments out of providing facilities. The decision for a mother to go to work is a personal decision and it should not be dictated by the morals of the community.

Dr. Stayton is currently at home raising her youngest child. She feels that "As far as day care is concerned, I think it is better for the child to be in the home. I see the parent-child relationship during the preschool years as being more critical."

Linda Odum, director for early childhood education for the Columbia Association, says, "The principal issue for day care on a broad scale must be the child's interests." She adds, on the freeing of women to work, "realistically, about 40 percent of the women want to work once their children reach age three. We have nowhere near satisfied the demands for personal freedom for women." Odum feels that within a New Town, the developer has an even greater responsibility to provide a variety of choices for people, particularly when it comes to educating children and bringing about opportunities to free women.

It is clear that there is an increasingly strong demand for service in the area of early childhood education and day care. None of the more developed New Towns—Columbia, Reston, and Irvine—has yet to meet this demand to its fullest extent. Columbia appears to have provided the most service to date, while all three have outstanding individual examples of model facilities and programs. The challenge seems to be to create an environment in which the children can learn and can enjoy proper nutrition and recreation, in balance with parental needs and responsiveness.

/ THE CHALLENGE OF COLUMBIA /

The form of Columbia from a design standpoint suggests function more than grandeur. The overall land use planning—the use of space for recreational, residential, commercial, and industrial purposes—is well balanced and almost without parallel in the United States. The Villages of Wilde Lake, Oakland Mills, Long Reach, and Harper's Choice are taking on distinctive identities.

The west side of Route 29, which bisects the New Town, is clearly the showcase. The developer is to be commended for boldly pursuing the development of the "downtown" and several Villages at the same time. The pace of development seems to be leading the people instead of the other way around. But what you see in Columbia is not what you get. Columbia is a highly serviced and dynamically interactive New Town, like Reston, developing a strong sense of community. Columbia is the people. This is the real magnetism. This is what can give Columbia staying power. This is what will keep the people coming—black and white; middle class, super rich and those of moderate income. Let us not pretend that the poor are being accommodated. They are not. The cross section of people is nevertheless broad.

The planning of Columbia has been under the direction of Morton Hoppenfeld since its inception. While some say that Columbia has outgrown Mort Hoppenfeld (as they do about his boss, Jim Rouse),

the Hoppenfeld influence is, as is Rouse's, both symbiotic and symbolic of what fruits can come from such a union. Hoppenfeld feels Columbia is "the success model which has enabled others to come behind us" and calls the architecture of the New Town "responsive". Hoppenfeld feels that the several hundred thousand dollars the developer spent on social planning has paid off and doesn't think that the New Town has any serious social problems: "The perception of social problems is a function of higher expectations. This is good because it raises problems to a level of consciousness where they get worked out."

The challenge of the New Town, however, is to create an environment in which the bonds between the people will be purposeful; in which the potential of all citizens can be realized; in which the dignity of man, as well as the dignity of woman, can command respect; in which the pursuit of happiness will not be inhibited; and in which mental, physical, spiritual, and economic fulfillment can be sustained.

When Jim Rouse addressed a conference on governance in the New Town in the spring of 1972, he spoke about community:

Here is a society in which we have this affluence and all of this freedom. We have run individualism into such a rampant state of social anarchy that we talk about community but don't mean it; we don't live it. We are not honestly going about making it work; we are not honestly going about using our freedom and our afflence and our concern about human dignity to make these things work in new community processes.[60]

/ NOT JUST ANOTHER NEW TOWN /

In North Carolina in the middle of what was once a thriving area for peanuts, cotton, soybeans, and tobacco, Floyd B. McKissick, a former national civil rights figure, is developing America's only rural New Town. McKissick—attorney, ex-director of the Congress of Racial Equality, farmer, philosopher, businessman, and organizer—has put it all together in his present role of developer, and asserts that he is "going to build Soul City because no one else will assume that task".

Soul City is not just another New Town. Soul City, to cite an editorial from *The Washington Post,* "is perhaps the most vital experiment yet in this country's halting struggle against the cancer of hectic urbanization".[61]

What is now about 5000 acres of farmland some 10 miles from the North Carolina-Virginia border will—as McKissick's plans become reality in the next 20 to 30 years—become a town for nearly 50,000 residents of all races.

The challenge of building this New Town is increased by the fact that the location is rural and in the midst of one of the poorest areas in the South, if not in the country. According to the Bureau of the Census, Warren County, where Soul City is situated, had a per capita income of only $1638 in 1970, compared to that of $3119 for the nation as a whole. In addition, while the national population grew by over 13 percent between 1960 and 1970, that of Warren County declined by almost 20 percent. The problem of poverty is compounded by that of race, and in the case of Warren County, over 60 percent of the population is black.

It is hard to conceive of anyone in the business of developing a New Town having to contend with as many obstacles as Floyd McKissick, but McKissick has the ability to turn a minus into a plus. He seems to thrive on adversity, and that has given Soul City a spirituality and a momentum that, at the least, seem miraculous. No obstacle has been too great for McKissick to tackle. No hurdle has been too high to clear. Unlike the Biblical Moses who led his people to the Promised Land, McKissick by his actions seems to be saying "This *is* the promised land."

/ McKISSICK'S PHILOSOPHY /

McKissick at age 50 seems more like a man in his twenties insofar as his energy is concerned; on the other hand, his wisdom suggests that he must be close to 200 years old. Growing up in Asheville, North Carolina, McKissick started out shining shoes. But he didn't shine shoes long. To hear him tell it:

> I learned that if I became a good shine boy, I would not have to shine shoes long. If I became a damned good busboy, I would not be a busboy long. If I became a damned good waiter, I would not have to be a waiter long. If I became a damned good bartender, then I had to go up to maitre d'. If I became a damned good maitre d', I would become the head waiter and then I would go into management and then I could control it and I then had the skills to do my own. That's what I learned a long time ago.

McKissick didn't limit his determination to his own personal ambitions. As an attorney, he was involved in the litigation of thousands of civil rights cases, and he organized and led many of the initiatives that turned the South around to respecting black people as first-class citizens. In talking about how things were in 1965 after the passage of national civil rights legislation, McKissick said:

In the South here, you couldn't buy fertilizer if you sent your kid to an integrated school. If you went to a Howard Johnson's or a Holiday Inn, the minute you went in to take advantage of your civil rights, there was a foreclosure on your house.

Floyd McKissick and some of his cohorts went around organizing buying clubs and managed to get the seeds and fertilizer that enabled the farmers to get their crops out.

McKissick's involvement in land goes back to his post-World War II days when he invested his savings in land in Asheville, after completing his military service. In this sense, he was putting his philosophy to work: "Power comes from the land, control of the land and use of the land." McKissick asserts that—

Land is also politically important. People don't understand that it's land ownership that creates political subdivision, starting with the village and then the neighborhood. It's land that ultimately ends up in a village, or a city or a county. . .and which creates the political substructures entitling it to more economic advantages. Land ultimately ends up as far as a state and then as a nation!

After buying property, McKissick went to law school at the University of North Carolina where, in 1952, he became the first black man in the school's history to graduate. His motivation for going to law school was in large part due to his recognizing that "you have to fight the law on two levels. . .law to save black people from oppression and law to really integrate them".

/ DEALING WITH THE FEDS /

Floyd McKissick and his longtime associate Gordon Carey approached the federal government in the summer of 1969 to get some support for his development proposal in the form of planning and financial assistance. At this time, except for his longtime friend and former civil rights attorney Sam Jackson, under whose office the new communities and planning programs came, few, if any, of the staff people took Floyd McKissick seriously. For the most part, those who had heard of Floyd McKissick knew of him as a civil rights figure and not as an attorney, a businessman, or a person with a substantial background in real estate.

Outside of HUD, where McKissick made his initial inquiries, a lot of concern was expressed by several members of the Congress, by the White House, and by political figures in his own state of North Carolina. In what can only be described as an atmosphere of political indifference, McKissick did not have the slick graphics and substantive reports that most of the other developers from around the nation had. The site for Soul City did not have a water system, the area was a pocket of poverty, its resident population was predominantly black, and the federal government through HUD had never supported a rural area New Town project.

What Floyd McKissick had was an idea, a few thousand acres of land with options on several thousand more, and about $300,000 in loans from the Chase Manhattan Bank. Within less than three years after he initially approached HUD, Floyd McKissick received what he had set out to get—a $14 million commitment from the federal government in the form of a loan guarantee to build Soul City.

Between his initial meetings in the summer of 1969 and the announcement by HUD Secretary George Romney and North Carolina Governor Robert Scott of the commitment in the summer of 1972, McKissick held scores of meetings with bankers in New York, the governor of North Carolina, the staff people at HUD, President Nixon's Domestic Affairs Assistant John Price, and others.

I first sensed the concern that the Administration had with the Soul City proposal when I was summoned to give a briefing at the White House along with the New Communities Office Director Bill Nicoson and Assistant Secretary Sam Jackson. I had prepared several charts and collected all of the substantive material I could before briefing John Price. Price was almost a stranger to me; we had only conversed a few times on the telephone, and I had expected the briefing session to be pretty cut and dried. The few times that I had had any direct contact with either the President's staff or the Vice-President's staff, I found the people whom I worked with to be exceptionally cordial, in contrast to the public image that often was less than favorable.

The meeting on Soul City was held in John Price's office and was limited to the three of us from HUD and Price. This provided for a rather relaxed atmosphere, and I proceeded to explain what the Soul City proposal was about. After nearly completing my brief, John Price interrupted and expressed what he said was the concern of "others", and that was with the name of "Soul City". I replied that "a lot of people are concerned with the name 'White House'".

It is difficult to objectively measure the political pressure that surrounded the Soul City proposal when McKissick initially made his request in the 1969-1970 period. From the perspective that I had as a federal official within HUD, I saw that it was the subject of almost constant inquiries that did not normally surround the applications for other New Town proposals. Even as late as the summer of 1972, after the HUD commitment was announced, *Newsweek* reported in the August 14, 1972, issue that "North Carolina Senator Sam Ervin has already questioned the propriety of channelling federal tax dollars into an essentially private enterprise." [62]

In spite of the frequent inquiries about Soul City and the general concern as to whether or not this proposal would result in an all-black town, I didn't fully appreciate the degree of political sensitivity until I had participated in a meeting in North Carolina with the governor of that state. I had accompanied Samuel C. Jackson, the Assistant Secretary for Community Planning and Management, to this meeting with Governor Scott to discuss the issue of HUD's providing planning assistance to the region in which Soul City would be located. The governor was present along with several aides. Floyd McKissick and his associate Gordon Carey were also in attendance.

The governor was a very cordial and friendly man, but made it clear that he wasn't any liberal by any stretch of the imagination and went about laying out the "ground rules" on how things would have to be with his office as far as the Soul City effort was concerned. The governor made three points. The first was that he had to deal with the opposition that many of the local citizens had expressed. Next, he made it clear that he wanted the planning assistance grant to be processed through the state's Office of Planning. Finally, he wanted things handled with a low profile as far as publicity was concerned. Other than this, he indicated that he didn't think the Soul City project would work but pledged his support. I came away from this meeting with a feeling of optimism because the governor was candid with everyone.

Most of the institutional framework that is normally required to allow for the receipt of federal program assistance was lacking in the area of the Soul City site. This meant that McKissick and his team had to structure the necessary institutions as they were needed in order to get federal support. The first such institution was the Warren Regional Planning Corporation that would carry out all of the substantive initiatives necessary to effect a comprehensive areawide plan. McKissick feels that the seriousness with which the planning was undertaken helped to turn around those in government who didn't think that he meant business. In addition to the regional approach that was taken to planning, McKissick demonstrated that his team had the ability to go out and get money and to meet deadlines on the numerous schedules that were imposed.

In February 1971, with the research and planning completed, the McKissick team returned to Washington, D.C., to make a critical presentation to HUD in order to receive consideration for support in the form of a loan guarantee. In order that no stone be left unturned, McKissick held a dry run the night before his formal pitch to HUD. He brought together his financial people, his own staff, and his planners. This dry run started about 6 P.M. and ended about 2 A.M.

The next day, McKissick introduced his associates who included the economic consultants of Hammer, Green, and Siler; several young, Harvard-trained black professionals; and his planner, Harvey Gantt. Like McKissick, Gantt had played an historic role in the integration of southern universities. In 1963, he attracted national attention when he became the first black student at South Carolina's Clemson University. After graduating from Clemson in 1965 with a degree in architecture, which he had started at Iowa State in 1960, and after a few years in professional practice, Gantt went on to the Massachusetts Institute of Technology and received his Master of City Planning degree. It is poetic justice at its best to find two black men who fought their way into the South's previously all-white universities over a period spanning 10 years joined together as planner and developer in the New Town of Soul City.

When HUD Secretary Romney and North Carolina Governor Robert Scott jointly announced federal support for Soul City in July 1972, it was a significant milestone for McKissick—but he didn't stop there. In taking what he calls a "total approach" to requesting federal assistance, McKissick sought support from every agency in Washington that could contribute to the development of Soul City. As of September 1973, McKissick's team succeeded in obtaining more support from federal agencies outside of HUD than any of the other New Towns guaranteed by the federal government. This support includes a $1.1 million grant from the Office of Economic Opportunity(OEO) to provide comprehensive health services to the two-county (Warren and Vance) area surrounding the Soul City site; a $90,000 OEO grant to provide for five people to effect social planning; a $500,000 OEO grant for economic development; a $98,000 grant from the Department of Health, Education, and Welfare under the Emergency School Aid Act to work with about 100 children at the junior high school level who are underachievers; and a $12,500 grant from the National Endowment for the Arts for a cultural arts program. All of these grants were requested by the nonprofit Soul City Foundation and, in some cases, were directed into other nonprofit organizations such as HEALTHCO, Inc., which were "spin offs" from the parent agency.

In addition to setting up the regional planning agency, the Soul City Foundation, and HEALTHCO, Inc., McKissick organized the Kerr Lake Utilities Company in order to become eligible for water and sewer grants from the Environmental Protection Agency. In setting up the Kerr Lake Utilities Company, McKissick as he tells it, "had to bring together the people in the region, blacks and whites, to come and sit down together and talk".

By mid-1973, three years after the initial meetings began, application was filed with the Economic Development Administration to develop a regional water system that would take in the counties of Granville, Vance, and Warren. In undertaking these regional efforts that go far beyond the boundaries of the Soul City site, McKissick asserts that "sometimes in order to help yourself, you have got to help others, and this was our belief. . .that we have to bring people together".

McKissick has had success with the federal government where others, especially blacks, have failed. In discussing his own experience in maneuvering through the bureaucracy, he says,

> We've had a great amount of cooperation on the part of federal agencies. I think we seek more, but when I evaluate the kind of cooperation that was previously given, it would indicate narrowness in our ability to go to various federal agencies and demand. . . .White people use all facets of the government. . . .we have been confining ourselves [black people] to OEO and sometimes HEW and HUD. . . .Our project opened up the avenues to really develop liaison and contacts in all the federal agencies. The cooperation we received demanded a hell of a lot of work on our part, and it required us to do the kind of work that they normally don't expect black people to even know how to do. I think we have measured up to that standard because we have measured up to a standard not set by blacks, but a standard set by whites.

The Soul City financial team consists of three general partners: McKissick Enterprises; the black-controlled architectural and engineering firm of Madison and Madison International Inc., of Cleveland, Ohio; and the National Housing Partnership. The initial financing was provided by the Chase Manhattan Bank and Irving J. Fain, a close friend of McKissick's from Providence, Rhode Island. McKissick is quick to point out that—

> Between Chase and Irving J. Fain, that really gave me a start to go forward. . . .when our outline of preliminary plans

went out to them, they immediately backed me. Irving J. Fain with $200,000 and, of course, Chase, with a series of interim financing to take the step-by-step through HUD.

/ PEOPLE MAKING A DIFFERENCE /

Aside from having a strong financial and management team, McKissick has added strength in the people who surround him. It is a credit to McKissick himself that he goes out of his way to point out the people who are working with him to make Soul City a success.

One of these is 30-year-old New Yorker, Stan Roman, who is directing and developing the comprehensive health program. A 1964 graduate of Dartmouth and a 1968 graduate of Columbia University's Medical School, Roman left his position with Harlem Hospital, where he was head of medical clinics, for the Soul City experience because he "believes in the concept of the New Town". He feels that a model health care program cannot be started in an urban area and that it is necessary to develop a model.

Stan Roman seems out of place in the rural setting of North Carolina. He is a bachelor, drives a Mercedes convertible, and has an urbane manner more befitting a society physician in Beverly Hills or his native New York City. In reflecting on the rural setting of the Soul City, he says, "Cultism can cause a deadening of creativity. Many of the people here have reverted to the life style that is peculiar to this area. What is needed here is an infusion."

Making a clear distinction between race and poverty, Roman stressed that "Nutritional problems are not black, they are poor; living conditions are not black, they are poor; lack of care is not black, it is poor."

Also involved in the day-to-day operation of Soul City is Lewis Myers, the associate director of the Soul City Foundation. Myers, a Franklin and Marshall College graduate in sociology and a candidate for a Master of Business Administration degree at the University of North Carolina, is married to Floyd McKissick's daughter Joycelyn. Joycelyn, who earned a master's degree in education from Harvard, is the director of community affairs for HEALTHCO Inc.

Next to members of McKissick's family, most of his current team is made up of the people he was closely associated with both as an attorney and as a civil rights leader. Some of these include attorney T.T. Clayton, Gordon R. Carey, and Charles Davis. In the three years I have known them, I have found nothing more impressive than their abiding faith in themselves, in their leader, Floyd McKissick, and in their purpose—to build Soul City.

Outside of his own immediate team, McKissick has received wide support from the academic community. This support has come from the University of North Carolina, North Carolina Central University, and the Massachusetts Institute of Technology. The Rouse Company, developers of the New Town of Columbia, Maryland, provided the training for the entire Soul City staff. Commenting on the relationship between the two groups, McKissick says, "We would have to call the Rouse Company about every week or so. . .and they responded."

Behind Floyd McKissick's drive and his ability to effectively bring together men, money, and material is his experience in the Army following the Second World War: "I saw how the Marshall Plan had sent millions and millions of dollars over to Europe, and I watched that process and I watched them organize." He further noted that the people went about the business of rebuilding, converting Army equipment for their purposes, and that before long they had rebuilt the entire town. He saw just a few competent people direct others to rebuild with broken bricks and concrete and to beautify with color. After this, McKissick said, "Man, with all of the dying communities in the South, what the hell we could do if we just really got together here."

Added to this, McKissick found that the missing link to the realization of the benefits that could have come out of the Civil Rights Act of 1964 was economics. It was 1965 when McKissick made up his mind to return to his native North Carolina and build a new community—

> . . .because integration cannot be carried any further just
> by means of direct action. . . .It was necessary for us to go
> through the image and the black power stage, but we should
> have fallen back on the solid foot with economic development
> rather than the destruction of economic forces.

A prime example of economic leverage cited by McKissick was the effort
to integrate the lunch counters in the early 1960s. According to him,
success resulted despite the store's initial assertion that: "Hell would
freeze over before a black man would be allowed to sit at the lunch
counter with a white man in the South. . . .After six months and about
five million dollars in losses, hell froze over."

/ PRAGMATIC POLITICS /

Floyd McKissick has been the subject of criticism in the black community
for supporting President Richard Nixon in his re-election bid during 1972.
McKissick feels that this criticism is unwarranted and says it doesn't
bother him. He says he is more concerned about whether or not he is
creating opportunities by his acts. He points out that he has received
"support from both political parties". McKissick asserts that "my politics
are pragmatic. They are based upon the desire to accomplish solutions to
problems, not rhetoric."

/ THE ESSENCE OF CITYHOOD /

In staging the actual development of Soul City, McKissick has been
sensitive to the local priorities of the region and accordingly will focus on
medical services, employment. and housing in that order.

McKissick feels that "industry is going to be the key to the
development of the southern city" and thus will center his own efforts
around a modern complex, Soultech I, that will consist of 40,000 square
feet of manufacturing and processing space and 12,000 square feet of
office space.

Soul City will offer its new residents a life style that is in sharp
contrast to the metropolitan areas that house the majority of the citizens
in the United States. It will also offer those within the contiguous area an
opportunity to enjoy the best of what the region can provide while doing
much to minimize the problems that have caused so many to
flee—namely, the lack of employment opportunities, poor health service,
and substandard housing. In addition to a pleasant terrain, the environs

of Soul City include large lakes suitable for recreational purposes. This is important because recreation has often been a key factor in the few rural counties that have enjoyed growth.

It is particularly appropriate that Floyd McKissick used the word *soul* in the name for his New Town for it was precisely this—soul—that the distinguished professor Arnold Toynbee wrote was "the essence of cityhood". [63]

6

PARK FOREST SOUTH

Chicago, Illinois, is the nation's third largest metropolitan area. About 40 miles south is the beginning of what its developers call "a whole New Town", Park Forest South. Approaching the site of some 8000 acres that will eventually contain 110,000 people, observers will see the strip development, the typical subdivisions, the small Midwestern towns, and the blight that has become the rule rather than the exception throughout urban America. To this there are two exceptions: Park Forest, Illinois, launched in the 1940s, one of the early attempts to build a New Town;

and Park Forest South. Park Forest today has a population of about 35,000 and is principally a middle class white community. Unlike its neighbor to the north, Park Forest South is developing into a racially mixed community and expects to provide up to 15 percent of its housing for low and moderate income families.

Many of the satellite New Towns developing in the United States, such as Reston, Virginia; Columbia, Maryland; Jonathan, Minnesota; and Irvine, California, to name a few, are being built on virtually unobstructed land, giving their planners a free hand in the approach to design. Park Forest South represents a development that is subjected to numerous constraints in that the site is bordered by existing highways, subdivisions, and Park Forest, and bisected by a rail line and underground utlity lines. The developers of this New Town are turning what to some might be a minus, into a plus. Interstate 57 forms the western boundary and provides access to downtown Chicago in about 40 minutes; it is also contiguous to the New Town's industrial park. The rail line will eventually allow for the New Town residents to commute to the downtown Chicago area in about a third of the driving time. Considering the new energy consciousness, this is a definite benefit. And unlike most of the other developing New Towns, Park Forest South has self-government.

Developer Lewis Manilow, son of the co-developer Park Forest Nathan Manilow, initiated the plans for Park Forest South in 1966; a year later, the development was incorporated as a village. During the same period an agreement was reached with the Illinois Central Railroad to extend a commuter line to the New Town.

By March 1971, Manilow and his financial partners—which include the Mid-America Improvement Corporation, a subsidiary of Illinois Central Industries; and the U.S. Gypsum Urban Development Corporation, a subsidiary of the U.S. Gypsum Company—obtained a guarantee from HUD for $30 million, the third such guarantee issued by the federal government and the largest issued as of that date.

Conceptually, the Park Forest South New Town represents a balanced environment of commercial, residential, recreational, and industrial land use, highlighted by Governors State University, a linear town center, the largest natural forest in northeastern Illinois,

well-designed community facilities, lakes, golf courses, and other
attractive open spaces.

/ A LINEAR TOWN CENTER /

Park Forest South's principal "showpiece" will be a three-mile-long town
center. This concept might be called a twentieth-century version of the
extended marketplace that was typical of the twelfth-century Zahringer
New Towns of Central Europe. This concept, which will segregate

automobile and pedestrian traffic, allows for commercial, cultural, and recreational activities. Although Manilow is not one to impose his will on the residents, this "Renaissance man" of the New Town movement has received a grant from the National Endowment for the Arts to commission sculptures. Manilow, who has contributed one of his own acquisitions, "Yes" by Mark DiSuervo, says, "I want to develop some sculpture that relates to what we are doing."

/ GOVERNANCE /

Unlike most of the other New Towns developing in the United States, Park Forest South is incorporated as a village and is run by an eight-member council. The village council has the power to tax, to zone within the village limits, and to object to development within 1½ miles of its boundaries. This is particularly important because most developing New Towns are not in a position to "control" development adjacent to their boundaries, some of which could be detrimental to the character of the planned development.

According to the vice-president of the Citizens Planning Council, the principal issues in the New Town are the process of planning, the schools and related sites, housing for low and moderate income families, and communications between the old residents in the existing subdivision of Woodhills and the new residents.

/ FOR SOME A NEW WORLD /

Chicago has been traditionally one of the most rigidly segregated large central cities in the nation. Its public housing is a national disgrace, and living conditions are among the worst to be found anywhere. Don Williams, former Chicago resident, describes Park Forest South as "almost like living in a new world". His old world was a 23-story high rise located at 64th and Lowe, on Chicago's South Side next to an elevated railroad line. "When we first moved here, we didn't feel right. . .we finally figured out it was the absence of the noise," says the Army veteran who is now completing his undergraduate studies at Governors State University. Williams added that—

> . . .this is a better environment for the kids. . .the people here are not uptight. The Chicago schools are notorious. Here we have an open school and our kids have taken a strong interest in reading and learning."

The New Town of Park Forest South is another case where the developer has taken the initiative to employ an affirmative action officer on a full-time basis. This area of responsibility rests with Walter Strothers who, behind his soft-spoken and friendly manner, has negotiated tough and substantive opportunities for both laborers and contractors to enjoy

the benefits of the New Town construction process. As a result of Walter Strothers' efforts and the backing provided by Manilow, nearly 20 percent of the labor force was black as of the spring of 1973, and it is expected to continue at this level. Strothers has also been instrumental in getting several large electrical and construction contracts awarded to black firms. In order to appreciate the full benefits of what the developer and his affirmative action officer have done, one must understand that the Chicago area has traditionally been a tough place to bring about significant racial breakthroughs in the building trades.

While the New Town is still in the early stages of development, Strothers is intent on pressing for substantive involvement of blacks and minorities as entrepreneurs in the commercial sector as the development of Park Forest South unfolds.

Leonard Juniel, the chairman of the Human Relations Commission for the New Town, says that his seven-member organization has not had any complaints regarding racial problems. Much of this can be attributed to the developer's initiative in the area of affirmative action.

/ GOVERNORS STATE UNIVERSITY /

The concepts behind Governors State University, which has been named in honor of the past governors of the state, is as innovative as the New Town. Located on a site of 750 acres, a $24 million modern facility, when completed, will eventually house over 10,000 students. Admission is open to graduates of junior colleges or equivalent institutions with a "C" average. The tuition is less than $500 a year for state residents, and the specific thrust is to provide educational opportunities for students in the low income category. The school year is comprised of 6 two-month sessions, allowing for either continuous or interrupted enrollment. Under a system where grades are not given and failures not recorded, students are in the unique position of not being able to flunk out. The average age of the students is 28; two-thirds are married and about 25 percent are black. By structuring the tuition and entry requirements to reach low and moderate income groups, Governors State University provides an opportunity for such groups to break out of an economic category that might otherwise be permanent.

/ HICKORY SCHOOL /

In keeping with the trend developing throughout most of the New Towns, Park Forest South has as its first elementary school a modern, open-classroom, $800,000 complex that houses some 645 students. The well-staffed school has three teachers for each grade level with two aides, a full-time psychologist, a music teacher, a social worker, a counsellor, and a nurse. In addition to a number of innovative programs for the children, the school also has a parent education program. In explaining the staff composition and learning conditions, the young principal, Gale F. Guyer says, "We deal in the realm of the reality."

/ THE MOUNTAIN CLIMBER /

The late Nathan Manilow built Park Forest. His son grew up with the development that was influenced by the short-lived "Garden Cities" movement in the 1930s. "Park Forest was like a mountain to be climbed. . . .it was there to be done and we did it. . . .the greatest influence on me was Park Forest." Lewis Manilow is now climbing another mountain, one that is more challenging than the first one. He calls his current efforts "the most exciting business" he knows. When Park Forest South is completed, Lew Manilow will have done his thing—he will have built *a whole New Town.*

7

JONATHAN

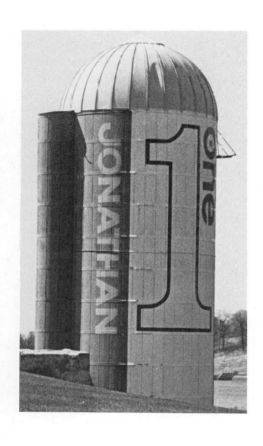

/ THE CONCEPT /

Driving west on Interstate 494, I was once again reminded of the sprawl that has afflicted most suburban areas in the United States. This interstate highway, which forms part of a circumferential highway around the Twin Cities of Minneapolis and St. Paul, is straddled by large industrial plants, shopping centers, hotels. and other forms of development that at times suggest a twentieth-century image of optical pollution. About 15 minutes after taking the Chanhassen turn-off, I found myself in the middle of what seemed to be farm country: rolling hills, winding roads, and pleasant pastures where cattle could graze undisturbed.

Here, in the quiet of rural Minnesota, only 25 miles or about 40 minutes from downtown Minneapolis is the New Town of Jonathan. Named after famed local explorer Jonathan Carver, this New Town was the first to receive the backing of the federal government. In January 1970, HUD approved the 8000-acre development that over a 20-year period will become home for some 50,000 people. As a result of the government's backing, the developer received a loan guarantee in the amount of $21 million.

Jonathan was brought into being by one of Minnesota's leading conservationists, former state senator Henry T. McKnight. When the senator died suddenly in December 1972, the population was approaching the 1500 mark. By this time, however, Henry McKnight had left his mark on the New Town and had set in motion things to come.

The location for the New Town is in the southwest growth corridor and is bisected by a main line of the Chicago-Milwaukee Railroad. This line is expected to pave the way for Jonathan to be the first New Town to have a rapid rail link with its nearby central city.

The Jonathan plan—which represents the collective efforts of Henry McKnight and the Jonathan Design Group and is headed up by planner-architect Ben Cunningham, calls for five villages of about 7000 people each and a town center that will have about 15,000 people. This brings the planned population to a level of 50,000. The town center will ultimately include an educational complex that will offer a full range of academic and vocational courses.

With conservation as its hallmark, the New Town will provide outstanding opportunities for recreation. The one man-made and three natural lakes combine to give nearly a square mile area for a variety of water-oriented activities such as swimming, sailing, canoeing, and fishing. About one-third of the total area of the New Town will be open space. The residential sections will combine to make up 30 percent of the area, and 27 percent of the area will be for industrial and commercial uses. The remaining 10 percent will be for roads and other public uses.

/ SOCIAL CONSIDERATIONS /

Jules Smith, the senior vice-president and general counsel of the Jonathan Development Company, says: "Far too many people look at New Communities as physical things; unless we get a sense of community, we are not going to build any New Towns."

The substance of the thrust toward a sense of community is suggested in the community goals that include the following:

> To develop a heterogeneous community with a balanced mix of income levels and unit types; to increase communication and understanding among diverse economic and social groups by involving them in the common purpose of building a self-reliant community; to make possible maximum opportunity for self-realization and development of individuals of all ages; to heighten the awareness of the individual as to his role within a working ecological system by preservation of natural features of the site and provision of an outgoing educational program; and to provide a man-made environment designed to enhance the general quality of life for community residents.[64]

Jonathan is one of the few New Towns in the United States that has a social development plan, commonplace in the European New Towns, and also that has been the subject of some efforts in social planning.

During the several days spent in Jonathan, I had an opportunity to discuss the development with about 30 people—not sufficient for scientific sampling, but enough to give a feel for issues and problems. Most of them were extremely pleased with their experience to date and expressed a sense of being pioneers in the New Town experience.

One black housewife and mother of three has lived in Jonathan for over two years. She and her husband moved the family to the New Town in order to get away from the inner city school system. Before moving to Jonathan, her son, in the fifth grade, had never been exposed to the new math. While she does not pretend to speak for other blacks, she is happy living in Jonathan.

Another housewife, white and also the mother of three children, moved to Jonathan because of the rental practices that, unlike those in Minneapolis, do not discriminate against prospective tenants on account of age or number of children. In her efforts to obtain suitable housing in Minneapolis, she had run into numerous situations where her family could not be accepted in a three-bedroom apartment or where her baby of only a few months was not allowed. Divorced and remarried, she also feels that Jonathan is less restrictive toward divorcees seeking houses than other communities.

Mrs. Pat Graham heads up the information office for Jonathan and previously held a similar position with the New Town of Reston. Both she and her husband Gene are originally from New York City and have made the move from one New Town to another. Because of her unique experience of having lived in these two New Towns, she has been able to play a role in many of the management and policy decisions of the Jonathan Development Company. She is concerned with "the shift away from a socio-economic mix and the thrust toward the $35,000 and above housing market". The economic constraints notwithstanding, Pat Graham in describing why more blacks have not been attracted to Jonathan says, "Minneapolis does not have ghettoes like the East Coast. . . .I think blacks find the city comfortable." She also feels that the 18-month housing moratorium effected by the Nixon administration in January 1972 has had a negative impact on Jonathan in that it forces the company to appeal to the higher income bracket to market housing.

Calvin Dirl, president of Dirwill Systems, Inc., manufacturers of roof trusses, is one of the few black entrepreneurs in Jonathan. After 13 years of experience in various phases of the construction industry, Cal Dirl decided to go into business for himself. His market analysis indicated that roof trusses were in demand in the Minneapolis metropolitan area. He subsequently prepared a proposal and submitted it to the Small Business Administration for a loan guarantee in the amount of $145,000. With the assistance of Charles McCoy, a black SBA executive, and Ed Welch, a white bank official, Dirl had his loan approved in about two weeks. Largely through the efforts of the late Senator Henry McKnight, the developer of the New Town, Dirl was provided with about $60,000 in front money. Of this, $45,000 was amortized through leasehold improvements, $10,000 was used for a down payment on machinery and equipment, and $5000 was made available for salaries during the first nine months of operation.

According to Dirl, his company will gross about $800,000 through sales during the first year's operation, which represents a margin of about 6.3 percent or $27,000 before taxes. He says, "At an estimated 20,000 starts in the metropolitan area, we need only six percent of the business to realize corporate objectives." Dirl feels that the cost of housing in this country is "ridiculous" and that through the use of roof

trusses, the costs can be lowered somewhat. He says that the only problem he has had after about a year in business is that of "overcoming the negative image" that has been projected about blacks. Dirl expects to pay off the bank and the Jonathan Development Corporation within two years of his starting date and then take his company public.

Steve and Nancy Reiner are a young, well-educated husband-and-wife team who were involved with the Jonathan New Town planning process as a political scientist and human resource planner, respectively. Nancy saw her function as one of "trying to influence the quality of human service delivery systems". She helped to start a Human Resources Center that included a child care center, a summer theater, a teen center, and an art center. She found that during the early 1970s, 17 percent of the families were female-headed households, and she expressed concern for the needs of women who were stuck in the house. Both of the Reiners think "that there is a difference of opinion about the worth of the social amenities package", in contrast to developer Dahlin who in expressing his views on social programs says, "nothing is more deceptive than building programs that cannot be sustained". According to the Reiners, a large segment of the Jonathan residents are articulate and well-educated and have high expectations: "They expect the developer to know what they need and to provide it. . .they don't expect to have to do anything to get it." Steve adds that "These expectations were expressed by a group of people and Nancy's job was to react in a constructive way and to harness existing energy." The couple's philosophy was "to create a framework within which specific programs could be developed". They feel that the management of Jonathan does not understand this philosophy.

/ THE MINNESOTA RENAISSANCE FAIR /

One of the highlights in the area of cultural events takes place each year in Jonathan: the Minnesota Renaissance Fair, which tries to recreate the life of sixteenth-century England. Each September it draws nearly 50,000 people from throughout the Midwest.

Hundreds of artists and craftsmen come colorfully attired in period dress from all over the country to exhibit their wares. The entertainment includes everything from jugglers to swordfighters to concerts by many of the local bands and orchestras. Inaugurated in September 1971, this event promises to become a Jonathan tradition. This type of rich social-cultural activity seems to be rare in the United States in the traditional suburban settings. I remember the Midwest fairs from my college days in Michigan, but I have not come across the type of festive and spirited activity that I experienced in Japan, Sweden, and Greece.

The New Towns such as Reston, Cedar-Riverside, and Jonathan, through their respective festivals, are filling a void that can go a long way to promote better interaction between the diverse peoples that make up this nation.

/ HOUSING /

Jonathan, like its sister New Town, Cedar-Riverside, has broken away from the traditional residential patterns that have resulted from a combination of biased marketing practices, federal program regulations, and restrictive zoning ordinances. Jonathan Senior Vice-President Jules Smith says he—

> . . .would never use the 235 and 236 programs [ownership and rental assistance programs provided by HUD] as they were originally conceived. . . .they are builder programs rather than people programs.

Smith feels that "the nationwide policies need to be changed so that the question of a person's income is not raised with respect to their housing".

The developers of Jonathan have mixed both styles and economic categories in the effort to promote a "sense of community". A mixture of single-family detached houses, townhouses, and apartment complexes will be interspersed to provide a range of homes to

accommodate families from the low and moderate to the upper income range. In one of the neighborhoods observed, $70,000 houses were sited just across the greenway from townhouses that cost less than $20,000. This is difficult to appreciate until the turndown of the Valley View proposal is brought into the picture. In this instance, the developer of the New Town of Irvine, California, sought to locate a complex of moderate income houses in a neighborhood where the existing homes had appreciated considerably, and the residents successfully fought the developer's proposal, which left the neighborhood homogeneous.

Some of the experimental efforts conducted by the developers have centered around modular, stacked, and expandable units. The Tree

Loft apartments are modular units which, in the spring of 1973, provided one- and two-bedroom rentals from $145 to $200 a month. These prices can be contrasted with a more conventional apartment complex, Lake Grace Manor, which offered one- and two-bedroom units from $177.50 and $207.50 a month, respectively.

Rental townhouses such as Carvers Green provide two- and three-bedroom units from $270 and $350 a month. In an effort to lower the cost of housing, the use of prefabricated "stacking units" was examined for mass production purposes. These units were constructed on a small scale but were not marketed on a communitywide basis.

Smith expects that each village will have a high rise for the purposes of identity—the building serves as a visual reference point.

/ COMMUNITY INFORMATION SYSTEM /

One of the most significant experiments and truly innovative efforts to take place in any of the New Towns is that of the Community Information System project that was conducted in Jonathan. This federally assisted project established a two-way capability between the central facility that has computer and television equipment and the information terminals located in hospitals, schools, offices, businesses, and homes. This type of an effort essentially wires the entire community for television, much like a city is normally wired for electricity.

The principal difference between the Jonathan experiment and normal Community Antenna Television (CATV) is that with the Community Information System program, you can "talk back to your television set". Former HUD Assistant Secretary Harry Finger has indicated that "The innovative use of telecommunications, including cable television, may well be another example of a new tool that will help determine and characterize the structure and functions of communities of the future." [65]

As part of the experimental program, doctors in a nearby clinic are using the system to talk with other doctors and to examine patients and x-rays. This use of two-way communications or "telemedicine" may prove to be of particular significance in rural areas where quality medical service is often not available. In another experiment, students at Chaska High School used the two-way capability in a career education project and were able to ask questions of various people on the job to become more familiar with what opportunities actually existed. I expect that it will be difficult to measure the potential of this system. The real challenge will be to ensure that individual privacy is guarded on the one hand, while human interaction and community needs are serviced on the other.

/ SENATOR HENRY T. McKNIGHT AND HIS SUCCESSORS /

The late Senator Henry T. McKnight was a man of great vision and commitment. In addition to Jonathan, where he was the president of the Development Corporation, he was also involved with the development of the New-Town-in-Town of Cedar-Riverside and the New Town of Harbison near Columbia, South Carolina. An editorial in the Jonathan newspaper *Appleseeds* described him as "an American Dreamer" and went on to say that—

> . . .the first forty-five years of Henry McKnight have no focus. We only see the vague outline of a wealthy young man wandering and searching. Private schools, Yale, selling advertising for the *New York Herald Tribune*, the war, ship

command, assistant to the publisher of *Look* Magazine, Washington, agriculture, travel advisory jobs. . . .Then he returns to Minnesota. The family business, Conservation, Politics. The idea of a New Town. Focus. The last ten years of Henry McKnight's life shine with clearness. A man has found a direction. It is never too late. He loves and he cares. The outdoors. Animals. The soil. Music and theater. Minnesota, Picnics. His friends. Innovation and experiment. Travel. Cattle. History. His family. Jonathan. Cedar-Riverside. America.[66]

By the fall of 1969, the presence of Henry McKnight was as familiar on the seventh floor of HUD as most of the staff members working for the Office of Community Planning and Management. He was never in too much of a hurry to share his views on his and other New Town developments. On December 27, 1972, Senator Henry T. McKnight died, leaving as his legacy his community—Jonathan, Minnesota.

His planner Ben Cunningham described him as a man with "great sensitivity to the land and a concern for the people who lived on this land".[67] Gloria Segal, the co-developer of Cedar-Riverside, said of the late Senator: "He had a creative forward imagination which incorporated different pieces of ideas, picked up on a national and international scale"; he was "a man of great complexity and high energy". [68]

Following the untimely death of Henry McKnight, the leadership passed to Robert J. Dahlin who was named the new president of the Jonathan Development Corporation. The transition seemed to be traumatic for both the community and many of the professionals associated with the design and management for the New Town.

An *Appleseeds* editorial on Dahlin described him as a "dollar and cents man". While noting that "he does not intend to change the basic developments of Jonathan", it stated that "he opposes the kind of social planning which he feels invades individual privacy and implies a Big Brother attitude". The editorial continued:

> We must say, however, that in our opinion Jonathan is not just a dollar and cents place, and that cash flow is not the only flow we have to be concerned with. There is also the flow of human beings—their needs and their aspirations. . . .If Bob Dahlin is against planned and regimented lives, we are in complete agreement with him. But if he opposes planning that provides facilities and opportunities for the community, then we think he misses the whole point of a New Town.[69]

If I had a second thought about whether or not Dahlin was a

dollar and cents man, they were put into perspective when I entered his office. His desk was clear except for three yellow legal pads, a desk calculator, and a telephone. He openly admitted his having "a basic predeliction against Big Brotherism". The 44-year-old new chief executive officer has a rich background in real estate management and development.

Bob Dahlin's real-world perspective is balanced by the more people-oriented concepts of Vice-President Jules Smith. At six feet eight inches, Smith is a towering figure. A graduate of the University of Minnesota Law School, he set up the first County Planning Commission in 1957 and was a city attorney in Chaska from 1961 to 1968. He is one of the few people in the New Towns movement who is sensitive to the combined problems of municipal finance, corporate finance, legislative affairs, and social requirements. Smith also serves as president of the Jonathan Association. Of all the people whom I have met in the New Towns business, Jules Smith is the one who could bring the most to the position of general manager of the federal government's New Town Community Development Corporation. Smith is also the only holdover from the original leaders who initiated the Jonathan New Town.

After the change in management, New Community Services, Inc., the planning and design firm made up primarily of staff members from the Jonathan Design Group, was dissolved. The firm was headed by Ben Cunningham, a gifted architect-planner who worked very closely with the late Senator McKnight for nearly seven years to bring Jonathan into being. Cunningham's efforts in Jonathan established him as one of the outstanding planners in the United States. After his departure from Jonathan, Cunningham joined the developers of the New Town of Park Forest South. Following his departure, *Appleseeds* wrote: "That it is happening at all is the achievement of Henry McKnight, Ben Cunningham, the Design Group and the new leaders and residents of the community which honors its land and its life." [70]

The efforts of the late Senator McKnight and Ben Cunningham have provided Jonathan with a good form as a strong departure point. Dahlin's skills along with those of Jules Smith certainly establish an effective management capability. I am, however, concerned that the words of the late Senator need to be taken quite seriously if the potential that is certainly there is to be fully realized. The words that I refer to were expressed by McKnight in a letter to *Appleseeds* in June 1972:

It takes more than a pioneering spirit to build a new town. It also requires, I believe, a strong participation from the new town residents whose wide interests, youthful energy and mellow experience can so significantly contribute to the process of the new town's development.[71]

   Jonathan represents an environmental envelope that will enhance the resident's ability to live in harmony with both nature and his fellow man. The lakes, open spaces, and wildlife preserves are complemented with what will become 44 miles of greenway paths. The differences among driving, bicycling, jogging, and walking are brought into sharp focus by the abundance of natural beauty that is encompassed within the site. Urbanization in the United States has shut many of our citizens off from the biological and cosmic forces that I feel come into play when man is exposed to the natural as opposed to the built environment. There is something that I cannot quite describe, something that is quite stimulating that you experience walking along a lake or under the trees in a light rain. . .or when you have the sun or even the moon rise over your body. Whatever this something is, it comes through in Jonathan.

8

CEDAR-RIVERSIDE

/ A BOLD EXPERIMENT /

One of the boldest urban experiments of the century is taking place in Minneapolis, Minnesota: the development of America's first New-Town-in-Town, Cedar-Riverside.

Initiated in the early 1960s as an attempt to renovate one of the city's oldest neighborhoods, the Cedar-Riverside project has grown from a small real estate operation in an area involving a population of 4000 people into a planned 340-acre community that will over the next 20 years become home to some 30,000 residents. But Cedar-Riverside's

importance lies not simply in the scope of its facilities—it will also provide a crucial test of the viability of the central city as a place to live.

In over two decades of increased activity in the area of development from all levels of government, the United States has failed to rebuild its central cities—that is, to make them livable. Yet leading planners such as Dr. Harvey Perloff, dean of the Graduate School of

Architecture and Planning at the University of California at Los Angeles, have consistently advocated the concept of New-Towns-in-Town. Insisting that urban problems must be faced head-on, Dr. Perloff has charged that "outlying New Towns are an escape from the social reality".

In June 1971, the federal government, through HUD, approved the request for assistance to Cedar-Riverside in the form of a $24 million loan guarantee. The decision represented more than the endorsement of the county's first New-Town-inTown; it was a bold and unprecedented step at the national level to address the plight of the central city. The risk is real. Developer Gloria Segal warns that "If Cedar-Riverside fails as a demonstration, then I am concerned with the viability of the revitalization of cities throughout the country." Cedar-Riverside's chances of success, however, are strengthened both by its location and by the talent that has gone into the planning.

The state of Minnesota has been among the leaders nationally in planning and conservation. It has provided the U.S. Senate with Walter Mondale, one of the nation's leading housing advocates. Similarly, Minneapolis, the fifteenth largest city in the United States,

provides a uniquely favorable atmosphere for urban experiments like Cedar-Riverside. Called by newspaper publisher Barry Casselman "the bio-magnetic center of North America", Minneapolis has an established and growing employment base. Its citizens are politically sophisticated and active; yet there is little political tension or other related problems that afflict most large eastern cities. The university community contributes an additional element of open-mindedness. Moreover, the Minneapolis-St. Paul Metropolitan Planning Agency has been one of the most progressive in the nation.

But perhaps Minneapolis' strongest asset is its rich resource of human talent. Joining Segal as originators of the Cedar-Riverside concept were developer Keith Heller, formerly with the Business School at the University of Minnesota, and the late Senator Henry McKnight, the developer of another of Minnesota's New Towns, Jonathan. As the New-Town-in-Town idea unfolded, the Heller-Segal team grew to include other Minneapolis citizens: Ralph Rapson, the project architect; Don Jacobson, the staff planner; and Dr. David Cooperman, supervisor of social planning. They, in turn, have drawn on the contributions of internationally prominent professionals such as the economic consultant firm, Hammer, Green, and Siler Associates; landscape architect Lawrence Halprin; and Heikki von Hertzen, planner of Finland's New Town of Tapiola.

/ THE NEIGHBORHOOD /

During renovation, the first phase of the Cedar-Riverside plan, the Heller-Segal team sought to save a neighborhood rich in ethnic heritage but sad in history. The story of Cedar-Riverside goes back over a hundred years. Occupied primarily by Scandinavian immigrants, the area reached its prime in 1910 with a population of some 20,000 Swedes, Norwegians, and Bohemians. As time went on, however, and freeways sprang up to the north and south, forming a three-way boundary with the Mississippi River to the east, the area was cut off from the rest of the city. By the 1950s, decline was evident. By the early 1960s, the place was a known haven for crime. Buildings with turn-of-the-century charm housed beer halls, and movie theaters specialized in "skin flicks"; the neighborhood resembled a skid row.

Now, less than 10 years after the Heller-Segal team went to work, the changes are dramatic: today, Cedar-Riverside reminds one of New York's Greenwich Village or Washington, D.C.'s Georgetown. I got my first taste of its old-world charm in April 1973, when at Gloria Segal's invitation. I traveled to Minneapolis for Cedar-Riverside's "Second Annual Snoose Boulevard Festival".

"Snoose Boulevard" (meaning Snuff Boulevard, named after a cheap and popular tobacco) recalls the area in Minneapolis where Scandinavian immigrants originally settled. The festival is a celebration of the cultural heritage that once flourished there. As I watched the festival officially begin with a colorful parade led by the Swedish language division of the Salvation Army, it was not hard to imagine what life must have been like at the turn of the century.

Continuing throughout the two-day festival were open-air songfests, public dances, jam sessions with Swedish and Norwegian fiddlers, concerts by the multi-talented Anne-Charlotte Harvey and her troupe of entertainers, as well as demonstrations of crafts such as spinning and weaving at specialty shops like "Depth of Field". Musicals, plays, and sing-alongs lured the public into landmarks like the Old Firehouse and Dania Hall, dedicated in 1886 as a community center and fulfilling its purpose once again.

Local merchants provided a variety of Scandinavian cuisine to the delight of some 10,000 festival-goers. Edna's Cafe, for example, featured Norwegian "fattigmand" and Swedish meatballs; Ellison's offered homemade Swedish sausage and fishballs, flatbread, and imported Scandinavian cheese. The bars, of course, served Scandinavian beer. The shrimp I sampled at the Fuji International rivaled any I'd had in Tokyo. Another international touch was the London double-decker bus, especially loaned to the festival for tourists too tired to tour any longer on foot.

I continued my trek, marveling at the dramatic changes I knew had taken place here. Of 33 bars that once lined what is now Cedar Avenue, only about half remain. The Cedar Theater, once known for the aforementioned "skin flicks", now houses the Minnesota Dance Theater. A former beer and dance hall has been converted to house Theater-in-the-Round, a 20-year-old community theater group. A former knitting mill houses the Guild of Performing Arts, which has schools of dance, music, and theater. In addition, many of the area's vacant lots have been transformed into mini-parks. And the walls of adjacent buildings, once barren and in disrepair, have been brought back to life with colorful super graphics—the likes of which I had never seen before.

Beyond the main streets of Cedar Avenue and Riverside Avenue are homes for the present population of about 4000 people. Many are two-story frame dwellings with front yards. Occasionally there is a white picket fence, recalling the age-old "American dream". Scattered among these single-family units are 3-story walk-up apartment buildings that house many of the students attending the nearby University of Minnesota. One resident, with whom I stopped to talk, reminded me of the rich mixture of Cedar-Riverside's people when he described his neighbors in an apartment building in the 400 block of Cedar Avenue as "young, old, Africans, whites, Chinese, homosexuals, and Jesus freaks".

Indeed, perhaps more exciting than the concerts, demonstrations, and delicious Scandinavian dishes were the people themselves. The festival attracted a rich cross section of the young as well as the old, the wealthy and the poor, Scandinavians as well as a variety of ethnic

groups and nationalities. The people took over, singing, dancing, eating, shopping, talking, laughing. Still others stood around on the street corners and sidewalks, as the old-timers did, watching the parade of people.

/ TWENTIETH-CENTURY REALITY /

But even in the midst of Old World celebration, the people of Cedar-Riverside never forget that theirs is the twentieth century—for dwarfing the landmarks of yesteryear is what has been called a "concrete phoenix", the complex of 12 high rise buildings comprising Cedar Square West, the first stage of the New-Town-in-Town. Reaching as high as 40 stories, the buildings of Cedar Square West remind us that Cedar-Riverside is not just a success story in the annals of urban renewal; it has a challenge yet to meet.

The heart of the challenge lies in the fact that Cedar-Riverside seeks to attain two diverse goals. The first is to develop high residential density in order to provide for the area's institutions. At the same time, the plan calls for the creation of a socially and economically integrated community out of heterogeneous population.

Five institutions make up the New Town's employment base: the University of Minnesota's West Bank Campus, Augsburg College, St. Mary's Junior College, St. Mary's Hospital, and Fairview Hospital. The combined visitor-working population is expected to amount to 75,000 daily. To meet this demand, five neighborhoods are planned surrounding a town center with a variety of shops, a hotel, and space for offices. More specifically, the development plan calls for the construction of nearly 13,000 units that will be interconnected by a series of elevated walkways and plazas.

In considering the pros and cons of high rises, pure theory must be weighed against the reality of the American urban experience where millions commute daily to and from the central cities, wasting precious hours and polluting the air with their automobiles, and where many find themselves cut off from a variety of educational, social, and cultural experiences and activities. Ultimately, however, the choice will be made by the people themselves. As University of Minnesota graduate student Curt Suplee puts it: "I didn't come here [to Cedar Square West] because of the architecture. I came because it is the cheapest and closest place to the University."

The simultaneous goals of New-Town-in-Town Cedar-Riverside—to create both social and economic integration in a heterogeneous community—provide another facet of the Cedar-Riverside "experiment". The prognosis for this aspect is good because "people-conscious" developer Segal is transferring much of her own social philosophy into the project. She wants Cedar-Riverside to be "a place for people who love cities". Consequently, of all the New Towns under way in the United States, with the possible exception of Columbia, Maryland, Cedar-Riverside has the strongest emphasis on social planning, cultural activities, and housing for mixed income groups.

/ EFFECTING A HOUSING MIX /

With rare exception, people who receive some form of assistance from the local or federal government to offset housing costs are made visible either by the architecture or by the location of their dwelling units. Even in those few cases where assisted housing is "scattered" throughout a neighborhood, it is usually given away by a less than stylish design and other features that suggest that the occupants are somehow "different" from their neighbors. The New Town of Cedar-Riverside is taking the approach of making those who are in need of and who will receive assistance from the federal government "invisible".

Through a unique combination of financing methods, the developers have created a plan that will allow for about 100 units of publicly assisted housing, over 500 units of federally assisted housing, and slightly more than 400 units of market rate housing to exist within the first stage. These units will not have any exterior characteristics that will distinguish between them. Problems have beset this unprecedented approach. For example, the developers were unable to get the support of a private mortgage company; instead, they had to work out a program with HUD, which meant additional bureaucratic hurdles.

But developer Segal believes Cedar-Riverside will prove that an economic mix can work. The New Town experience can then be shared by students, the elderly, professionals—everyone, no matter what his tax bracket.

/ SOCIAL PLANNING /

To provide social services for such a diverse group of people is no small job. Kathi Connell is a human resources/social planner who was associated with the Cedar-Riverside project during its early stages of development as a New Town. Young, well-educated, and energetic, Connell asserted that "The essence of social planning is livability—that is, the creation of space that not only reflects people's needs but allows them to mature." According to her, it is the social services component that will eventually link Cedar-Riverside to the lifeblood of the city of Minneapolis.

Each of the five neighborhoods that will make up the New Town will have a facility including a child care center and a 24-hour health clinic. Both the child care centers and the health clinics will have fee schedules that, in effect, will be scaled to accommodate the needs of all income groups.

Special steps have also been taken to address the needs of the handicapped. In addition to individually designed living units, ramps are being provided from the grade to the plaza level to allow complete access for those who are dependent upon wheelchairs. Because it is expected that 10 percent of the total population will be elderly, the social planner is working through a variety of task forces to ensure that their needs are answered as well.

/ ACCEPTING THE BURDEN TO INFORM /

The New-Town-in-Town of Cedar-Riverside has provided a range of opportunities for blacks that spans finance, employment, construction contracts, and business in the commercial sector. Behind this effort is Charles Williams, a skillful affirmative action officer who, like his counterparts in Park Forest South, Columbia, and The New York State Urban Development Corporation, spends his full energies in this area. At 34 Williams has succeeded in bringing about some changes for blacks that, at the least, must be described as dramatic.

In 1973, the black-owned Nash Construction Company completed a 30-unit, $615,000 building that is part of the first stage of the massive New-Town-in-Town. After completing this job, the Nash Company went on to perform a contract for another client in the amount of about $2 million. Another black firm, the Munson Plastering Company, completed a job for about $240,000 in the first stage of the Cedar-Riverside complex. In addition to these, contracts have been

awarded to a black carpeting firm for about $40,000; to a black-owned landscaping firm for over $100,000; and to a black painting contractor, Napue Painting, for about $85,000. In addition to this, the developer maintains over a million dollars on deposit with a local black-controlled bank, First Plymouth National.

In spite of these successes, Charles Williams still has to "go to the businesses" and often finds that potential contractors or entrepreneurs will say, "You're jiving", or "You're just here 'cause the government sent you." Williams takes it upon himself to "accept the burden to inform", as he puts it, "if it is misinformation" that must be countered. Williams is critical of the Small Business Administration and feels that "with all of its stringent criteria—it is not geared to the needs of the black businessman".

Charles Williams is an extremely sensitive person who is understanding but not hung up on the issue of race. Part of his sensitivity stems from his experience of having been born and raised in what he calls "the gutter" of St. Louis, Missouri, as a member of a family of nine. While there is a visible record of achievement, Williams is not at all content to rest on any laurels. The complimentary newspaper articles and photos have not found their way to the walls of his modest office; they are buried deep beneath the papers on his desk. He freely admits to having to bargain internally with the developer and other members of the staff. He finds that it is necessary to compromise and adds that compromising comes easy. "In the ghetto every day is a compromise." When a problem arises internally, Charles Williams frequently goes right to the top to get policies changed. He feels at this level that "If you have to compromise with the President, at least you will be on a par with other areas in the company."

/ THE ARTS /

In any community the arts provide a priceless avenue for social and spiritual harmony. In an area as rich with artists and cultural interest groups as Minneapolis is, Cedar-Riverside's efforts are as important in forming the spiritual strength of the community as the steel beams and millions of tons of cement are in forming the structural strength of the "concrete phoenix". In fact, like John Coiner, an activist craftsman in the area, the residents are vocal in their demands for development of all kinds of social, recreational, and especially cultural activities.

In answering this challenge, Cedar-Riverside Associates has added another "first" to their list of New Town innovations. Assisted financially by the National Endowment for the Arts, the development

team includes an advocate arts planner, a sort of ombudsman-organizer who acts as initiator and liaison with the artists and cultural organizations in the Minneapolis area. Filling this role is Ann Payson, holder of master's degrees in English and art history from the University of Minnesota, as well as being a dancer and musician who also enjoys archaeology.

Since March 1972, Payson has sought to "represent the realistic cultural needs and potential of the community" by working with the Minnesota Opera, the Minnesota Dance Theater, the Guild of Performing Arts, the Theater-in-the-Round, Shakespeare in the Streets, the West Bank Arts Gallery, the Dudley Riggs Brave New Workshop, and a host of other groups to ensure that the rich artistic and cultural resources of the area are fully developed. In addition to the normal space requirements that the development team must deal with, Payson is also working to obtain a sufficient number of housing units for resident artists to accommodate those in the present neighborhood and those who might want to become a part of the New Town.

Cedar-Riverside, as an urban experiment, faces unexpected challenges every day. And like anything so new, it demands flexibility and varieties of talent from its leaders. It is noteworthy that the Cedar-Riverside team, unlike most working on New Towns in the United

States, draws heavily on the resources and involvement of young people, blacks, and women. Considering that the accomplishments of Gloria Segal, it is lamentable that she is one of the few women in executive positions in the New Town movement.

Cedar-Riverside is probably the closest that any U.S. development comes to representing the ideas initially espoused by the late Le Corbusier. Rather than to side with either Corbusier, the advocate of the vertical city, or Doxiadis, who asserts that "high rises work against man", I view Cedar-Riverside as an alternative to automobile dependency insofar as adults are concerned. Although material on the adverse effects of high rise living is rather thin, it does seem logical to conclude that it will be to the disadvantage of young children to live above the first few floors.

Further, it is essential that our large central cities be given new life. While Cedar-Riverside represents one approach, it is by no means the only alternative. The New-Towns-in-Town like Cedar-Riverside, Roosevelt Island, and Fort Lincoln are potentially the most responsive to the pressing issues of the central city and, because of their locations, the developments with the highest density. They will probably become the New Towns with the greatest accessibility to a wide range of activities and diversity.

Paradoxically, the solution to revitalizing existing cities and building new ones that are viable lies between the vertical and horizontal alternatives; in this regard, Cedar-Riverside has sought no middle ground.

/ THE LARGEST PRIVATELY FINANCED NEW TOWN IN THE WORLD /

Irvine, California, is the largest privately financed New Town being developed anywhere in the world. The total area of 83,000 acres or 130 square miles is expected to have a population in excess of 400,000 people by the year 2000!

I first visited Irvine in the spring of 1970 at the encouragement of architect-planner William Pereira and one of his top associates, Ben-Ami Friedman. Irvine had not received much attention in the East, where Reston and Columbia dominated the discussions on New Towns. I had low expectations and some reservations as to whether Irvine was pursuing New Town objectives as I had come to understand them. After several days with Ray Watson, then the executive vice-president; Dick Reese, the director of planning; and Tom Ashley, an economist—and a complete tour of the site and surrounding area—I found the Irvine undertaking mind-boggling.

Much of the thinking within HUD is that "the private sector just doesn't function without guidance from the government". Reston wasn't respected because of its financial difficulties, and Columbia was regarded as something that happened only because of Connecticut General's backing, something that would probably never happen again. Within HUD a prevailing notion was that the federal government would set the course for New Town development in the nation.

Irvine and other New Towns, especially in Southern California, have proved this "thinking" untrue. My first impressions of Irvine centered around its scale, site, sophisticated management, planning concepts, and socio-economic profile. During the period from 1970 to 1973, I have had occasion to visit Irvine almost a dozen times and have been able to experience more than what initially met the eye. More importantly, I have met many of the students and residents who provide a more balanced point of departure for an interpretation of what Irvine is about.

An advertisement that appeared in the *Los Angeles Times* on October 1, 1972, indicated: "Only six places in the world have that perfect combination of coastal beauty and kindly climate known as 'Mediterranean'." The six places noted were Nice, France; Botany Bay, Australia; Capetown, South Africa; Vina del Mar, Chile; the Dardanelles; and Irvine, California.[72]

What is said of Irvine might hold true for a large part of Southern California which, with its Mediterranean climate, is the most intensive area of New Town development in the United States. Within the short span of the 150 or so miles between Santa Barbara and San Diego, there are eight large-scale developments that some refer to as New Towns. These developments include Valencia, Westlake, Irvine, Rancho Bernardo, Laguna Niguel, Rancho California, Mission Viejo, and Rancho San Diego. The sizes of these developments range from 4000 to 83,000 acres and the planned populations from 30,000 to over 400,000. Collectively, these developments represent a total area of about 130,000 acres and a projected population of almost 800,000 people. Almost without exception, these developments are middle and upper class economically, with a strong emphasis on residential and recreational uses. The development that is pursuing the greatest challenge in "city building" is Irvine.

In 1864, the Irvine site was originally purchased by James Irvine and combined with some Mexican ranches and a Spanish land grant to form the Irvine Ranch. Irvine's son, James, Jr., put the ownership and management of the entire ranch under the Irvine

Company in 1894. The land remained primarily agricultural for the next 60 years. In 1937 the James Irvine Foundation was formed and was assigned 51 percent of the stock of the Irvine Company. In 1960, the internationally prominent architecture and planning firm of William L. Pereira & Associates was retained to develop a master plan for a large segment of the Irvine properties. During the same period, the Irvine Company donated 1000 acres to the University of California for the site of a new campus. In December 1971, the city of Irvine was incorporated, representing about 18,000 acres and some 20,000 people. In June 1974 the city had expanded to approximately 26,000 acres and 29,300 people.

The Irvine property extends from the Pacific Ocean inland 22 miles to the Lomas de Santiago Mountains and is within the sphere of influence of the cities of Santa Ana, Costa Mesa, Newport Beach, Laguna Beach, and Tustin.

Company President Ray Watson calls Irvine "a city of villages". Within this "city of villages", the Mediterranean climate, coastal location, and topographic features provide for a wide range of activities and land uses.

A principal focal point is Newport Center, a 622-acre commercial complex situated on a bluff overlooking the Pacific Ocean. Within this well-designed complex of space-age architecture, there is a shopping center with four major department stores and about 60 shops, a financial center that houses 90 or so firms, a modern medical complex, restaurants, and a 1350-seat theater. Twin 9-story high rise office towers, along with the 18-story Union Bank Building, the 16-story Avco Financial Center, and the 10-acre headquarters complex for Pacific Mutual Life Insurance Company, give a distinctive urban character and sense of permanence in an "age of transience".

Another focal point is the 1500-acre campus of the University

of California at Irvine. The buildings, like those in Newport Center, are well spaced and reflect an urban character. This campus opened in 1965 with 1600 students and has an enrollment that in 1973 was approaching the 10,000 mark. In addition to the nine-building fine arts center which was completed in 1971, the University of California at Irvine will contain a major engineering school and the California College of Medicine. Although a relatively new campus, the athletic teams have succeeded in capturing an impressive number of National Collegiate Athletic Association championships in swimming, tennis, baseball, and golf. In early 1973, Olympic decathalon champion Bill Toomey was appointed head track coach at UCI. Toomey's abilities and interests extend well beyond the area of athletics and into community affairs, public relations, education, and business, where his talents also command respect. Bill Toomey also represented the President of the United States at the 1972 Olympic Games in Munich, Germany. From the conversations we have had, I expect that he will internationalize track and field at the New Town

in that he has expressed an interest in training athletes from developing nations at the Irvine campus.

The Irvine industrial complex is "the fastest growing industrial park in the nation", according to its president Tom Wolff. Formerly with the Howard Research and Development Company, developers of the New Town of Columbia, Maryland, Wolff now oversees the development of a 4000-acre site that has over 1000 diverse companies as tenants. This

complex, where over 30,000 people work, is served by three freeways and two railroads, and is within 30 minutes of the Los Angeles and Long Beach port facilities. The significance of the industrial sector of a New Town is often not appreciated. Regardless of the form of a New Town, it is the industrial sector that provides the opportunity to realize a broad tax base, in addition to creating more jobs in the commercial sector. The unparalleled success of the Irvine industrial complex gives added support to the expectation that Irvine will become a viable city.

In addition to these focal points, there are six shopping centers serving the nine Villages presently completed or under development, a 336-acre regional park, an 18-hole public golf course, a 185-acre county park, the Big Canyon Country Club which includes an 18-hole championship golf course, a lake in the mountain foothills, a 700-acre motorcycle and trail bike course, and other recreational and cultural amenities.

/ THE FIGHT TO HOUSE MODERATE INCOME FAMILIES /

In the midst of opulence and an environmental envelope that commands envy worldwide, there is controversy on providing housing opportunities for moderate income families.

During the early stages in the process of developing New Towns, it is not unusual for development companies to favor the middle and upper income sectors of the market in an effort to improve the flow of cash and offset some of the high front-end service costs. When this happens, however, the risks are that a negative inertia will build up and that the people who get in during the early stages and realize rapid appreciation in the value of their houses will not be favorably disposed to additional units with prices that either approach what they paid originally or are lower. A clear case of bias against possible residents who might occupy moderate income housing has emerged in this New Town.

The developer's proposal to provide housing for about 11,000 people on a site of about 484 acres, 200 acres of which would be developed in the first phase, brought forth the wrath of home owner groups in the area in early 1973. The housing would have been for families with incomes from $8500 to $12,000 a year, and the units were initially priced from $20,000 to $32,000. The complex was to include a townhouse section of 912 units, 375 apartment units, and 504 detached homes with respective densities of 12, 25, and 7 units per acre. The opponents of the project argued that the density was too high; that it would adversely affect the school population, traffic, and surrounding property values; and that it would incur costs for flood protection.

In March 1973, the Planning Commission voted 6 to 1 to approve the project with a recommendation to lower the density by reducing the total number of units from 1791 to 1358. In one of the numerous hearings held to discuss the Valley View Village project, the following questions were asked: "Will the people who buy here be on welfare and/or government support?" "Has there been a study on minorities who will move in, and will those minorities make an imbalance in the schools, necessitating busing to other schools?" "Why does the Irvine Company feel this area is important?" "If it fails, will it wash its hands of it or move the entire project to another location intact?" One person commented, "I came from Covina where the majority of these kinds of people were on food stamps." [73]

In February 1973, the City Council of Irvine voted 3-2 to reject federal assistance for housing for low and moderate income families, and subsequently voted against the Valley View project, which would not have been federally assisted, thus closing the doors of the New Town to moderate income families. In rejecting the use of federal assistance, one councilman reportedly said, "Almost every case of federally subsidized housing we know about has proved to be a disaster." [74] In contrast to this dissenting councilman is Councilwoman Gabrielle Pryor who supported the use of federal housing programs and decried the council's attitude toward this type of housing assistance as a "socialistic bugaboo". [75]

The City of Irvine Planning Commission approved the forming of a study committee to develop alternative means of housing moderate income families. Councilwoman Pryor has suggested a goal of 15 percent of the total New Town for moderate income housing on a basis that would scatter the units throughout the entire development with no more than two houses being built next to each other.

The issue of providing increased housing opportunities within the city of Irvine was brought into sharp focus by George Leidal who wrote an editorial in a local newspaper, the *Daily Pilot*:

> Evidently there are some in the city of Irvine who do not share the general view that this most blessed of future cities will someday become a "model urban environment".
>
> Worse than the mounting attacks on the Irvine Company's proposed Village of Valley View and its "moderate priced" housing–from $20,000 to $30,000 per home–it appears these same "some" do not care to share whatever Irvine is to become with blacks, Chicanos, widows or divorcees with children. [76]

Of Valley View, Leidal went on to say:

It meets the needs of families earning from $9,600 to $12,000 a year—teachers, journalists, postmen, policemen, young executives, truck drivers, plumbers and many others. But, at recent meetings on the proposed new Irvine village, there have been those who've objected to making room in the new city for these people, and Marines from El Toro or Santa Ana, and "welfare" clients, and divorced women "with all those children" and transient young people.

If these views prevail, one may only wonder who will be the next group of people to be excluded from the model urban environment?

People below a certain IQ? Others with too many college degrees? People who limp? Jews?

How about blue-eyed blond males over six feet? That includes me. Of course, were Hitler alive today he would welcome me into his society, so I wouldn't need Irvine, or its restricted $50,000-plus inventory of homes.[77]

The Leidal editorial correctly points to the areas of race and class that may be more descriptive of the real motivations than the arguments of density, traffic congestion, school crowding, the costs for flood control, and federal assistance.

The people of the New Town must come to grips with this issue and consider the obsession with promoting a life style against the disadvantages that can arise by excluding the school teachers, the policemen, the firemen, the hospital aides, the enlisted military personnel, the factory workers, the elderly, the artists, the handicapped, the divorcees with or without children, the young married couples, the blacks, the Chicanos—in short, the full socio-economic spectrum of society.

If Irvine cannot provide housing for those who represent all of society, it will greatly compromise its worth as a city, its growth will be stunted, and it will not serve as an appropriate legacy to those who have labored arduously to give it the potential for greatness. Perhaps more than this, Irvine, without a balanced representation of its region, will risk becoming unnecessarily sterile and masked in environmental opulence.

What has happened in Irvine is typical of what has happened in most of the suburbs in the United States. What is different is that there is an astute Planning Commission, a developer with a sense of purpose, and an emerging leadership from some of the elected officials to deal substantively with the issue. Therefore, the fight goes on.

In the New Towns of Columbia, Reston, Jonathan, and Park

Forest South, the provision of housing for low and moderate income families was initiated very early in the development process. This probably minimized the level of resistance that might have resulted. In addition, for the most part, the people in these New Towns knew what they were becoming a part of conceptually—a New Town that was being developed for a broad range of income categories.

The Irvine City Council, perhaps for different reasons, is not entirely wrong for opposing the concentration of housing for moderate income families. Also, there is much truth in the assertion that federal housing programs are a "disaster". In the New Towns of Columbia, Jonathan, and Cedar-Riverside, the developers successfully fought existing federal regulations and were able to effect a mix of units for low and moderate income families within areas of market rate housing.

In Sweden, the housing for low and moderate income families is completely indistinguishable from the market rate units. The mix effected in Cedar-Riverside comes closest to this practice. In the British New Towns, an individual or family can, within the same unit, go from being subsidized by the government to paying market rent to assuming a mortgage.

The negative image of federally assisted housing projects in the United States is, to a large extent, a result of the federal government's forcing concentration without providing the full range of support services necessary to ensure a reasonable quality of life for the residents. This has resulted in poor or no maintenance, the bankruptcy of administering housing authorities, and, in many instances, an insalubrious environment.

In contrast to the poor neighborhoods of many of the large central cities where the jobs are nonexistent and municipal services are lacking, New Towns offer a much more realistic alternative to providing housing for moderate and low income families. In this situation the employment and educational opportunities and services are more supportive of people trying to get a new lease on life.

An alternative to subsidizing the unit is providing a subsidy to the family or the individual. This provides for a smoother transition toward enabling others to enjoy the full range of benefits that prospective residents of the New Town seek to enjoy.

In early 1974, representatives of the Irvine City Council under the leadership of Councilwoman Gaby Pryor met with the developer and worked out a proposal called "Executive Homes". (Since the proposal covers moderate income housing, the choice of "Executive Homes" is a wise one because it serves to alleviate the stigma that is often attached to this type of housing.) The latest proposal calls for small clusters of 30 to 40 units within a cul-de-sac type of setting scattered throughout the New Town. This would take the form of an add-on zone that could be applied in any Village and would allow densities of 10 to 15 units per acre, even in a normal single-family or townhouse neighborhood that might have anywhere from 5 to 12 units per acre. The increased density for "Executive Homes" is necessary to reduce the per unit cost. The use of small clusters avoids concentration in any one Village. The developer has indicated that the City Council would have to allow these add-on zones in a sufficient number of places to permit an annual volume of 100 to 150 units in order to realize economies of scale from mass building. This proposal has been accepted by the City Council, and the developer is proceeding with efforts to apply it to a number of Villages.

In contrast to the countless number of local elected officials whom I encountered while with HUD who felt they would seriously jeopardize their political careers by dealing forcefully with efforts to provide housing for low and moderate income families in their communities, there is the example of Irvine's Gaby Pryor. As a member of the City Council, she has led the fight to provide housing for moderate income families, and it is to her credit as well as that of the New Town that she was the top vote-getter in the March 1974 elections when all five incumbent members of the City Council were up for election. As a result, she was elected mayor.

/ URBAN PLANNING IN PRACTICE /

The Irvine Company maintains a staff of nearly 40 people to carry out its planning activities under the direction of Dick Reese, vice-president for planning. The planning operation is, indeed, one of the most sophisticated efforts of its kind and is complete with scale models, maps, renderings, a computer-assisted data base, alternative schemes, numerous substantive reports, and, most important, a staff of exceptionally talented people. Most of the urban planners in the United States are philosophers and analysts. Dick Reese is one of the few practicing professionals; he is also the vice-chairman of the New Communities Council for the Urban Land Institute.

One of the unique aspects of the Irvine planning concept is the system of "activity corridors" that weave throughout the massive site, holding the principal focal points together. Within the activity corridors will be a concentration of recreational and neighborhood-oriented commercial activities, along with footpaths and bicycle trails. Ultimately, Irvine will consist of about 40 Villages of which 9 are already in existence.

In implementing the master plan for Irvine, Reese points out that the company must deal with political jurisdictions representing the cities of Irvine, Newport Beacch, Tustin, Laguna Beach, Costa Mesa, Santa Ana, and Orange, in addition to Orange County and the State of California. They also must deal with four school districts, four public utility companies, and the South Coast Regional Commission. Although Irvine is within the five-county jurisdiction of the Southern California Association of Governments (SCAG), the company has not had any appreciable involvement with SCAG because it has not applied for any federal funds.

In the process of developing the Irvine properties, a garden environment is being created out of a semi-arid climate by a sophisticated water management system. Irvine has a current water management program with a five million gallon per day capacity for total reclamation at the primary and secondary levels of treatment. Currently used for agricultural irrigation, it is proposed that the system provide reclaimed water for the irrigation of all major planned open spaces.

To fully appreciate the planning initiatives that have taken place at Irvine, one need only look out of the window of an airplane after departing from Los Angeles International on one of those rare clear days. In contrast to the sprawl that seems to go on for endless miles, there is Irvine, a form that suggests the work of a giant sculptor who wanted to show that there is an alternative to strip development, leap frog development, overhead utility lines, physical blight, freeways that look like spaghetti overlaid on an erecter set, billboards, and the smog that results from the misuse of the automobile.

In asserting the policy of the company, Dick Reese says, "In the design of Irvine, we are intent on dealing with the psychological as well as the physical."

/ COMMUNITY ASSOCIATIONS /

A resident of the New Town talks of how "people occupy themselves with community affairs and recreation". The backbone of this New Town–and perhaps, after money, the life blood of Irvine–is the interaction of its citizenry. In terms of voluntary activity and organization, the Irvine Community Association is a model that other New Towns might seek to emulate.

The community association concept has been in use since the inception of the New Town and has proved successful both in bringing people together and in effectively maintaining common properties. No small by-product of this activity is that through effective maintenance, the value of properties in developed and undeveloped areas has been preserved and increased.

The Community Association of Irvine functions more like the cluster associations in Reston than like the Columbia Association. The purposes of the community associations in Irvine, which are compulsory for home owners, are to "maintain common areas, . . .effect architectural control, . . .enforce community rules governing use of the common areas, . . .carry out cultural, educational, recreational and social activities, . . .involve youth in responsible planning, prepare and distribute newsletters, . . .and take other actions deemed to be in the best interest of the community". [78]

The community associations have been outstandingly successful in organizing club and group activities, such as drama, bridge, and athletic events. There are also similar activities for teen-agers.

The Irvine experience has shown that it is important to structure the size of each community association in relation to the amount of the common area that has to be maintained so that the dues and assessments are equitable. It has also been revealed that vandalism is reduced in areas where teen-agers participate with community associations in planning and other functions.

/ CULTURAL SHOCK FOR SOME /

The racial integration that exists in Irvine centers, for the most part, around the University of California at Irvine. By the end of 1972, the population of the University reached about 8000, of which almost 10 percent are black and Chicano.

Steve, a black student from Los Angeles, describes his new surroundings as a "wig out". His immediate reaction was one of cultural shock since the Irvine environment was a sharp departure from his former neighborhood.

Another black student from Watts describes the surroundings as "machine oriented" and feels that the university environment is "very controlled". He did find that for the first time in his life, however he got "all the food" he could eat.

A female student talked of how negatively "the sisters" reacted to "brothers" dating the white students. "Sisters got into powder puff football just to take out frustrations on the white girls."

Floyd is a 21-year-old black pre-med student who has been at UCI for over two years. He points out that there is a big difference between the campus area and the city of Irvine, but adds, "I am not concerned with socio-economic diversity. I would like for Irvine to stay small."

Eugene is 25, works in Irvine but lives in nearby Santa Ana, and earns about $10,000 a year by working two jobs. "I think it would be good to live in Irvine; I just don't want anyone to bother my property. I want a nice place to live and don't want our twins to be hassled."

The black students indicate that there is little interaction between the campus and the rest of the New Town area. There are usually small parties given on weekends, and quite a few of the students drive back to Los Angeles to visit their friends in their former neighborhoods. The mood of one black student seemed to reflect that of many who have opted for a good educational opportunity at the expense of social fulfillment. "The first year was the roughest. I never worked so hard in my life, but I have never learned so much either."

An outlet for the many who are frustrated in the new environment comes in the form of a black theater group—THE BODACIOUS BOO-GORILLA—where they can participate as actors or audience.

/ TOWARD VIABILITY /

Irvine is exceptionally planned, well managed, suitably located, and environmentally appealing. There are no monuments in Irvine to suggest that the days of grandeur may have passed. Irvine, with the University of California campus, is sure to become academically stimulating. With the abundance of open space including golf courses, lakes, ocean front, riding trails, even tot lots, it is the best of playgrounds for all ages. Certainly one cannot argue against the success of Tom Wolff and company with the Irvine industrial complex or the success of any of the other well-trained, highly motivated, super-educated members of management and their related organizational areas. They are good guys whose "real world" experience establishes the "bottom line" as the point of departure.

But something is missing in Irvine. The university community notwithstanding, Irvine is a place more for those who have "made it" than for those who "want to make it". It is, therefore, essential that the efforts of Mayor Pryor and writer George Leidal continue toward effecting housing opportunities for all members of society. Diversity is, at the least, an essential ingredient in the make-up of a community seeking viability. As Irvine becomes more diverse with respect to representing the ethnic and economic groups that exist within its region, it will then realize its full potential as a viable community.

10

AN INTERVIEW WITH LUD ASHLEY

Thomas Ludlow Ashley is and has been a major figure in the Congress of the United States as a supporter of New Towns. In addition, since his election to the 84th and each succeeding Congress, he has been involved with legislative efforts to provide housing for low and moderate income families, the elderly, and the handicapped. Ashley recognized the significance of the Housing Act of 1968 that provided some support for New Towns, and in 1969, along with other members of Congress and the business community, he toured the New Towns in Europe.

After further study and liaison work, which involved the National League of Cities and the Conference of Mayors, a report on New Towns, sponsored by the Ford Foundation, was released. Ashley subsequently took the initiative to form an ad hoc subcommittee of the Subcommittee on Housing to deal with New Towns and urban growth. Special hearings on New Towns followed and then the drafting of the Ashley bill that subsequently became the Urban Growth and New Community Development Act of 1970. It was this piece of legislation that provided a major impetus toward launching the New Town movement within the United States.

An interview I held with him on May 23, 1973 reveals the quality of his involvement and leadership:

Campbell: What was your motivation for putting the New Community package together, and how did you sell the idea?

Ashley: My interest goes back 8 or 10 years to when I became thoroughly disenchanted with the traditional development process. Traditionally, it has taken place without planning, without consideration of the fundamental needs of people, and, in many respects, it is the worst example of a private enterprise system which, of course, is calculated upon the profits of mortgage, and on occasion (in this situation, particularly) with regard to the building of housing and neighborhood type facilities, it seems to me that our history has been a very, very oblique one—and it is the worst of what the private sector can do.

Blacks, for the most part, have not been able to afford to live in other than the lowest priced housing which has been within our central cities and economic racial ghettos. The people who have been able to move to the suburbs and join the out migration have been those who could afford to do so. As a matter of public policy, this is absolutely wrong. That these kinds of developmental aberrations were, in considerable respect, promoted by the federal government through FHA, particularly since the post-World War II period, does not alter the fact at all. In retrospect, this was a bad public policy.

I wanted to try to take on the traditional development process. It was very clear to me that this would be impossible for me to do alone or even in concert with like-minded members of the Congress because of the entrenched interests which were far too strong, and I am speaking now of the National Association of Home Builders and the National Association of Real Estate Boards. Our full concept of private property militated against a sharp departure from the traditional development process. Land speculation has been a part of the American process for a hell of a long time, and it would be stoutly dependent on the basis of our concepts, legal and otherwise, of private property. Of course, these are subject to change by the courts as we have seen and will continue to see, but 10 years ago they were pretty sacrosanct.

Success in this kind of effort could not be obtained by any kind of direct frontal assault on the established development proccess. That meant that we would have to find a different mechanism, a different kind of approach, and the new communities which have enjoyed a considerable experience in Europe and elsewhere seemed to lend themselves to this. In other words, the idea would not be initially to take on the kind of suburban growth that we have seen take place, and which continues to take place; the idea would be to pose an alternative form of development that, on the basis of sheer competition, would so lend itself and would be so much superior to the living opportunities to the extent that they exist at all for people of lesser means, that this form of development would begin to enjoy a considerable reputation—and that continues to be the essential strategy.

Campbell: As part of that strategy, it seems that you wanted to get into the total process of development, to improve the quality of life, and, perhaps, to provide a vehicle for housing low and moderate income families. Are these valid observations?

Ashley: Absolutely! Again, it was only an assessment and an analysis of the shortcomings of the type of development that we have by virtue of the private approach, the traditional private approach, that suggested areas that in new community legislation should be addressed as positive requirements under the program.

Campbell: What about the business of experimentation and innovation?

Ashley: I had in mind that there be no stereotype or single prototype for a new community. We live at a time when the sum total of human knowledge is doubling every five years, although, to be sure, you would not know it by looking at the suburban developments that are going up outside Toledo or where-have-you. What I had in mind was a real demonstration city program similar to what we tried to come up with in 1966 or whenever it was, and it turned into Model Cities and instead of a dozen or so, it became 148; and to the extent to which we really learned some meaningful lessons, it was considerably diluted. To encourage a whole spectrum of innovation, we did not specify the kind of innovation, but it obviously lends itself to education, communications, and the kinds of physical input structure that might be involved.

Campbell: What about the role of the federal government in terms of leadership in this area? What is an appropriate role for the federal government to play?

Ashley: Well, going back to the basic legislation that was passed in 1970, Title VII, which is now largely identified as the basic authority for new communities, there are two parts—A and B. Part A dealt with the necessity and, as a matter of fact, authority for an evolving national growth policy. Part B addressed itself to the need for federal assistance to new community developers, but the pecking order is very important. Part A did address itself to the necessity for an evolving national growth policy of which new communities, in Part B, would be an essential tool.

It is widely accepted that there has been no assumption of responsibility with respect to Part A. There has been no effort whatever really to come to grips with something like a national growth policy. It has been construed, inaccurately, to involve something like a federal growth policy—that is to say it would be determined here in Washington and foisted on the rest of the country. Well, there is a difference between federal and national. This is national, and I think it would have to involve state and local communities as we know through land use planning and other such activities.

Campbell: The federal government spends billions of dollars through the General Services Administration on military construction and through leases and other forms in acquiring facilities each year. There is no planning policy in this regard, and there seems to be a permissive attitude toward the location of federal facilities and the leasing of federal spaces. Do you think it would be appropriate to have these decisions take place more within a structured planning framework?

Ashley: Absolutely so. The fact of the matter is that it has been acknowledged, not only in the legislation in Part A of Title VII but by the President himself in his 1970 State of the Union message where he commented on the broad migrational trends that have taken place, that there is the need for something in the nature of a settlement policy, and, God knows, people are drawn not really to where the welfare is the most generous but to where they think jobs are going to be available. The federal government has taken the view that this really should be subject to logrolling on the part of the Congress; that decisions are made on the basis of who is the committee chairman and who is in a position to curry political favor with the Administration decision makers as far as location of facilities is concerned. This is all clear to us; we know that this is the basis upon which these decisions have been made. But decisions haven't been made on the basis of where, in fact, it is desirable—from an energy standpoint, from any one of a number of standpoints—for these jobs in fact to be located.

The wrong criteria have been used not only under the [Nixon] Administration but in previous administrations, Democratic as well as Republican. This most certainly would be a very important and very appropriate kind of element in the decision making that should occur at the federal level.

Let me just address myself to the role of federal leadership in this whole area. As I said, *There must be a much more assertive role of leadership at the federal level with respect to a national growth policy generally.* There is not going to be a coherent national policy in the absence of federal leadership. We can't rely on the states to do this on their own volition, although some states are moving ahead in advance of federal leadership. But this is not rational, it is not coherent, and, certainly, if the other countries of the world are any criteria or present any evidence, then there must be, in fact, some game plan in which the players include the federal government, partially for the reasons you indicate because the decisions made at the federal level are enormously important, but also incorporating the states and the local communities— all working together to plan and to carry out a growth strategy.

As far as new communities are concerned, the federal government really is the only level of government that has the capacity to absorb a considerable amount of contingent liability. Is it reasonable to expect that contingent liability that will be billions upon billions of dollars be undertaken by the states or by subunits within the state? The answer to that is No. The only state that has done anything with regard to this is

New York. So what has turned out to be the fact, which we anticipated, is that this is an appropriate role for the federal government, but it is essential that the federal government develop requirements and criteria, as a quid pro quo for their financial support in terms of the grants that were also a part of Title VII legislation.

In other words, it really is a matter of national policy that we want. We want communities to be not just bedroom communities, not just all white communities, not just high income communities, but communities that reflect the pluralistic quality of America itself.

It is an appropriate role and, I think that the proof of that is in the pudding, because if there are some 75 developers who have indicated a very manifest and intense interest, then there are 75 in back of them and they might well be interested in Title VII. At no time has there ever been, to the best of my knowledge and understanding, any criticism of the requirement that there be a racial or income mix in a new community. That has never been raised. If we talk about an existing suburb and whether it will be appropriate for the federal government to say to an existing suburb whether it is at Gross Point, Michigan, or at Ottowa Hills just outside Toledo, that they have to make provisions for an economic and racial mix, they would be stoutly resisted.

There is something very different about doing something new in the way of a new community, in the make-up, the composition of the new community, and insisting with respect to an existing suburb and again, because I know I don't have the votes, I have steered away from a direct conflict on the basis of taking on existing suburbs of existing communities. The courts have addressed themselves to that. It is possible to write legislation—I found this to be true the hard way—that is going to insist that existing communities better reflect housing opportunities for the industry that they have, that housing opportunities be available to lower income as well as medium and upper level income families, that it is not impossible in new communities and I think that this is enormously important. The life style of America is changing. The young people today don't want to live in a lily white suburb; I think that they are much more interested in the real America, and this is being offered in the new communities that are being developed today.

Campbell: That is an interesting term. You used the "real America"; Jim Rouse uses the term "next America" which refers to an attitude of working positively and constructively to overcome existing problems. Is this the type of attitude that you would like to see unfold in new communities?

Ashley: Yes, very much so, because as we have discussed before, new communities aren't the ultimate answer in themselves. It isn't the housing solution at all—new communities provide some basic requirements in the way of decency of living environment, but that just scratches the surface. There is a hell of a lot more to be done to really make this a viable *living* environment, and this has to do with the real problem, which is the people.

What about that six-year-old kid, black or white, Jewish or Catholic, who has the behavioral problems? Is there any kind of community mental health facility that can be helpful in recognizing the symptoms at an early enough time to be effective, to save the kid and his family and other people who might be hurt in the absence of this? That is just an example. Obviously, it goes much further—the whole educational structure, the real ability of people, in a reasoned kind of way, to address themselves to their own problems. New communities don't offer a problem-free avenue to the better life; those problems are going to be there because it is part of what we are going through as a society in a worldwide society.

Campbell: Do you have any thoughts on high rises? Apparently there have been studies made in some of the European countries that have suggested that when families live above the fourth floor, the children may have their development retarded, and, regarding adults, nervous breakdowns and other disorders become much more acute. Have you given any thought as to whether or not it would be appropriate for the federal government to have a hard and firm policy that discourages families from living above the fourth floor? Or do you think it ought to be researched more substantively and a hard case made?

Ashley: I think it probably should be researched more, although there has been a hell of a lot of research done on this, as you indicate. We went last year to six European countries looking not at new communities particularly, although that was a part of it, but trying to get a fix on how they evolve national growth strategies. In the process we found that the Poles have been doing unusually good work in the whole research area. They export their research. They exported it to England, to France, to Germany, and even Romney was interested in using some of the counterpart funds for this purpose, but he did come down on that. But what they found, Carlos, was really very interesting because they were very frank to admit that in their post-World War II building program, they went for high rise, somewhat quality high rise, damn good stuff we thought. They certainly were comparable to our high rises; they don't go more than about 8 or 9 stories as a general rule. What they had found was that the fourth story is maximum, and the reason they got at this was to do a very, very broad-gauged survey of families living in these apartment complexes. And the number one problem that they found, and the number one wish of the people living in there, was not necessarily lower density as such, but to get away from the high rise. And what they figured on the basis of this and on the basis of psychological ramifications that began to emerge is that about four stories was all that they would pursue in the future.

Whether we should mandate this kind of limitation gets into a difficult area because, obviously, the feasibility of an undertaking involves the poor in large measure. Certainly in Cedar-Riverside, for example, with limited acreage, any such limitation on high density would wipe out the viability of the undertaking, and it never would have gotten off the ground. I really have a fear of this for a Cedar-Riverside. What we are really saying is that maybe the rest of the world has found this out, that maybe if we found it out along with some other things. . . .

Because this is a New-Town-in-Town, it really does try to address itself not only to the physical structure, but to the software, to the whole psychology of neighborliness in a neighborhood type environment. Maybe it will work, but we certainly don't know. At the present time we are saying, "OK, go ahead and shoot the dice. We will back up your bonds." In other words we just don't know whether all the requirements for a new community are going to work sufficiently well so that the danger that is attendant in high rises can be sufficiently obviated to make them viable.

Campbell: What are your thoughts on Reston or Columbia and the other New Towns presently in the development stages?

Ashley: I wish that Reston and Columbia were Title VII undertakings because even the severest critics of new communities would have to say that, on balance, they have been remarkably successful. They are far from perfect. A lot of people get killed trying to get to Reston from Washington, D.C., or from Columbia to Baltimore. The transportation considerations were given very short shrift—that is a very, very substantial limitation of the element of viability, and I am sure that in time to come, this problem will be addressed after the fact, just as we sewered most of America after the fact. Both of these new communities have been enormously helpful in terms of lessons learned. Simon learned a hell of a lot, and some of it not very pleasantly, as far as Reston is concerned. I saw him the other day, and he said that Reston, for the first time, is now in the black. So you see it really is possible to accommodate people of different income levels, even with transportation and other difficulties, and on a paying basis.

Rouse, of course, discovered this long since. His testimony is valuable because he says, as you know, east of the Mississippi River *there will never be a New Town where acreage has been assembled as the acreage for Columbia was*. In other words, it simply isn't possible any more to do it in the dark of night—which, of course, he did to keep land speculations down, etc. He did it without eminent domain and that simply isn't possible anymore. We have got to come to grips as a nation with land speculation, and that being the case, eminent domain is essential. It really isn't an answer to land speculation, but at least you have the ability to put it to a jury as to whether or not it has been a really outrageous kind of speculative mark-up that is involved. No, as I say, I think that these two communities have been enormously helpful. They have not been perfect, and you learn from the imperfection. We also learn very good lessons from the areas where they have been successful, but I think we learn much more from the mistakes and oversights which are bound to take place in what really is a fairly new direction as far as development is concerned.

Campbell: Do you think your experience—we talked about this a year or so ago—as a pilot has given you a greater sense of awareness and appreciation for both the natural and built-in environment?

Ashley: Yes, I don't think that there is any question about that; particularly since a private plane does not go very high, above 8000 or 10,000 feet and starts gasping a bit—I fly a lot lower than usually because I do want to see what is going on. At least I did for two years and then it was really very, very discouraging. It really underscores, as you fly over America at 3000 or 4000 feet, what the hell we are doing to this country of ours. It is really a crying shame. Because if there was any good that was coming out of it, if people were getting decent housing, that would be one thing, but the housing really isn't any good and the land use is so destructive and wasteful, it is really the rape of America today, and we are not addressing ourselves to it. It is very discouraging and very frustrating. We are obviously not going to be able to go on indefinitely in this direction. Quite often we, as a country, will have to get badly burned before we learn the hard lesson.

Campbell: Do you think that this will happen in terms of the whole environment issue?

Ashley: Yes, I do, and the energy crisis is a part of it. The mass of ugliness that we see now in most parts of the country is going to become an outrage to more and more people, mainly because it is so selfish. It is the product of banality, of greed, of crass money grabbing—the attitude and conviction in many respects that it is my land, I bought it, and I can do any damn thing I want with it and the hell with generations to come. That is not an attitude that we are going to tolerate indefinitely as a society—we are just not going to.

One of the things that can be helpful is the kind of good land use planning that is implicit in new communities. There is nothing the matter with growth; growth is fine, but it has to be planned with a sensitivity toward the environment and toward the fact that we have limited resources in this country, including land. It has to be treated right so that people can derive benefit from them, but that is not the situation at the present time.

11

AN INTERVIEW WITH ED LOGUE

The New York State Urban Development Corporation was created in the spring of 1968 by the state legislature as a result of leadership exercised by then Governor Nelson Rockefeller. This happened during the period that followed the April 1968 assassination of Dr. Martin Luther King, Jr. The King assassination triggered riots in many of the nation's large cities and heightened public concern for the conditions that existed in the ghettoes.

UDC was established as a public benefit corporation and as a state agency to "develop and finance housing for low, moderate and middle income families; to assist industrial and commercial development; and to provide needed educational, cultural and other civic facilities".[79] To meet its objectives UDC was equipped with special powers. These included the power of condemnation or eminent domain (this is the right to take private property for public purposes in exchange for just compensation); the right to override local zoning ordinances; and the power to use the state building code in place of local ones when the use of the latter would make development projects economically unfeasible.

The state legislature gave UDC an initial authority to raise money up to $1 billion through the sale of tax-exempt "moral obligation" bonds. By 1974 this authority was increased to $2 billion. The moral obligation bond was a pioneering financial expedient designed by a Wall Street bond attorney named John Mitchell. The moral obligation bond is a public debt device that is technically known as the legislative make-up. Under this process, which does not commit the full faith and credit of the state, the governor agrees to ask the legislature to make up any deficiency which may arise in the debt service reserve fund, a common element of revenue bond financing.

By its sixth anniversary UDC became the nation's largest producer of federally assisted housing for low and moderate income families. Over 33,000 units were occupied or under construction in more than 50 communities throughout the state as of the fall of 1974. Included in UDC's achievements are the initiations of three New Towns: Roosevelt

Island in New York City; Radisson, near Syracuse; and Audubon, near Buffalo.

/ THE UDC NEW TOWNS /

The most publicized of the three UDC New Towns is Roosevelt Island. On a 147-acre island site in New York City's East River, is the $350 million development that will eventually house 18,000 people. This New-Town-in-Town features an automobile-free environment, an aerial tramway on which passengers can ride to Manhattan Island in three minutes, and a refuse disposal system that will compact garbage and remove it via a pneumatic tube. Completion of the first 2100 of the 5000 total apartment units is expected by the end of 1975. Of these 2100 apartments, 1100 are for middle and upper-middle income families and 1000 are for moderate and low-income families.

The New Town of Radisson is located 12 miles northwest of Syracuse, New York, on a 2700-acre site. Construction began on this New Town in October 1971, and it has a planned population of 18,000. Radisson has an 800-acre industrial park. The major tenant so far is the Jos. E. Schlitz Brewing Company which will have a 6 million barrel brewing operation annually in a 1.3 million square foot plant. Scheduled for completion in early 1976, this is the largest new brewery in the world.

Audubon is the largest, in terms of planned population, of the three UDC New Towns. Eventually, 27,500 people will live in some 9000 units on the 2000-acre site, which is about a 20-minute drive from downtown Buffalo and 5 minutes from the new campus of the State University of New York. The first residents began moving in during September 1974. The development period for Audubon is estimated to be between 10 and 15 years.

/ ED LOGUE /

During the first six and a half years of UDC's operation, the agency came under the direction of nine directors and a president named Ed Logue. When he was appointed by New York's Governor Nelson A. Rockefeller to head the state agency in July 1968, Logue brought with him some 15 years of experience in development administration. He had previously administered urban renewal authorities in New Haven, Connecticut (1953-1960) and Boston, Massachusetts (1960-1967). In 1967, Logue ran for mayor of Boston and placed fourth. Logue's combined records of achievement for the three agencies he has headed up represent over $5 billion dollars in construction.

A by-product of Logue's leadership has been the number of

construction contracts awarded to black and minority firms. This amounted to about 20 percent of the contracts let by UDC, or some $80 million in New York City alone, from 1971 through mid-1973. UDC's affirmative action officer, Don Cogsville, is quick to credit Logue for the success to date: "One thing you've got to have is a guy at the head of the organization who says, 'God damn, it's going to be done', and then gives the freedom to do whatever is necessary to get things done."

I interviewed Ed Logue in his New York City office on June 12, 1973.

Campbell: What is your philosophy regarding the development of New Towns?

Logue: I believe in the idea of New Towns. I believe that it is time we got back to it in America. We used to be building New Towns at an enormous rate, probably faster than almost any country in the world. But we've pretty well stopped that process now. Generally, what we are doing now is expanding the existing urban areas. There have been very few really new communities founded.

We ought to go back into that process and begin again for lots of reasons having to do with ordering our national urban growth, saving the land, and using our resources economically. It is perhaps our last chance to demonstrate that people of different incomes, races, and ethnic origins can live together. I also believe that a lot of the pathology of the cities can be eliminated by new community life styles. By that I don't mean just harm and disorder, but also the very foolish expenditures of energy and resources. Having seen some New Towns, I fell in love with them.

Campbell: I understand you visited new communities in Scandinavia and other parts of Europe.

Logue: Yes, I visited England, Scotland, France, Holland, Denmark, Sweden, and Finland.

Campbell: You indicated in one of your articles that you think all Americans should visit these New Towns. Do you think that would have a major effect on changing the thinking toward development in this country?

Logue: I wish I could get a lot of people in a jet airplane and take them just to Tapiola [the New Town in Finland], just that one, or maybe Stockholm and its New Towns.

Campbell: In terms of the mix, do you advocate mixing incomes within a particular building or within clusters?

Logue: Within a cluster, not within the same building. To an extent I believe you can mix moderate and low income families, but the price of housing is such that you can't mix low income and middle income in the same building because I, for one, can't justify giving lower income families the same quality of accommodations that people get who pay two or three times as much for it. On the other hand, you can't work it the other way. You can't get the upper income families, who have the widest range of housing choices, to take less than they otherwise deserve.

Campbell: To what extent will your profile of housing that would be available normally be affected by the Nixon administration's moratorium?

Logue: I wish I knew. It just so happens that in the last three weeks I've been to a groundbreaking in Harlem, a ribbon-cutting in Harlem, and a groundbreaking in central Brooklyn. If we can get Secretary Lynn and some of these other people who have no particular background in housing and who are now making housing policy for the country to see that, and to see how people live, we might get them to do what the Congress says is the law of the land—to administer the housing acts instead of trying to destroy them.

Campbell: What do you think accounts for the negative attitude of the Nixon administration?

Logue: Well, the so-called "new conservatives" in the academic community, largely from Harvard and MIT, originally helped to sell distorted urban renewal. To them, "urban renewal" was only the process of tearing away slums occupied by poor people, often poor black people, and replacing them with luxury housing in which no poor black people live. That was the image that they quite deliberately painted of the urban renewal program. I always believed that that was the fault with it. That went on, but it was by no means the full story or even the balance of the story. Those folks started it, the "now" administration of the 236 and 235 programs by the federal government—not by state government and not by city government, but by the federal government.

Under Secretary Romney, FHA managed to get more housing started for low and moderate income families than under 30 years of Democrats. They also managed to have the government cheated on a somewhat larger scale, I think, than the Democrats ever managed to do. I never have believed in throwing out the baby with the bath, and I think that's what they did. Also, I think this Administration does not really feel that the users of low and moderate income housing are a part of its constituency.

Campbell: Do you think they are motivated politically?

Logue: I think they are trying to make clear, in a variety of ways, that the idea of government as the solver of social problems is an idea that has been around long enough, and they want to try some other idea. I think that the recent events that happened have muted that. God knows what they would have done if it had not been for Watergate. What has come out in the last three months—I'm not trying to talk about that subject—but what has come out is that what was on the statute books didn't matter. I believe that the housing moratorium is an unlawful act. I happen to believe you do not have the right to stop programs that the Congress has passed and appropriated money for.

Campbell: Do you have a policy on high rises for families? Do you have any policy that would restrict them to the lower floors?

Logue: No, but for $1.50 you can go see what our policy is. Right around the corner, in the Museum of Modern Art. I am serious. We just opened a show there last night. It is called "Low Rise—High Density". We haven't built a hell of a lot of very high rise housing; we are trying to get away from that. I don't believe and never have believed that it is a good thing to put low income families in elevator buildings.

Campbell: What about families in general?

Logue: Well, I don't think my children like it. They live on the thirteenth floor of an apartment building. They are not New Yorkers; it's the first time this has ever happened. Most of the time, since my daughter went away to college, I see her somewhere else, with some friends or relatives. She doesn't like the city. My son just gets used to it, but I know damn well my wife doesn't like it. I would rather live in a house.

Campbell: What do you like?

Logue: A row house. I was born in a row house. I lived in Boston in a row house on Beacon Hill. That's my idea of a good life, and you have a place to go on weekends.

Campbell: What about your sense of priorities in terms of where New Towns should best be located? How do you weight the New-Town-in-Town as opposed to satellite new communities?

Logue: Well, I cast my eyes on the biggest New-Town-in-Town site in America two weeks ago–10 days ago. It is 20 years old, a disastrous urban renewal project in Philadelphia, west of the airport. I am not sure that it wouldn't hold 40,000 families; it's a huge thing, but it is hard to tell it from the rest of Philadelphia today. I suppose if I had my druthers, the concept that has the most validity, and certainly the most value for the money, would be to do what the British call *extended towns*. It is a funny thing, I am a Philadelphian by birth, had my early schooling all in Philadelphia and was parochially patriotic about it. This is silly, but it comes to a point. I was always somewhat perturbed that Philadelphia, which was at the time of the signing of the Declaration of Independence the second largest city in the British Empire, believe it or not, fell so far behind New York so fast. When you look at this map, it is very clear why. You can't go west from Philadelphia easily; it is an awful, awful chore. This is the way this country grew–it is that simple. The result: upstate New York became the first great grain export area in America. The first great wine producing area in this country was also upstate New York. Comparatively speaking, a very large manufacturing base resulted in the area, and that, to a large degree, is why upstate New York doesn't grow very much. What we frankly need to do, if we are going to do anything in this country, is to mandate industrial location decisions.

Campbell: President Nixon signed an Executive Order, as did President Kennedy, that encouraged the location of federal facilities in New Towns. There has only been one–the Geological Survey in Reston. There are no federal facilities in any of the others.

Logue: That came too late to keep Bob Simon from going broke.

Campbell: Stewart Udall [Secretary of Interior during the Kennedy and Johnson administrations] was responsible for that decision.

Logue: Well, I was annoyed with a hell of a lot of my friends in Washington saying–I know it is Bill Finley. He was one of the people who were very annoyed. He is a very talented guy who was then director of the National Capital Planning Commission, and he came out; he was the author, I believe, of the plan for "Washington in the Year 2000". I told him that I had a very proud copy of it. I said what a terrible thing that assumption was, and it was a valid assumption that the federal government go on growing in Washington. I believe one of the things wrong with our federal government is that it is too damn big. One has the impression around the Whitehall area of London, or the Kremlin, that the heart of the Executive Branch of most national governments is rather small. But at any rate, I believe that the government's decision-making power atrophies if it is not possible for the people at the policy-making levels of government to move in a community, socially and casually, in a way that brings them to easy contact.

As an exercise, I went through a directory of federal offices in Washington figuring out which ones didn't have to be there. We could substitute for the location of armed services installations, the location of large parts of HUD, and the regulatory functions of FHA. There is actually no need for these to be in the District of Columbia or the capital area. They could be in Indianapolis. The Veterans Administration has no reason to be in Washington. I remember one time when I was in a discussion with the chief planner of Moscow and I was teasing him about questions asked of congressional officials in Moscow. When asked, "What is the population of Moscow?"–"8 million." And "What's it going to be in 10 years?" He said very proudly, "8 million, we have it under control." I said to this guy–I had done some homework–

> How did you, when the Soviet government first thought about this, decide Moscow was going to be 3 million. And then about 20 or 30 years later you decide it was going to be 5 million. Now you tell me the size is going to be 8 million, how did this happen?

He said,

> I'll tell you. The Ministry of Fisheries is in Moscow and the Minerals Research Institute is in Moscow, and there is absolutely no reason for that–there are no fisheries anywhere near Moscow and there is no mineral worth looking for anywhere near Moscow–but the minister in charge wants that demonstration of his importance somewhere in Europe and the officials of the institute or the agency want to be as close as possible to the throne room where the decisions are made.

So when you figure that even there that's a sign, they've got a problem. In fact, the only society that has licked it is the Chinese. That is by deciding that your children and mine are not going to live with us and go over the hill and live somewhere else.

Campbell: Which one of the three New Towns do you feel is the most important in terms of urban development?

Logue: Welfare Island.

Campbell: Why?

Logue: Because it has higher stakes. We are trying to demonstrate that people of high and low and middle and moderate incomes can all live together on 50 acres on a 150-acre island, and that they can send their children to the same public schools, and that two things are possible—racial and economic integration and the public schools can be a magnet.

Campbell: What about the New Town of Audubon? What do you see there as a major factor in getting ahead?

Logue: Well, the university is going to be key. The most difficult thing, the most exciting thing, is the part of the new community which is supposed to go to the heart of the campus. There we want to create some of the enchantment of Harvard Square as it used to be before it got overwhelmed with trash. Have you seen Harvard Square recently? It's terrible. I used to enjoy going over there. The thing that shocked me the most is what happened to Charles Street. . . .

Campbell: Do you see some principal differences between the development of new communities in the United States and the way in which New Towns were developed in England?

Logue: Oh, yes indeed.

Campbell: Would you care to comment on any of those?

Logue: Well, in the United Kingdom the New Town policy was a policy which began at the top level in the national government and was administered from there. That is not true in any way of the United States. All of the leadership in the New Towns has come from private individuals for the most part, except for us.

Campbell: Do you think that this would be one way that other states could effectively move forward with the development of new communities?

Logue: Yes, I can give you the location in 10 minutes for new communities in Massachusetts, for example.

Campbell: Well, do you think the state of Massachusetts will, say, structure an urban development corporation? Do you feel that if you enjoy success here, which apparently you are, other states will follow suit?

Logue: No.

Campbell: You don't?

Logue: No, we took a step backward.

Campbell: What was that?

Logue: Well, our powers in suburban areas were restricted. UDC residential projects in towns or villages can now be defeated by a vote of the local governing body.

Campbell: This was done by the state court?

Logue: By the legislature, God bless it. I got a letter in the mail this morning from some fellow in the town of Manans, outside of Albany. He said, "We told you we didn't want you. Now that the legislation has passed, I can tell you that the town board will be against it so why don't you go away and stop bothering us."

Campbell: That's terrible. Do you think that attitude has more to do with race or class?

Logue: I sure as hell would like to believe it is class, but I don't.

Campbell: Do you have any comments about the future, the development future, of this country? Say in the next 10 to 15 years? Where do you see us headed?

Logue: I don't see us headed anywhere. It is just stumbling around.

Campbell: Would you ever accept the position of Secretary of HUD? And, if so, what would your major thrust be? I would go so far as to say that I could not think of anybody in the country who would be more qualified than you. If we had a President who really wanted a qualified person, you are obviously the most experienced developer.

Logue: I don't really think that is very likely. I would just like to know that the President who offered me the job would say, "What I want you to do, fellow, is carry out the law." Everything we have been talking about is in the books. I can't imagine being Secretary of HUD for a President who said, "Now I want you to get these things under control and cut those programs back." No point to that.

Campbell: Would you take it provided that you. . . .

Logue: The law is good enough; the law really doesn't need a damn thing. I don't happen to think that 236 [a federally assisted low rent housing program] is too sensible. The housing laws in this country are as good as they are anywhere in the world; it is just that we keep changing them instead of trying to enforce them.

/ FINANCIAL TROUBLES SET IN /

Up until the middle of 1974, UDC did not encounter any serious problems in raising money through the sale of bonds to support its construction program. At this time, UDC began to experience cash flow problems, and in July 1974, Logue so advised the bond underwriters. In the summer of 1974, UDC postponed the sale of $100 million of short-term notes because of high interest rates. The rates were about 9 percent; prior to the summer of 1974, UDC's average cost of money was 6½ percent. In September 1974, when UDC sold $225 million worth of bonds, it had to pay 9.4 percent interest.

In order to strengthen UDC's posture and increase confidence in the agency from the financial community, Ed Logue recommended a five-point program in December 1974 to Governor Wilson and Governor-Elect Hugh Carey. This called for a state appropriation for UDC of $18.5 million, compared to a 1974 level of about $11 million; a 10-year deferral on a UDC loan obligation of $48 million to the state; creation of a $50 million stand-by debt service reserve fund; creation of a $50 million stand-by project loss reserve for a period of 10 years; and an increase in the UDC $2 billion debt ceiling.

On January 8, 1975 Governor Hugh Carey stated on the UDC situation:

> The UDC is facing an imminent exhaustion of funds. All of its ongoing projects will grind to a halt within four or five days unless we take immediate action. It takes $1 million a day, seven days a week, to keep UDC running. But UDC is out of funds, and the financial community, with which we have been working over the few days since my inauguration, will not lend UDC any more unless its house is put in order.

Carey called for "an immediate change in the top management of UDC" [80] and sought an emergency legislative appropriation in the amount of $178 million to keep UDC operating through the end of the fiscal year.

Eight days later, Ed Logue addressed the New York State Senate Committee on Housing and Urban Development. After citing UDC's accomplishments and commenting on the financial problems which included recommendations, Logue focused on what he called "the real issue": "The anonymous claims of lack of confidence by the financial community are a smoke screen. The UDC cash flow problem was presented by me to the underwriters in July of 1974 as an urgent problem." Logue went on to say:

> Last summer and much more emphatically this past December, it was made clear to me what the banks wanted. They wanted a stop on any new housing construction by UDC. They wanted a stop on completion of our three new communities. The first recommendation was socially irresponsible, the second financially incompetent. UDC's present financial crisis basically stems from the determination of the banks to accomplish that result.[81]

In concluding his testimony, Logue said:

> The real issue is, Will the financial community provide adequate mortgage funds at reasonable rates or will federal authority have to be invoked to require that or shall we forget about housing as a priority. . .? We cannot allow basic public policy of this importance to be made in corporate board rooms and issued to public men by fiat.[82]

Three weeks later, on February 5, 1975, Ed Logue resigned his position as president and chief executive officer of UDC.

On February 25, 1975, UDC was unable to meet a bond anticipation note of about $100 million and $4.5 million due in interest payments. This resulted in UDC's becoming the first statewide agency in modern history to default on its payments. In order to avert the collapse of UDC, Governor Carey proposed that the state legislature provide $250 million and wanted banks to put up another $350 million. This would allow UDC to complete projects under construction and repay its outstanding obligations. By March 1975, the state legislature provided about $110 million for UDC while some 80 New York savings banks, according to the *New York Times*, "indicated interest in buying $275 million in bonds to help out UDC".[83] Also, eleven major commercial banks in New York City proposed the establishment of a $140 million revolving credit fund to assist UDC.

Publicly there were reports that the UDC financial crisis was caused by banks refusing to lend the agency additional money. The banks reportedly were dissatisfied with UDC's internal management. There were, however, at least three factors that aggravated the UDC crisis that cannot be overlooked. First, there was the 18-month moratorium on federal housing subsidies declared in January 1973. The lack of such subsidies that were vital to UDC's housing program caused some projects to have an uncertain future. Next, there was the weakening of UDC's relationship with the state, in that the legislature in May 1973 provided towns and villages with the power to veto any UDC residential project. This, of course, raised questions with respect to the state of New York's confidence in UDC. Finally, there was the soaring of interest rates that caused UDC to pay 9.4 percent for money in September 1974, compared to an average cost of 6 ½ percent a few months earlier.

More was at stake than the some 6000 UDC jobs and the 16,000 housing units under construction and the three New Towns. The larger issues were the integrity of the state of New York and the future of the municipal bond market that suffered a serious blow because of UDC's troubles. Although the UDC management under the new leadership of builder Richard Ravitch has an uphill fight on their hands, they will probably succeed in keeping UDC alive long enough to complete the projects that are presently under construction. Beyond this, the future of UDC is open to speculation.

12

THE DEVELOPERS

Within the process of developing New Towns, the developer is key. It is the developer who must collectively deal with the residents, the elected officials, the financial partners, and the public interest groups.

The business of developing New Towns in the United States has created a small but highly select "fraternity" of people who are devoting much of their lives to the projects they are involved in or to the development of New Towns in general. Several of the developers like Robert E. Simon and Lewis Manilow are sons whose fathers were associated with earlier efforts to build New Towns in America. Simon's father was associated with the effort to develop Radburn, New Jersey, into a New Town in the late 1920s and Manilow's father was a co-developer of Park Forest, Illinois, which forms the northern border of Park Forest South.

Within this select group, it is not unusual for executives to move from one New Town to another, which was the case with two executives connected with the New Town of The Woodlands, located near Houston, Texas. The present general manager was formerly with the New Town of Columbia, Maryland, and his assistant was formerly with the New Town of Gananda, located near Rochester, New York. Tom Wolff, now in charge of the rapidly growing industrial park for the New Town of Irvine, California, was formerly with the New Town of Columbia, Maryland. Ben Cunningham, now the planner for the New Town of Park Forest South, was the planner for the New Town of Jonathan, Minnesota. This group is as diverse as the towns they are associated with, and for the first time in the modern history of development within the United States, blacks and women are playing an increasingly significant role in the development process.

/ ROBERT E. SIMON /

Robert E. Simon can rightly be called the "Father of New Towns in America", in the modern sense, for it was he who pioneered the movement when he initiated the development of Reston, Virginia, in 1962. Simon, in addition to being an internationally known developer, has a rich background in cultural and social activities. From 1938 to 1960 he was the president of New York City's famed Carnegie Hall. He

has also been a director of the Washington Opera Society. Although we have been friends for years and he continues to return to Reston, the first time we discussed his philosophy and thoughts on New Towns in depth was in his mid-town Manhattan office in the fall of 1972. Simon's office had two round tables, some green plants of varying sizes, and walls covered with renderings and site plans for his latest venture–the New Town of Riverton. We discussed the role of the developer with regard to New Towns; Jim Rouse, the developer of Columbia; social issues; and the involvement of residents.

Bob Simon sees the developer's role as that of a catalyst which is the principal function in the social sense, and he repeatedly uses the word *appropriate* with respect to this role being carried out. He describes Columbia's Jim Rouse as part Messiah and part organizer. He says that Rouse is a better organizer but questioned some of the things that Rouse did and in particular his leadership of the ecumenical effort: "I thought it was inappropriate for Jim Rouse to lead the Columbia ecumenical effort."

Another field Simon says the developer must stay out of is that of communications. He does, however, feel that the developer can enter into the area of education, and he initially subsidized the Lake Anne Nursery and Kindergarten School (LANK), which has been a success story in itself. Bob Simon feels strongly about providing a maximum opportunity for individual expression and thinks "cluster associations are very important because they give people an opportunity to work together to decide on self help". Simon further asserts that "people should not be robbed of their initiative".

Social relations officers are not normally included as part of the New Town management staff within the United States as they are in England. Simon is supportive of social relations officers being part of the community associations staff with U.S. New Towns.

Simon's Reston has been an "open" community from its inception in that individuals were not subjected to discriminatory practices on account of race. The first residents who moved into Reston in December of 1964 and early 1965 included blacks. At this time, there was no national fair housing legislation. Part of the Civil Rights Act of 1968 included a provision for fair housing, or that which was open to all regardless of race.

In 1965, according to Jane Wilhelm, Reston's director of community relations from 1964 to 1969, "both the local banks and HUD were indifferent toward Reston" because of its open occupancy policy. Simon admits that for three weeks after the first black family bought a lot in Reston in 1963, the Virginia banks were deciding whether to cut him off. Wilhelm points out that "part of Simon's financial problem centered around the fact that he had planned Reston as an integrated community" and "Simon never backed down on the subject of integration. His only compromise was to maintain a low profile on sales and advertising. He said he 'would close down for five years if necessary'."

Simon was critical of Rouse for saying that he was going to recruit qualified blacks to move into Columbia, asserting "That's not a developer's function. . . .he should concern himself with opening up the doors."

Today, Reston is about 9 percent black and relatively free of acute race problems. In 1972, Simon said, "I think the black situation in Reston is about as good as one can expect."

Robert E. Simon left Reston in the fall of 1967 when a subsidiary of the Gulf Oil Corporation, Gulf-Reston, Inc., took over. Simon's accomplishments, however, are not forgotten. He normally returns to Reston each year for the Spring Festival, and amongst the old timers he remains somewhat of a folk hero. In addition to the town, sporting events and a learning center bear his name. Simon has received and continues to receive awards for initiating the development of Reston. In the spring of 1974, in my capacity as a member of the Board of Directors of the American Society of Planning Officials, I had the privilege of presenting Robert Simon with our Silver Medal for his outstanding efforts in planning and development.

/ JIM ROUSE /

Jim Rouse is the developer of Columbia, Maryland, which is the fastest growing New Town in the United States. He is also the head of the nation's tenth largest mortgage banking firm. His office, in the American

City Building, is well decorated, colorful, yet modest. Jim Rouse was a very easy person to talk with because he himself is relaxed and at ease. I asked him if he was satisfied with Columbia as "a profile for the Next America", the term widely used for marketing purposes. His reply was:

> I feel pretty good, I feel pretty hopeful. The most important change is the forward attitude among people that things can be different. . .and expecting that we can make things work. What this attitude really means is that the source of the attitude. . .the physical plan and the scale promote community. . .and this is, in turn, reinforced by the Community Association and the legal structure. People have been given the power to effect change. The Village Associations are the voice of the community. The fundamental intent of Columbia has worked.

Rouse credits Columbia's success to prior planning for several reasons. The physical plan emerged from a series of requirements as to what worked and what didn't work. Information was provided during the development process that equipped the developer to deal with race, education, health, and religion. Social and institutional things were fully integrated. The product was environment. Rouse feels "the integrity came through to the people and the plan", but concedes that "an area where we have fallen down has been in communicating the ethos [the qualitative character resulting in the present product] of Columbia at a central point".

Columbia appears to have the widest racial and economic mix of any of the New Towns under development in the United States and also has the most successful community association. Rouse says that "the remarkable thing about Columbia is its diversity".

Some have accused Jim Rouse of being overly involved in the development of Columbia. As for the others, Zeke Orlinsky, owner and publisher of the *Columbia Flyer*, a local newspaper, says:

> In the earlier years, the developer was synonomous with Columbia. Jim Rouse as a person was extended to be a type of symbol of what Columbia is. . .that was the image. As Columbia got bigger, it began to outgrow Jim Rouse.

Rouse does not feel that a developer can be overly involved but that he can be overly "dominant" and asserts that "If I have performed a function, . . .it is in insisting that we understand and deal with the full fabric of city."

Jim Rouse openly admits that he has had a good financial partner in Connecticut General Life Insurance Company without which he "would not have made it". Although he has long been a giant in the building industry, having developed almost 30 shopping centers throughout the nation, and the village of Cross Keys in Baltimore, it is Columbia that seems to have given him the greatest challenge and satisfaction.

/ LEWIS MANILOW /

Lewis Manilow is the developer of Park Forest South. In his early forties, he is one of the youngest developers in the New Town business. A graduate of Harvard Law School, he is also a civic leader in the arts and theatrical areas. Lew Manilow has been the producer of off-Broadway plays; he is a tennis buff, a collector of oriental rugs and sculpture, a wearer of fine shirts, and a person of unending energy and managerial skill. In addition to his wide cultural and civic activities, he was the first chairman of the League of New Community Developers, which is no small indication of the respect that he has gained among his colleagues. Manilow has been described as having the "arrogance born of professional skills and financial muscle".

Lewis Manilow grew up with Park Forest, which was developed by his late father Nathan. Park Forest, which is just north of Park Forest South, was one of the leading planned developments during the 1940s. Lewis Manilow feels strongly about what he calls "the ultimate vitality of the community", the growth that comes from the residents doing things. Manilow says,

> . . .we tend to be a little wary about romantic presentations. . . .I want to be sure that I can deliver. *If you give me a blank piece of paper, I can plan the most incredible New Town in the world. . .but it's much tougher to make the parts work economically and socially.*

I asked him about the business of the developer's role and specifically related it to both Rouse and Simon, and he said,

> I don't think there is that much difference between Simon and Rouse. . . .we all would like to be pure catalysts. I am very deeply involved in the hospital program here. Right or wrong. . .we get more involved in some areas than others.

Manilow's development company has received $60,000 from

the National Endowment for the Arts to commission some sculptures for the town center. He has also contributed one of his own pieces which is presently located near his farm house on the development site. To appreciate what Lew Manilow is doing, one must consider that he could retire to a life of luxury, but instead he has chosen to build a New Town in the midst of constraints that would drive other men away.

/ RAY WATSON /

The New Town of Irvine, California, will ultimately house close to 500,000 people on about 70,000 acres. This, the largest New Town development presently under way in the United States, is being carried forth under the direction of Ray Watson.

When I first visited Irvine in 1970, Ray Watson gave me a tour of the New Town which has exceptional design and landscaping. Much of this comes from Watson's basic discipline as an architect and from the efforts of the William Periera firm that did the initial planning. Watson has a large modern office which overlooks the city of Newport Beach and the Pacific Ocean. On one wall is a three-by-five-foot color carpet replica of Irvine's master plan that Watson made with his teenage son.

Although Watson is an architect, he is not the type to be caught up with lofty dreams; he understands the bottom line and business of finance. He has available to him some of the most sophisticated management tools that allow for decisions to be made on a rational basis. Some of the computer-assisted input enables him to make decisions that will allow for construction starts to be adjusted periodically according to market forecasts. He says,

> What is worth observing in Irvine is the governance. . . the involvement of the people. *A sense of community comes out of the involvement in the community.*

Although his efforts were not successful, he pushed for housing for low and moderate income families during the incorporation of the city. Watson feels that the physical attracts, and that because New Towns are visible, they are good places to show what can be done. I have made about 10 trips to Irvine since my first trip in 1970. The most notable change is that Ray Watson has built a strong and exceptionally talented staff. The promise of Irvine rests as much with the management as it does with the people.

On September 16, 1971, Ray Watson appeared before the Housing Subcommittee of the Committee on Banking and Currency of the U.S. House of Representatives to testify on Irvine and New Towns in general. At that time he stated:

> The New Town of Irvine, I wish to stress, is not and will not be an isolated New Town, removed by miles from an existing metropolitan area. It is, instead, and was designed purposefully so, part of the greater Los Angeles regional fabric. It has been described by others as a "satellite New Town." The *New York Times* calls it "an outer city". It is not to be—and cannot practically be—a city in isolation.[84]

/ WILLIAM H. MAGNESS /

William Magness' exposure to New Towns goes back to the late 1930s, when he was a student at the University of Tennessee working in a training program with the Tennessee Valley Authority. He subsequently continued his efforts with New Towns in South America where he was a chief engineer and manager of services for Gulf Oil Corporation, Venezuela, operating during the early and mid 1950s. He later went to the Middle East on loan from Gulf to the International Oil Consortium. There he was responsible for all of the planning, engineering, and development activities for the Iranian Oil Exploration and Producing Company and the Iranian Oil Refining Company, the largest in the world. The planning, design, and construction of completely New Towns as well as modernizing old ones came under his responsibility. The Shah of Iran

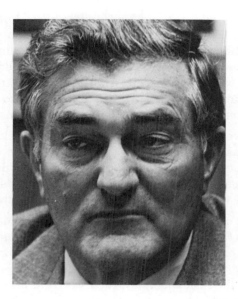

decorated him as an officer in the Order of Homayoun and the French government decorated him as a Cavalier in the Order of Arts and Letters.

Magness became president and director of Gulf-Reston, Inc., in January 1968, and was elected chief operating officer in June of 1969. Eighteen months later, Gulf-Reston, Inc., realized the first profit-making year in the history of Reston's development.

Magness calls New Towns "an important antibiotic to an urban crisis of international proportions". When he spoke at the dedication ceremonies for the International Center at Reston on September 29, 1973, he underscored the importance of innovation and universal cooperation:

> The seriousness of providing decent accommodations for anticipated populations up to the year 2000 is known in every land and tongue, and is as important to the future well-being of a nation as finding new and better sources for energy and raw food materials. Just as in our space program, technological innovations in the housing field must come through universal cooperation and the willingness to share scientific and industrial advancements.[85]

With respect to Reston, Magness feels that environment and education are two factors that must be predominant. The well-traveled Magness feels that *"Reston has no peer in the world."* Reston has led the communities of the county in providing housing for low and moderate income families—and not without difficulties from the federal government. Magness points out that it took about four years to process the first assisted housing complex, Cedar-Ridge, and almost two years to do the next, Fellowship House. He says, "we[Gulf-Reston, Inc.] have had so much trouble with FHA [Federal Housing Administration] that we'll never go FHA again". Magness feels that the only way to provide housing for moderate income families is through condominiums.

On governance, his position is that the developer should turn the community association over to the citizens at the earliest possible moment. Residents of Reston and other New Towns ought to take note of this point because once the development period is complete, the developers will leave and the residents will be left on their own.

No one questions the financial genius of Bill Magness, but from time to time he is the subject of criticism for his development practices or for his failure to provide services that residents feel they deserve. In his four years to date, I find that the gap that existed between the developer and his staff and the residents has closed, and that his management has become more responsive to the total needs of the community.

Just as Simon had to deal with indifferent bankers and federal officials at HUD, Magness has had to deal with indifferent local elected officials. Magness is to be credited for his efforts in keeping the Reston concept alive in the difficult times of the "anti-growth" movement. It is also to his credit to have recognized the international significance of Reston as he has through the dedication of the Dag Hammarskjöld Plaza and the International Center within the New Town.

/ FRED JOHNSON /

From 1971 to 1974, Fred Johnson was the head of the development corporation responsible for building the New Town of Harbison, just seven miles from Columbia, South Carolina. A graduate of Morehouse College, he decided to stay in the South when the great majority of his classmates pursued positions in the Midwest and the North. Johnson, a former mortgage banker and insurance executive, feels—

> . . .that if you really believe in the capitalistic system, you will find that *the real opportunities are in the South.* The southern white will work with you on a sound economic development plan and will give you the kind of cooperation that you can't get anywhere in the country.

The Harbison idea was initially conceived in 1970 by James Costen, dean of the Johnson C. Smith Seminary in Atlanta, Georgia. The

United Presbyterian Church was the catalyst in putting together the feasibility money—$50,000. Johnson was selected over more than 30 candidates, largely because of his outstanding record in the business community. As an insurance executive, he was one of the first blacks to become a member of the Million Dollar Round Table. He subsequently became associated with Atlanta Mortgage Company in the late 1960s and made it one of the largest black-controlled mortgage companies in the country. At the suggestion of T.M. Alexander, Jr., then acting director of new communities with HUD, Fred Johnson began to give this area of involvement serious consideration.

Under Johnson's direction, Harbison has had its application processed through the federal government in the record time of 12 months. Johnson and his associates have gained the support of the governor of South Carolina, the local business community, and the principal institutions in the state that are concerned with development.

/ GLORIA SEGAL /

Gloria Segal is the co-developer of Cedar-Riverside, the New-Town-in-Town located in Minneapolis. She feels that while the thrust of the new community program is supposed to be experimental and innovative, it is really operating within the constraints of what has happened before. For example, she points out that one of the objectives is to create a socio-economic mix, but that there is no program to really accomplish this. She and her staff had to work almost a year to bring about this type of housing mix she feels is essential to the new community program. Widely respected among her colleagues, Segal has put together a professional staff of about 25, of which 9 are women.

Gloria Segal and company are researching and dealing with just about every element that is part of what Jim Rouse might call "the full fabric of city". Segal, whom Washington, D.C. architect John Courtney calls the "Gloria Steinem of the New Town movement", says, "The challenge is to make Cedar-Riverside attractive to people who live in the suburbs. . .that is, to make them give up the suburban home."

Her presence and participation also lend a sensitivity that is long overdue in the American development experience. Women are probably more aware of the community in the total sense because they tend to make more use of the services. Consequently, they are usually in a better position to make some of the subjective judgments that enter into the decision-making process for developments such as New Towns. Gloria Segal provides a leadership that is refreshingly sensitive.

13

LEARNING FROM
THE EUROPEANS

/ THE BRITISH EXPERIENCE /

In the fall of 1969, I traveled to England as part of a nine-member delegation from HUD to study the British experience with both New Towns and systems building. Our delegation was headed by George Romney, Secretary of HUD during the first four years of the Nixon administration, and we were hosted by the Ministry of Housing and Local Government.

Our tour in the Greater London area consisted of visiting the New Towns of Bracknell, Harlow, and Stevenage; eight industrialized building sites; and the Building Research Station. In addition, we held discussions at the Bear Inn in Woodstock, a twelfth century New Town in Oxfordshire next to Blenheim Palace where Winston Churchill was born.

The large-scale twentieth-century British experience with New Towns started with their New Towns Act of 1946. By mid-1969, they had housed over a half million people in 12 "first generation" New Towns (designated between 1946 and 1950). In the period between 1961 and 1968, 10 additional New Towns were designated to house an eventual population of over one million upon completion.

Following the Second World War, the British were confronted with housing shortages in London, as well as a number of adverse conditions such as overcrowding, air pollution, and traffic congestion. The problem of population growth and concentration in London, which had surfaced before the War, was still at hand. In a deliberate attempt to disperse both population and industry, eight New Towns were situated around London about 30 miles from the central business district. This distance was thought to be close enough to encourage migration and far enough away to discourage commuting. The eight London area New Towns are Stevenage, designated in 1946; Crawley, Harlow, and Hemel Hempstead, designated in 1947; Hatfield and Welwyn Garden City, designated in 1948; and Bracknell and Basildon, designated in 1949. The initial target population for each of these "London Eight" was in the area of 60,000 but has since changed to more than 100,000.

The most impressive aspect of the British New Towns is that they were planned and located with several purposes in mind. All are instruments of national policy and planning. In the case of the "London

Eight", the purpose was to relieve the population concentration in London.

Corby, designated in 1950 in Northamptonshire, was developed to provide housing for workers at the Stewarts and Lloyds Steel Plant. Peterlee, designated in 1948 in Durham County, drew its population from surrounding mining areas. Since 1967, several of the New Towns have been designed and located to further address the problem of population concentration in the Greater London area. These include Milton Keynes, which will have an eventual population of 250,000; Petersborough, designed for almost 200,000 people; and Northampton, which is designed for 230,000 when completed.

Housing in the New Towns is about 80 percent single-family attached and principally oriented toward the blue collar worker. Initially, some 90 percent of the housing in the New Towns was publically assisted, but this later changed because of a policy to effect 50 percent home ownership. As the New Towns program evolved, it has undergone many other changes, showing that the British are not wedded to any particular concept in their thinking. The "London Eight" New Towns were located within largely undeveloped areas surrounded by open spaces. Most of the subsequent developments were located near existing centers of population. The size of the developments has also changed over the years. The initial thinking was that populations of 50,000 within built-up areas and up to 80,000 within a radius of about 10 miles were optimal. It was felt that in cases where the populations exceeded 80,000, many of the problems that the New Towns were designed to solve—i.e., the long journey to work, the loss of touch with the countryside, and the lack of a sense of community—would again surface.

The efforts undertaken in the late 1960s were much larger in size. Milton Keynes will have a population of about 250,000, and in central Lancashire a proposal was designed to increase an existing population from 250,000 to 500,000. The thinking here was that car ownership and the increased mobility of the family would permit large undertakings without suffering a loss of community. (It must be kept in mind that the energy crisis was not at this time a major factor in decision making among the planners.) Thus, the idea of small-scale New Towns with population limits seems to have been abandoned in favor of recognizing mobility patterns and the benefits from providing a wider variety of choices for employment, education, shopping, and leisure.

Town planning in England is both a respected profession and a process. The process is supportive of New Towns through regional policies that eliminate or minimize competition with respect to commercial, industrial, and residential activities. The effectiveness of the

British planning system causes me to think that it is almost totalitarian. The government-sponsored Development Corporation carried out the development in conjunction with the private sector, which did much of the actual construction. Within the New Towns structure, there were social development plans and professionals assigned full time to deal with social problems. Also of special significance is the fact that there was a program to link jobs with housing. This effort was carried out by the Ministry of Labor and the Ministry of Housing and Local Government in conjunction with the Greater London Council for their particular area of jurisdiction.

The development of New Towns in England appeared to unfold in an atmosphere of rationality. This is not to say that there were no problems with local jurisdictions. There were. I expect that my impression stems, in part, from the planning process, the facts that the government-sponsored Development Corporation played the key role in coordination, and that the Ministry of Housing and Local Government is staffed entirely by civil servants, except for the Minister who is a political appointee. (In the United States, the Secretary, the Under Secretary, and all assistant secretaries are appointed by the President. In addition, special assistants, deputy assistant secretaries, major office directors (such as that for New Community Development), and many division directors are subject to White House approval.)

When we visited Bracknell, the population was only about 33,000. I was impressed with the scale that resulted principally from two-story row houses, the separation between pedestrian and automobile traffic, and the large open spaces. The population of Harlow at the time of our visit was over 75,000. Of particular note was the existence of heavy industry and a large sports complex. Stevenage's population was slightly more than 60,000, and the town had a particularly impressive Town Center with well over 200 shops. Collectively, our impressions were based on what we could see, the reading material we were provided, and the comments from the people whom we could talk with. Mine were positive and I expect that if any of us had any doubts about the potential for New Town development in the United States, we were relieved.

/ NEW TOWNS AND PLANNING IN GREATER STOCKHOLM, SWEDEN /

I visited Stockholm, Sweden, first in the summer of 1971 and again in June 1972 while attending the United Nations Conference on the Human Environment. I found the city, which was founded in the thirteenth century, to be a dramatic departure from the large cities in the United States. There are no slums, the old town *Gamla Stan* has been restored, the central business district has undergone renewal for two decades, and a public rapid transit system affords easy access to the entire metropolitan area. New Towns house suburban populations, in contrast to the strip development and sprawl that are commonplace in America.

I was particularly fortunate in having as a host Campbell Cyrus, an American architectural designer/planner who has been living and working in Stockholm for over 10 years. Because of his language facility and personal contacts, I was able to get many of my questions answered and to meet with many government officials and private citizens who were extremely helpful.

The Stockholm metropolitan area represents the best example of regional planning, urban redevelopment, and New Town building of any metropolitan area I have visited in the United States, Europe, or the Far East. It is probably the best example of planning within a regional context anywhere in the entire world. What is seen today, however, dates back to the turn of the century insofar as government policies and practices are concerned.

In 1904, the city of Stockholm began purchasing land outside of what then were the city limits, and by 1964, it owned about 70 percent of the land within its present boundaries. In addition, as of 1970, the city owned some 200 square miles of land outside of the present city limits. This amounted to about twice the area of the present city. American government officials and citizens alike ought to take note of this practice because of the negative impact that land speculation has had on planning and development in the United States.

Another major decision involving the public sector took place in 1941 when the population of Stockholm was less than 600,000. The city decided to build a subway, and by the end of World War II, the project was under construction.

New Towns in the greater Stockholm area were started in the early 1950s as part of a regional plan. In the northwest sector is Vallingby where occupancy began in 1954. This New Town had a 1970 population of about 50,000 and is less than 30 minutes from downtown Stockholm by rapid rail transit. Approximately 92 percent of the nearly 20,000 dwelling units are multi-family. The first of the three major New Towns in the Stockholm area, Vallingby has an impressive and highly functional town center. A pedestrian plaza is situated over the rapid transit station, and the town has cobblestone streets with circular designs and reflecting pools. As in the British New Towns, pedestrian and automobile traffic are separated, and there is emphasis on open space.

To the south of Stockholm's city center, and less than 20 minutes away by subway, is the New Town of Farsta. Occupancy began here in 1957, and by 1970, the population was about 23,000. Of some 7500 dwelling units, 87 percent are multi-family. The layout and design are not dramatically different from Vallingby, and the overall environs are equally attractive.

Southwest of Stockholm's center, and about 23 minutes away by subway, is Skarholmen, the latest New Town to be built. Occupancy began here in 1963, and the 1970 population was about 37,000. Of 12,000 dwelling units, 86 percent are multi-family. The design of Skarholmen dramatically departs from that of the other New Towns. The regional center is much larger than those of Vallingby and Farsta, and the central area is home for about 8000 people who live in huge residential blocks ranging from three to eight stories in height. From a distance, the area around the town center looks like file cabinets neatly stacked on the side of a gradually sloping hill. From within the town center, the excessive use of unfinished concrete, along with the rectangular design patterns, gives the impression of a scene from Orwell's *1984.*

Unlike the communities developed in the United States, the New Towns in greater Stockholm are highly serviced. Nowhere is this more apparent than in the provision of day care facilities. In Vallingby, there is about one day care/nursery place for every 10 dwelling units, in Farsta, there are about 1.2 day care/nursery places for every 10 dwelling units, and in Skarholmen, this figure has increased to about 1.7 day care / nursery places for every 10 dwelling units.

Since 1946, about 90 percent of all housing produced in Stockholm has had some form of government assistance. This is usually in the form of grants, reduced interest rates, and rent subsidies. Unlike government-assisted housing in the United States, it is impossible to distinguish which families or individuals receive government assistance from the design and location of their housing. This type of invisible assistance, along with a high level of community support services, has provided neighborhood stability and has minimized management and maintenance problems. It is perhaps here where we in America stand to learn the most from the Swedish experience. In contrast, housing programs within the United States have been builder oriented and built in areas without adequate support services, in addition to segregating people by income and race. I doubt if the billions of dollars experienced in defaults on federally assisted housing by HUD would exist today if our practices in planning and providing support services and assistance were similar to those in Sweden.

It would be wrong to conclude that all in regard to planning and development in Stockholm is "hunky dory". There are numerous groups actively involved in criticizing and otherwise commenting on the planning process. The most popular of these groups are Alternative Stad (Alternative City) and Miljoskyddsradet (Guardians of the Environment). These groups emphasize the pedestrian domination of the central downtown area and the use of public transport; the preservation of trees such as the large elms in the Kungstradgarden (Kings Tree Garden), the main park in downtown Stockholm; and other views not necessarily consistent with the public planners. During the United Nations Conference on the Human Environment, these groups set up displays in the Kungstradgarden protesting many of the public plans and development practices.

14

FEDERAL EFFORTS SUPPORTING NEW TOWNS

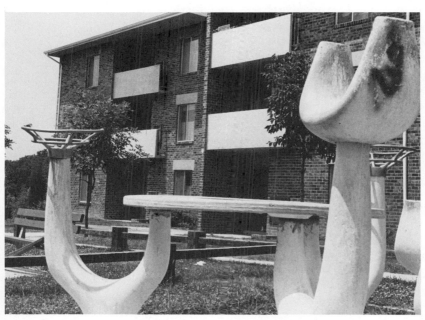

/ THE FEDERAL GOVERNMENT'S ROLE IN NEW TOWNS /

The involvement of the federal government in efforts to develop New Towns can be traced back to a 1936 "demonstration program" that led to development of small-scale "suburban resettlements" loosely following "greenbelt" concepts. These developments—Greenhills, Ohio; Greendale, Wisconsin; and Greenbelt, Maryland—ranged between 3000 and 6000 acres and were essentially residential in character. The 1936 "demonstration program" did not succeed in effecting the development of "New Towns" on a large scale or within the context of regional planning.

The case might be made that "New-Towns-in-Town" resulted in some instances from the Housing Act of 1949 which introduced "urban renewal". A case in point is the "New Southwest" in the nation's capital, Washington, D.C. While there are some provisions for housing low and moderate income families, this development did not begin to rehouse the great majority of the poor people it removed. The main thrust of urban renewal programs throughout the nation was commercial, and those related efforts that were residential provided middle and upper middle income housing opportunities, ignoring low and moderate income families. Because of the failure to respond to the combined needs of a large cross section of the citizenry, and to deal with the "full fabric of city", the case for New-Towns-in-Town resulting from the urban renewal program is rather weak.

The third opportunity for the federal government to get involved in New Town development came in 1965 when the Congress enacted legislation to allow HUD to insure mortgages for land to be developed and for improvements up to $25 million. This program, known as "Title X" in bureaucratic jargon, was either never sold to or never bought by the development community and was only sparsely used. Interestingly enough, it is designed to fit the scale of planned unit developments and might represent the fall-back position for the federal government if the present programs are scrapped.

In 1968, the first legislation directed specifically at New Towns emerged in the form of providing long-term loan guarantees for large-scale developments with a limit of $50 million per development. This program resulted in two New Town commitments—Jonathan, Minnesota, and Park Forest South, Illinois.

In 1970, the most comprehensive piece of legislation directed at New Towns, the Urban Growth and New Community Development Act, was passed which gave a new impetus to the role of the federal government in the development of New Towns. This legislative initiative which expanded on the earlier New Communities Act of 1968 stated among its purposes:

> To promote the general welfare and properly apply the resources of the federal government in strengthening the economic and social health of all areas of the Nation and more adequately protect the physical environment and conserve natural resources. . . .[and to] Refine the role of the federal government in revitalizing existing communities and encouraging planned, large scale urban new community development. [86]

The new legislation also expanded the guarantee authority up to $500 million, established a Community Development Corporation with a general manager, and provided for a number of key supplemental grants to state and local public bodies to support New Town development. These included programs for urban mass transportation, highways, airports, public health facilities, open space, libraries, recreation, neighborhood facilities, and public works facilities. Of particular significance was the fact that the legislation recognized the need for an urban growth policy and addressed the development of New Towns within this context. Between the time of the enactment of the Urban Growth and New Communities Act of 1970 or, as it is more popularly known, Title VII, and February 1973, a total of 15 New Town developments were approved. In November 1973 another New Town, Newfields, Ohio was approved by HUD. This brought the total to 16 as shown in Table 2.

The combined population projected for the 16 federally supported New Towns is 850,900; this covers a range from 18,000 to 150,000, with the average population being 53,000. This is close to the initial British ceiling of 60,000. Excluding the New-Towns-in-Town, the acreage ranges from 1740 to 17,000, with 10 of the 16 sites around the 5000 mark. As of November 1973, of the maximum guarantee authority provided of $500 million, $325.5 million has been committed, with the average loan guarantee amounting to about $23 million.

Twelve of the 16 sites are in metropolitan areas that experienced population growth between 1960 and 1970 at rates higher than the 13 percent national average. Of these, four New Towns (St. Charles, Shenandoah, The Woodlands, and Flower Mound) are located in metropolitan areas that grew during the 1960 to 1970 period at a rate

Table 2
SUMMARY OF NEW TOWNS GUARANTEED BY HUD

name	metropolitan area	state	projected population	guarantee amount		date of guarantee
Jonathan	Minneapolis	Minnesota	50,000 in 20 yrs.	$21	million	Feb. 1970
St. Charles	Washington, D.C.		25,000 in 20 yrs.	$24	million	June 1970
Park Forest South	Chicago	Illinois	110,000 in 15 yrs.	$30	million	June 1970
Flower Mound	Dallas	Texas	64,000 in 20 yrs.	$18	million	Dec. 1970
Maumelle	Little Rock	Arkansas	45,000 in 20 yrs.	$ 7.5	million	Dec. 1970
Cedar Riverside	Minneapolis	Minnesota	30,000 in 20 yrs.	$24	million	June 1971
Riverton	Rochester	New York	25,600 in 16 yrs.	$12	million	Dec. 1971
San Antonio Ranch	San Antonio	Texas	88,000 in 30 yrs.	$18	million	Feb. 1972
Woodlands	Houston	Texas	150,000 in 20 yrs.	$50	million	Apr. 1972
Gananda	Rochester	New York	50,000 in 20 yrs.	$22	million	Apr. 1972
Soul City		North Carolina	44,000 in 30 yrs.	$14	million	June 1972
Harbison	Columbia	South Carolina	23,000 in 20 yrs.	$13	million	Oct. 1972
Radisson	Syracuse	New York	18,300 in 8 yrs.		*	Aug. 1972
Roosevelt Island	New York City	New York	18,000 in 7 yrs.		*	Dec. 1972
Shenandoah	Atlanta	Georgia	70,000 in 20 yrs	$40	million	Feb. 1973
Newfields	Dayton	Ohio	40,000 in 20 yrs.	$32	million	Nov. 1973

*Issued a finding of eligibility for 20 percent grant from HUD supplementing 13 basic federal grant programs.

nearly three times the national average. Within the 16 federally assisted developments, there are two cases in which a metropolitan area has more than one New Town. Rochester, New York has the "satellite" New Towns of Riverton and Gananda within its metropolitan area and Minneapolis, Minnesota has the New-Town-in-Town of Cedar-Riverside "paired" with the "satellite" New Town of Jonathan within its metropolitan area.

Soul City has the distinction of being the only rural-based New Town. Cedar-Riverside and Roosevelt Island are the only New-Towns-in-Town approved to date under federal New Town programs.

In addition to the number of New Town proposals approved by the federal government by the fall of 1972, there were nearly 50 in the processing pipeline awaiting consideration. This demand and interest resulted from Title VII, the visible New Towns initiated in the private sector such as Reston and Columbia, a growing demand on the part of consumers for recreational amenities, and changing attitudes in the financial community toward long-term investments. The record achieved during the 1970-1973 period is commendable, but it was too closely tied to the personalities of the Secretary of HUD, the part-time general manager of the Community Development Corporation, the director of the Office of New Community Development, and several key advisors with HUD. The HUD organization and Administration practices were not entirely responsive to the demand for New Towns and failed to continue the momentum that had built up by the time the first dozen New Towns were approved.

Within HUD, top management relating to the New Towns program—the Secretary, the Under Secretary, the general manager, the special assistant monitoring the program, the director and deputy director of the Office of New Community Development, and several of the office directors—were either appointed or approved by the President of the United States. This is unlike the British system where all within the Ministry of Housing and Local Government with the exception of the Minister are civil servants. Of those working in the Office of New Community Development, which had a technical staff of less than two dozen people, less than 10 had substantive academic credentials and development-oriented work experience. None of the Office of New Community Development staff had executive-level experience with the private sector, and only three had any experience relating to large-scale development—that is, had worked within development corporations.

As the demand for federal assistance for New Towns peaked around early 1972, concern began to increase regarding the extent to which the Nixon administration supported the program. The Office of

Management and Budget had still not released the supplemental grants available for new community projects guaranteed by HUD. In late spring of 1972, William Nicoson, the director of the Office of New Community Development within HUD, resigned. Within months of his resignation, the internal management of the new communities program began to weaken. The staff morale throughout HUD was generally poor as the department was, in the words of one sub-cabinet official, "the Administration's guinea pig on special revenue sharing". The New Communities Office was particularly hard hit because after Nicoson resigned, about 10 key people followed, and by fall of 1974, the few experienced professionals remaining were noticeably overworked from carrying the extra load of assignments.

On November 30, 1972, shortly after resigning from HUD, I wrote a letter to Congressman Ashley inviting his attention to the conditions within HUD and the Office of New Community Development. This letter pointed out the low morale, the general confusion, the resignations, the limited staff capability, and the need to take steps to restore integrity to a very promising program. In particular, it was suggested that the next general manager serve on a full-time basis; that a quality professional staff be pulled together, that an inter-agency liaison be created to take advantage of the benefits of Executive Order 11512 (encouraging the location of federal facilities in New Towns), that greater emphasis be placed on New-Towns-in-Town, that the Administration be persuaded to free up the supplemental grant funds, and that attention be paid to areas of social concerns, particularly that of providing housing for low and moderate income families.

By January 1973, the key decision-makers on the guarantee process for federally supported New Towns—the Board of Directors of the Community Development Corporation—resigned. This was to be expected in view of the President's re-election and the beginning of a "new" Administration. What perhaps was not expected was the long delay in appointing a new Board of Directors and a new general manager. This process took about six months.

In addition to the staffing problems and the delayed processing of applications for New Town guarantees, a review of the decisions made by the late spring of 1973 indicated that there was no collective effort on the part of the Domestic Affairs Council to fully support the development of New Towns with the assistance of other federal programs. For example, there is little or no coordination between the Department of Transportation's Urban Mass Transit Assistance Administration and the Office of New Community Development to link satellite New Towns to downtown metropolitan areas with rapid rail transit. There is little or no effort made to coordinate the location of New Towns under consideration for federal assistance with the locations of growth centers determined by the Department of Commerce's Economic Development Administration. In addition to these deficiencies in inter-agency coordination, federal facilities or offices have not been located in any of the federally guaranteed New Towns. This is encouraged in an Executive Order 11512.

/ AN ASSESSMENT OF THE FEDERAL GOVERNMENT'S NEW TOWN EFFORTS /

Decisions on what New Towns would be approved, where they would be located, and what they would seek to prove were not based on objective criteria. The location decisions, especially, do not reflect any part of a national growth policy as called for in the 1970 legislation. Of particular significance is the fact that very few New Towns are located along rail lines (exceptions being Jonathan, Minnesota; Park Forest South, Illinois; and Riverton, New York). This considerably reduces the opportunity to restrict dependency on the automobile. In contrast, all of the three Stockholm area New Towns (Vallingby, Farsta, and Skarholmen) are connected to the central city by rail, by far the best example anywhere of New Town planning within the context of regional development.

Bill Magness, president of Gulf-Reston, Inc., the developer of Reston, Virginia, cites four years of processing time with HUD on an application for one assisted housing project and two years on another.

Jim Rouse, the widely respected developer of the New Town of Columbia, says, "rather than special programs, the government needs to realize that the building of New Towns is good".

Mort Hoppenfeld, vice-president for planning and design for Columbia and one of the major forces in New Town planning within the United States, criticized Title VII for falling short:

It does not select areas where New Communities would be useful; some are too small and contribute little to the region. The government lays on criteria without providing the means to achieve those conditions. The supplemental grants were never forthcoming; consequently, the opportunity for institutional development and social change is lost.

As a result of such criticism, the Housing Subcommittee of the U.S. House of Representatives held "Oversight Hearings" on the HUD New Towns program. Developers, mayors, city administrators, the Secretary of HUD, and others, including myself, participated in these hearings, held May 30 and 31, 1973.

Chairman William A. Barrett (D-Pa.) indicated that the hearings were called because the subcommittee's attention had been called to "a considerable number of administrative and substantive problems in the implementation of the program" and further indicated:

> . . .there are reports, for example, of excessive delays in approving projects due to the shortage of skilled staff, as well as reports of problems likely to be faced by new communities if certain supplemental federal aids are not made available as intended by the 1970 legislation. [87]

William Nicoson, former director of the Office of New Community Development within HUD, stated:

> At the beginning of 1971, for a few brief months, it appeared that the enormous potential of the Urban Growth and New Communities Development Act might be realized. The new communities programs had established credibility among developers. A small but dedicated staff had been assembled to administer the programs and was being expanded. High officials at HUD spoke enthusiastically of the programs both privately and in public.
>
> The Office of Management and Budget, however, was not enthusiastic. No funding for public service grants, innovative planning grants or interest-differential grants was reflected in the 1972 budget. When Congress nevertheless appropriated $5 million for innovative planning, the funds were impounded. [88]

Lewis Manilow, chairman of the League of New Community Developers and the developer of the Park Forest South New Town, noted that—

> Rather than merely making development decisions on the basis of the market, new communities developers are making these decisions in a broader context. Thus for the first time in history, consideration of such elements as the community's impact on natural resources, the environment, local governments, and the economic stability of the area are made before hand. This is a more comprehensive approach than traditional tract development and it insures to a large extent that the communities developed through this process will go far toward achieving sound and rational metropolitan growth. [89]

New Orleans Mayor Moon Landrieu said, "The only major tool available today giving us a chance toward producing a better tomorrow is the New Town concept." [90]

In my testimony before the Housing Subcommittee, I pointed out that—

There is a great inconsistency between the reality of the character of the American development experience and where we are as a nation in terms of technological advancement and wealth. Our metropolitan areas are characterized by polarization along the lines of income and race. There is a great disparity between the health profiles for blacks and whites in the areas of infant mortality, maternal death, and life expectancy. Millions of our citizens waste precious hours each day commuting to and from work. Monolithic megastructures and other anti-human structures are beginning to dominate our urban skyline. Each year over 200 million tons of pollutants are wasted in our skies. Our suburban areas have been overtaken by sprawl, strip development, leap-frog development, and other forms of inefficient land use. [91]

Most Americans probably expect that when the legislative branch of government mandates certain program activities, such as that for New Towns, the executive branch will carry it out. In theory, this is the way the process is supposed to work; in practice, it is quite different. Clearly, the Nixon administration did not carry out the congressional mandate in the areas of New Town development and national growth policy. The Administration's position was at best cautious. There is concern among top officials in the executive branch as to what the role of the federal government in regard to New Towns ought to be and also whether or not the New Town concept is a viable one.

New Towns can and are being built exclusively by the private sector without any federal assistance. Examples of such New Towns are Westlake and Laguna Niguel, both in California. There are other large-scale developments that loosely fit the New Town description elsewhere in California as well as in Florida, Texas, and Arizona. The main shortcomings of these New Towns are that they are of little value insofar as providing housing opportunities for low and moderate income families; they are located principally where they will market well, as opposed to where they are needed; they are not tied to any regional or national growth strategy; and they are not connected by rail to downtown metropolitan areas. If left entirely to the private sector, New Towns will not be at all socially responsive, and development in the United States will continue to polarize our society along the lines of income and race.

The attitudes of many of the top government officials associated with the New Towns program range from enthusiastic optimism to indifference to cautious conservatism. HUD Secretary George Romney, who served during the first four years of the Nixon administration, in a meeting following our trip to visit the New Towns in Europe in the fall of 1969, suggested developing just one New Town on an experimental basis. I argued at that point that we didn't have the luxury of doing that and needed to move forward with a large-scale program.

Sherman Unger, who was the HUD general counsel at the time, was more concerned with the qualitative as opposed to the quantitative aspects of the program. Had he been listened to, some of the economic shortcomings that resulted during the 1974-1975 period might have been avoided.

Sam Jackson had a sound knowledge of the program, but he served only part time as the general manager of the Community Development Corporation. He was also the general assistant secretary of HUD, along with being the assistant secretary for community planning and management. To no avail, I tried to get him to drop his other positions and devote his full energy to his position as general manager.

In December 1974, I interviewed John Ehrlichman, former President Nixon's top advisor on domestic affairs, on my Reston-based television show. His comments on the New Towns program helped to clarify the actual relationship that existed between the White House and HUD. He described the relationship with Secretary Romney as being difficult. The relationships at the assistant secretary level and below were described as being excellent. The reason that the relationship with Secretary Romney was difficult centered around a reported personality conflict between the Secretary and the President. Apparently, Secretary Romney wanted direct access to the President which he did not enjoy. In addition, Romney reportedly wanted White House staffers to deal directly with him, and this practice was not followed.

Personality is a key factor in decision making. This is particularly true at the top levels of government where there are so many political implications. The reported differences between Secretary Romney and President Nixon over "access" and personality probably hurt the furtherance of the New Towns program. My impression of John Ehrlichman's posture toward New Towns was that he did not have a hard and fast position one way or the other. He was concerned with the optimistic expressions about New Towns in many of the position papers submitted by HUD to the White House, and with the real commitment that the federal government would have to make to fully support the program.

During the recessionary period of late 1974 and early 1975, the HUD-assisted New Towns encountered serious financial difficulty. In a report to the Congress, "Getting the New Communities Program Started: Progress and Problems", by the Comptroller General of the United States, several projects were discussed with respect to not meeting their forecasts of revenues and costs. For example, Jonathan "had predicted net losses of $394,000 and $373,000" for 1971 and 1972, respectively, but the actual losses were "$800,000 and $867,000, respectively".[92] During this same period, "revenue from land sales was only $1.7 million compared with a projected revenue of $3.4 million".[93] Also, the developer of Park Forest South "had projected income of $2,699,000" for 1971 and 1972 but realized a net income of only $867,000 for this period. "The developer's financial position as of December 31, 1972, was substantially below that projected. Net working capital was $661,000 compared with the projected capital of $7,828,000."[94]

In January 1975, the *Washington Post* newspaper carried a week-long series of articles on New Towns. In this series it was reported that Riverton recently "closed its doors and laid off its staff when it was unable to reach agreement with HUD on the terms of a new guaranteed loan of $4 million"—and further that "A week later HUD dropped conditions on which it had previously been insisting and the loan went through, enabling Riverton to resume operations."[95]

Also in January 1975, James Lynn, Secretary of HUD under President Ford, announced that no additional applications for New Town guarantees would be accepted by the department and that four pending applications would be returned. HUD instead turned its attention to the matter of refinancing many of the New Towns to which it had earlier issued guarantees.

In the short run, the action taken by Secretary Lynn may be shocking, but if the New Towns program is to have a chance for success, the public sector, particularly the federal government, will have to reassess and strengthen its position. I expect that most developers would feel that they were led on by HUD in that the full benefits contained in the 1970 legislative package were expected to be made available at some point. In addition, the average guarantee commitment of $22.8 million was less than half of the $50 million maximum established in the 1970 legislation.

If HUD succeeds in effectively refinancing those New Towns that need assistance and then reopens the program with realistic financial support, the Lynn decision may prove to be a success. Considering the opportunities missed during the 1973-1974 period, I have no reason to believe that the federal government will—in the immediate future–provide support for additional New Towns. I expect that the federal government will proceed with a policy to "protect its investment" and to use this as an excuse to stay away from providing additional guarantees for New Towns.

15

THE CASE FOR NEW TOWNS

In arguing for New Towns and rational development, I expect that many will conclude that I am anti-city. I am not; rather I am pro-people. In this nation the large cities and the major metropolitan areas are becoming increasingly less attractive places to live for more and more people. The combination of polluted air, long journeys to work, increasing taxes and declining services, poor housing, crowding, and a host of other negative circumstances is getting to be unbearable. Add to this the isolation and the inability to have an impact on decisions in the public sector, and top it off with economic and racial polarization, and the city of chaos comes to life!

New Towns represent an alternative to the city of chaos, which is descriptive of most metropolitan areas in the United States. The final points on suggesting New Towns as *another way to live* are made with respect to governmental responsiveness, urban planning and national growth policy, survival of the central city, the human environment, economic and racial integration, housing for low and moderate income families, citizen participation; community services, and beyond the year 2000.

/ GOVERNMENTAL RESPONSIVENESS /

The performance record to date clearly shows that the federal government has failed to live up to the mandate for the development of New Towns as established by the Congress in 1970. In the Urban Growth and New Community Development Act, the Congress found—

> . . .that the national welfare requires the encouragement of well planned, diversified, and economically sound new communities, including major additions to existing communities, as one of several essential elements of a consistent national program for bettering patterns of development and renewal. [96]

By January 1972, HUD had approved loan guarantees for a total of six New Towns, and top officials were predicting that as many as 15 New Towns would be receiving loan guarantees annually. By August

257

1972, a total of 10 loan guarantees for New Towns had been issued by HUD. The August 1972 issue of HUD's *Challenge* magazine reported:

> . . .within three years of operation under the New Communities Program, the United States has moved into a position where developers, in partnership with various levels of government, can double the number of new communities initiated in England during the last 25 years. [97]

The implications of this assertion are that HUD was geared up and moving with developers "in partnership with various levels of government" and that the number of New Towns initiated in Great Britain since their Housing Act of 1946, which amounts to 44, would be doubled. An examination of the HUD performance record shows that 14 New Town guarantees had been issued by HUD as of September 1974 and that two New Towns were given findings of eligibility. This includes all of the activity resulting from the 1968 and 1970 legislative acts. The most productive period for HUD was between June 1970 and June 1972 during which 10 loan guarantees were issued for New Towns. This is to the credit of George Romney, Secretary of HUD during the first four years of the Nixon administration; Samuel C. Jackson, general manager of the Community Development Corporation within HUD; and William Nicoson, director of HUD's Office of New Community Development. Only three New Town guarantees were issued during 1973 after the change of Administration (Nicoson, Jackson, and Romney all departed HUD between mid-1972 and early 1973). In the almost a year after October 1973, there was no activity on the part of HUD with respect to completing the issuance of addition guarantees. This puts the boastful words of August 1972 in their proper perspective and raises serious questions about the capacity and integrity of the federal government with respect to carrying out the congressional mandate for New Towns.

The failure of HUD results from a combination of poor internal management and lack of support from the Office of Management and Budget. The Office of Management and Budget has failed to allow for the use of supplemental grants authorized in the 1970 legislation. This—along with an 18-month moratorium on federally assisted housing issued in January 1973 by former President Nixon, and along with environmental and economic problems at the local level—has seriously jeopardized the existing New Towns that have HUD guarantees and threatens the future of the entire New Town movement. It must be recognized, however, that the failure of the federal government to support New Towns as mandated by the Congress is the principal cause for the present conditions.

Given the congressional mandate for New Towns, the question must be raised as to why the federal government has not been responsive. It also must be recognized that in the absence of federally supported programs to house low and moderate income families, those New Towns that have been initiated will continue to accommodate those who fall within the middle and upper income categories. While the public reason for the Nixon administration's impoundment of funds had to do with an effort to curtail inflation, I expect that there is more to the lack of support by the Office of Management and Budget (which comes under the office of the President) than what is public knowledge. The lack of support may very well stem from a lack of understanding of what New Towns are, as well as a reluctance to deal with the issue of a national growth policy. In addition, I expect that there are those in government who are uncomfortable with a so-called partnership with the private sector because of the latter's profit motivation. Further, government tends to minimize or even eliminate risks in development, whereas the private sector assesses risks and invests accordingly. It would be a major step forward in the development of New Towns, if the executive branch of the federal government would respond to the Urban Growth and New Community Development Act passed by Congress in 1970.

/ URBAN PLANNING AND NATIONAL GROWTH POLICY /

My introduction to urban planning came as a graduate student where the emphasis was on "highest and best land use"; development control tools such as zoning; the process of planning which included citizen participation, zoning review boards, and "planning" commissions; and alas, the "master plan". This gem called the "master plan" was a graphic representation of land use, color coordinated with red for commercial, purple for industrial, yellow, brown, and orange for residential, and green for open space. About three years after graduation I was permitted to sit for oral examination for admittance as a full member of the American Institute of Planners. This oral exam consisted of my responding to questions based on my experience and interpretation of a rather lengthy reading list. All of the authors of the material just happened to be white males reflecting a bias that permeates the entire planning profession.

In almost a decade since my introduction, I have come to regard planning as both a nonprofession and a nonpractice. Planning commissions and zoning boards are nothing more than smoke screens for the real decision makers—bankers, politicians, and bureaucrats. If planning does exist, then where are the results? Look at metropolitan San Jose, California; Los Angeles, California; Chicago, Illinois; East St. Louis, Illinois; Fairfax County, Virginia; metropolitan New York City; or just about any of the some 65 metropolitan areas in the United States with populations over 500,000.

What is often called urban planning is, upon closer examination, scheming. Scheming explains the almost total absence of blacks and women in the profession, as well as the absence of young people and the elderly in the decision-making process. Scheming explains, in part, the results of a decision-making process that left cities and suburbs divided along the lines of race and class. Scheming may even shed some light on the "professional's" concern with the year 2000 while his hand moves quickly across a chart, coloring green a dilapidated building housing a mother and five children who are unsure as to where the next meal is coming from. Enough said on scheming.

The need is for development policies and coordinated efforts to deliver services to people and to achieve balanced growth. Of the 65 metropolitan areas that had 1970 populations above 500,000, some 33 had populations in excess of one million people. The three megalopolitan corridors—between Washington, D.C., and Boston; Pittsburgh and Chicago; and San Francisco and San Diego—combine to represent over half of the U.S. population. The concentration of population in these three areas only serves to diminish the quality of life by causing excessive demands on limited resources (land, water) and imbalanced demands for community support services (health, education, transportation, and recreation), let alone the quality of the air.

The federal government has, at best, paid lip service to the matter of developing and implementing a national growth policy. We are in an age of interdependence so it would be folly to discuss independence. The problems of energy consumption, environmental quality, and conservation are very much tied to whether the nation's growth is either irrational and unplanned or controlled. The question of where we locate New Towns might be less important than dealing with why New Towns are located in central cities, in metropolitan areas, or in rural areas, as well as how such location decisions can be brought about.

It seems to me that the federal government, particularly the Domestic Council, could play an effective role in shaping a national growth program by designating areas for new economic growth that take into account amenities and resources, and by supporting such decisions with infrastructure (roads and utilities) and transportation funding priorities, along with tax incentives to encourage private enterprise to locate and operate there.

Given a positive growth policy and financial incentives to overcome front-end and long-term holding costs, private enterprise can do the job. Federal and state governments could provide an extra incentive by giving the developer a vested position in an approved development plan that could preclude changes resulting from local legislative whims. A New Towns program within the context of a national growth policy is a prerequisite for decisions on what emphasis is appropriate for locations, as well as the number of such developments in central cities, metropolitan areas, and rural areas.

/ SURVIVAL OF THE CENTRAL CITY /

The central thesis of many who are urban "planners" or more precisely "schemers" is that the large American cities must be saved. In considering whether our large cities are worth saving, the following questions might be asked: Are our cities too big? Are buildings too tall? Have big cities outlived their usefulness? The answers to these questions might very well be Yes!

It is "in" to be pro-city. Even though the post-nineteenth-century cities with their industrial enclaves have given way to mid-twentieth-century service centers that become ghost towns at night, the "Emperor's Clothes" syndrome prevails, and few choose to recognize the many who live in squalor. Rather than cities per se, the emphasis must be on the people who presently live in cities and the steps that are necessary to create an environment in which they can best function.

An alternative to reconstituting central cities as desirable living places is that of introducing into the second growth cycle those aspects of human settlements that are provided the first time around in New Towns. This means introducing into central cities public elements that provide a hierarchial sense of place and personal identity offered by the neighborhood, village, and town levels. Such elements might serve to effectively increase the confidence of investors to the point where existing owners would be motivated to rebuild or rehabilitate what they have rather than to turn to the government for massive acquisition and renewal. The creation of a hierarchial sense of place might also assist in providing greater opportunities for participative decision making by the residents, which is often necessary to improve the delivery of municipal services.

The New-Town-in-Town is no panacea for urban ills. It is an alternative that encompasses services for people as well as dwelling units for their habitation. Cedar-Riverside is an experiment. It is not to be applauded. It must, however, be assessed by those who occupy it in terms of whether or not it is a quid pro quo for being free of the automobile. The same holds true for Roosevelt Island in new York City.

/ THE HUMAN ENVIRONMENT /

The environmental movement has been effect-oriented rather than cause-oriented. People are the cause of the problems that are often called "environmental", and it is within people that the solution exists. Little research has been done on technology misuse and abuse. We seemingly live in a switch-flicking, knob-twisting, handle-turning, dial-setting, button-pushing, totally mechanized and dehumanized generation. Those who live in metropolitan areas—about 75 percent of our total population—have become corridorized with the city at one end and suburbia at the other. Within this corridor we become isolated and unable to sense the feelings of our fellowman. On a hot summer day we wake up in suburbia in an air-conditioned home. After flicking a few switches, turning a few knobs, twisting a few dials, and pushing a few buttons, we get into an automobile (alone) which is also air conditioned and ride down a freeway (or is it "slaveway") to an air-conditioned office building. The horizontal corridor experience is now transferred into a vertical one by an elevator which in response to the push of a single button welcomes us into its silent chamber and lifts us to the floor of our choice. This experience goes on to reverse itself and then repeat itself day in and day out except for those 48-hour interludes that we call weekends.

Futurist Victor Ferkiss suggests that "Human beings flourish in a dynamic, moving equilibrium in which humanity changes and changes its environment, physical and social, at the same time." Ferkiss further states that "Unless our psychosocial needs are satisfied, we are crippled in our inability to function as complete human beings. . . ." [98]

With New Towns representing an attempt to build an environment for the total needs of people, some consideration must be given to the long-range effects that this might have on human behavior. Three points that might be considered are the need to ensure that New Towns are not overly serviced to the point where the challenge for adaptation ceases to exist, which might be a cause for regression; the period of time necessary for individuals to fully absorb the benefits of the New Town with respect to their behavioral patterns; and the time period necessary for a town to become a viable community, which might include a sense of community, the provision of institutional services to support the residents' needs, and attitude of respect toward the members of the community, and an identity with a particular place.

In the absence of hard data, I can not suggest that New Towns per se are the best example of places that are responsive to the human environment. It can be said, however, that the pedestrian-dominated plazas; the elimination of the automobile in New York City's Roosevelt Island New-Town-In-Town, the separation of automobile and pedestrian traffic in Reston, Columbia, Park Forest South, Jonathan, Irvine, and other New Towns; and the preservation of natural growth all seem responsive to people rather than buildings. In addition to these areas, there is the matter of scale and density, and except for the New-Towns-In-Town, there is a growing trend away from high rises and megastructures.

/ ECONOMIC AND RACIAL INTEGRATION /

There are many who may wish to think that the struggle for civil rights and equality is over in America. It is not. While the New Towns have failed to service the poor, they have in numerous instances allowed for racial integration. Traditionally in American development, whites have fled their neighborhoods when blacks moved it. In the case of Reston, Columbia, and Park Forest South, the integration of blacks and whites has proceeded without a repetition of past practices. Interestingly, in the case of Park Forest South, real estate sales persons have reportedly steered blacks to the New Town in an effort to keep surrounding suburban neighborhoods from integrating.

The significant feature of New Towns is that people know "up front" what they are getting into, and, at the same time, the newness of the town virtually precludes the establishment of rigid patterns along the lines of race. Considering the breakthroughs in housing, business activities, and management, the potential, although slight, exists for New Towns, provided they are developed on a sufficiently large scale, to act as a powerful vehicle to counter economic and racial polarization.

/ HOUSING FOR LOW AND MODERATE INCOME FAMILIES /

Unlike the British New Towns that are primarily for "blue collar" workers, the U.S. New Towns are principally housing middle and upper income families. I do not support a continuance of builder-oriented housing programs that, by their appearance, single out low and moderate income families. Conversely, I support people-oriented rent supplement programs that allow prospective tenants to acquire housing on the open market. Such programs are well suited for New Towns because families that rent with government assistance can enjoy many of the community support services that are provided for residents living in market rate housing. If New Towns are to succeed in realizing the social objective of providing housing for low and moderate income families, it is imperative that rent supplement funds be made available for prospective tenants and that dwelling units be set aside for such occupancy. In those cases where builder-oriented programs continue—that is, where the subsidy goes to the builder rather than the owner or renter—such dwelling units must be scattered and dispersed throughout the development.

The real benefits of good housing are less physical and more social and economic with respect to providing opportunities for upward mobility. It would be worthwhile for someone to research the difference in the patterns of upward mobility between residents receiving housing assistance in well-serviced areas such as New Towns and those living in poorly serviced areas in the central cities such as San Francisco's Hunter's Point.

If people are to enjoy the benefits of good housing, such housing must exist within the context of adequate community support services. Failure to approach housing as part of a total development program has resulted in widespread abandonment in many of the large central cities and has caused the federal government to become the nation's biggest slumlord. It is this total approach—one which recognizes the interdependence among housing, schools, employment, health and recreation facilities, and transportation—which makes New Towns particularly worthwhile in providing assistance to low and moderate income families.

Citizen participation has caught on in New Towns. Why? Because people are not playing games. There is both a need for achievement and a combination of money and talent available to get the job done right. The need exists because services are lacking, particularly during the early stages of development. The Reston commuter bus resulted from a need, and several talented people found a way to provide point-to-point commuter service within the paying capacity of the passengers serviced. The same is true for the Robert E. Simon Early Learning Center. The community associations such as those in Irvine, Columbia, and Reston, along with home owner's and/or cluster associations, have budgets and responsibilities large enough to attract strong interest and participation from their respective constituents.

The citizens, in participating in efforts to shape the development of New Towns, have a special role that is separate and apart from those of the elected official, professional staff, and developer. This role includes the identification of goals and objectives for the community, the level of services and public facilities desired, the support of bond issues and financing programs, the support of political candidates who are responsive to their needs, the determination of levels of economic and racial diversification, and the support of long-range growth programs to ensure the provision of housing, services, and jobs for future generations.

It is important that both developers and residents realize early on the benefits of working closely together to support each other where possible. This is especially true during public hearings in those jurisdictions where the New Town is not incorporated. In such instances, New Towns may have to compete with other developments for limited support services and other resources.

/ COMMUNITY SERVICES /

The provision of adequate community services can be a major problem during the initial phases of New Town development. This problem tends to exist because of the heavy front-end requirements for development—that is, the provision of a full range of support services when they cannot be justified on the basis of the existing market but only in terms of the potential market.

The provision of such services as day care, health care, and education along with the amenities of golf, swimming, and tennis is a strong marketing point; consequently developers can be damned if they do provide such services and amenities before the costs can be offset by income from sales and rentals, and damned if they provide them too late to attract the initial buyers and renters. It is important for the developer to identify what is going to take place with respect to community services and facilities, and where they will be located when they are provided, even if the "when" is expressed in terms of number of people rather than time. If problems are encountered by the developer in meeting schedules or with location changes, it is important that such changes be shared with the residents. They may even help to attract new people in order to gain the facilities at an earlier date.

/ BEYOND THE YEAR 2000 /

I do not expect anything dramatic to happen between 11:59 P.M., December 31, 1999, and 12:01 A.M., January 1, 2000. In the minds of urban planners and urban schemers, the year 2000 is a very real thing. In the lives of those who have the most pressing needs, I doubt if the year 2000 ever crosses their minds. An urban schemer suffering from a case of myopic elitism might consider—in terms familiar to him—dealing with the metamorphosis of megalopolitan megalomania and realize that neither trend nor history is necessarily destiny.

Just as the cities of the past have been located near navigable waterways and transportation terminals, or in the midst of a farming area, or for the purpose of satisfying military defense needs, the cities of the future may be shaped by the need to use new forms of energy such as solar or magnetic, or located under the ocean to harvest food supplies, or situated beneath the earth to allow an escape from air pollution. In addition, there is the possibility that communications technology and new transportation systems such as high speed hovercraft and personal rapid transit will cause cities to be reshaped. The technological challenge in the development of future cities seems formidable. This, however, is not the great challenge. This challenge exists today, it existed in the past, and it will exist in the future. The greatest challenge is to structure and maintain an environment that will serve the needs of people without destroying their initiative, one in which human potential is enhanced, and, finally, one where people irrespective of age, sex, race, religion, or economic condition can positively interact with each other and nature. This is what is happening in New Towns, and this is why they represent *another way to live.*

EPILOGUE
by Margaret Mead

New Towns are necessary to a society that has lost its way--lost its way in building segregated suburbs, in driving freeways through the centers of old neighborhoods, in tearing down the heart of cities and leaving only a gaping vacuum of high rise office buildings where people once lived. New Towns are necessary as we take our first groping steps towards righting the havoc that has been wrought by letting our railroads fall to pieces; our trolley cars fall into disuse; our theatres, libraries, and shops that once invited people into the city give way to scattered suburban centers or to abandoned buildings with their unused windows barred with iron gates. New Towns are a kind of light that beckons us ahead, that shows that it can be done; they are a reassuring first step.

It isn't that very many people are going to live in brand new towns, even though by the turn of the century we will have to build or rehabilitate as many dwelling units as we have now. Still most of us will live in rebuilt cities, or suburbs and developments that have been turned into communities again. But it is the New Towns that can tell us how to do these things, too--how to bring a slum to life, how to turn a suburb from a bedroom town where people are alienated and separated from their neighbors into a place where people work and meet and know each other.

It is in the New Towns that we can experiment and find out what we won't know how to anticipate. If you look carefully at the ways in which parts of suburbs have been designed, or the way plumbing and kitchens have been designed, or the idiocies in most modern hotels everywhere, you will see the result of designing at a distance, designing for a piece of an unknown whole, designing for people the planner never met who live in a way the designer never lived. The whole country is full of teapots that won't pour, of light fixtures that don't work, of doors and windows that let out the heat and let in the cold. Except for the very rich--people who live in homes they plan themselves--those who live in modern suburban developments or modern high rises in cities have absolutely nothing to do with how they are designed, or the shape of the community into which they move. They find a house they can afford, that seems about the right social level for the kind of people they are, that isn't more than 50 miles away from work, and move in and put up with it until they make enough money to move somewhere else, or lose enough money so they have to move somewhere else, or become superannuated about the time the house begins to fall to pieces. Everything in the house from the teapot that won't pour to the oven that turns on backwards and the door knobs that all fall off at once is unrelated to the lives of the people who live there. Mass production, mass building, and mass planning at a distance have taken their homes and their towns right away from them.

But if we want to get human communities back again, we will have to experiment. And a lot of the bright ideas will turn out to be wrong. Just because the legislation says that a New Town has to be integrated doesn't mean that the integration may not fail after all if attempted too late—as Carlos Campbell has told us. While it may be mandatory to include housing for different income groups, the shops may be too expensive and dazzling for those whose housing is subsidized. The planners may forget to find out whether there is any industry nearby, or whether a highway—not yet built—will come that way. If people buy their houses, there may be a sudden real estate boom, and all the original residents may sell out. The management may be democratic and lose control, or become autocratic and make the people apathetic. Or people who were actively concerned, tough-minded citizens when their houses were owned by a developer may become possessively preoccupied with the protection of their homes against outsiders once they become home owners. All these things have happened, and may happen again, unless New Towns are built slowly, a piece at a time, with a careful record kept of what the mistakes were, and time to correct them before it is too late.

For a hundred years Americans have been building their towns and cities by many blocks at a time; hundreds of houses are built all alike, that go wrong because there was no small-scale way of testing how livable they were. For houses and towns belong to a class of situations that cannot be programmed in advance. You can do something with a single house—at least build just one and let a family and a cat and dog live in it for a year to get the bugs out of it—but this testing can only be done for whole communities by building real whole communities and letting the people who live there take part in the process. It can only be done if the focus is on a framework for human lives instead of on customers buying preplanned houses.

Carlos Campbell has pointed out that we need a national growth policy and a will to carry out the laws that are already on the books. He has demonstrated vividly the relationships that exist between income and racial segregation; the greater participation of women; a better, more coordinated relationship between the private sector and government leadership. No one can have read these pages without a sense of sweep and frustration, of possibility, and of hope deferred. If all of the positive steps described within these pages were to be taken—and with the help of Watergate and the energy crisis, they may be—we would have a much greater clarity about scale, and the next step would lie, I believe, in the provision for people to choose each other as well as to choose housing and towns suitable to their individual needs.

We need to understand, far better than we do now, where to plan internationally, where continentally, where nationally, and what should be left to the smallest units of community, cluster, and neighborhood. We need to know whether providing a physical framework—one in which an income mix, and therefore a racial mix, and a full participation of women at every level of planning and execution—is enough. Can the hardware all be planned if the software is good enough? I don't think we are at all sure. It may be that restoring to smaller groups the actual decisions about the size, shape, and material of their homes is a necessary condition of full humanity. Or it may be that an extension of participation at the top, a receptivity to black business, or a willingness to give women a hand in the planning may be enough. Perhaps the reins of choice have slipped forever from the hands of those who would like actually to control the place within which they make their homes. If so, working at many different levels, with a real mix of economics, race, age, sex, and ethnicity at every level, must be the answer for the future. What would make the greater difference: more blacks and women in HUD, or more possibilities of redesigning mass planned houses—on the spot? Or must we try for both?

But one thing seems certain to me. The next step must be the early involvement of the future residents, and not only in the planning and in the hearings on policy; the future residents must be allowed to choose each other before the New Town, or the New-Town-in-Town, or the satellite town is built. There is no need to treat New Towns as if they were voyages from one port to another, with passengers who have never met. Old kin and neighborhood and friendship ties could be maintained, and the human fabric of the new or rehabilitated communities could already be partly woven before a foundation stone is laid or a single unit goes up. It takes only a brief three or four years to build New Towns when it is brick and mortar that we use, but ties between people take longer. Too much effort in New Towns goes into trying to make people into communities. Instead, friends and neighbors, kindred and work companions should be able to move together within a framework that has been prepared for them to make just such choices.

FOOTNOTES

1 / Edmund N. Bacon, *Design of Cities* (New York: The Viking Press, 1967), p. 13.

2 / Constantinos A. Doxiadis, *Ekistics* (New York: Oxford University Press, 1968), p. 5.

3 / Alvin Toffler, *Future Shock* (New York: Random House, 1970), p. 165.

4 / John F. Kain, "A Short Course in Urban Economics," in *Municipal Yearbook 1968*, eds. Mark E. Keane and David S. Arnold (Washington, D.C.: International City Managers' Association, 1968), p. 245.

5 / Kenneth B. Clark, *Dark Ghetto* (New York: Harper and Row, 1965), pp. 63-64.

6 / Robert Conot, *Rivers of Blood, Years of Darkness* (New York: Bantam, 1967), p. 239.

7 / Lyndon B. Johnson, "Address to the Nation on Civil Disorders, July 27, 1967," in *Report of the National Advisory Commission on Civil Disorders* (New York: Bantam Books, 1968), p. 539.

8 / United States Housing Act of 1937, Basic Laws and Authorities on Housing and Urban Development (Washington, D.C.: U.S. Government Printing Office, 1969), p. 225

9 / Excerpt from The Housing Act of 1949, Basic Laws and Authorities on Housing and Urban Development (Washington, D.C.: U.S. Government Printing Office, 1969), p. 1.

10 / Excerpts, Demonstration Cities and Metropolitan Development Act of 1966 (Washington, D.C.: U.S. Government Printing Office, 1966), p. 349.

11 / Patterns of Disorder, Report of the National Advisory Commission on Civil Disorders (New York: Bantam Books, 1968), p. 142.

12 / Housing and Urban Education, Special Cue Report (New York: Center for Urban Education, 1971), p. 8.

13 / Gurney Breckenfeld, "What the President Should Have Said About Housing," *Fortune*, November 1973, p. 39.

14 / The Quality of Life Concept, U.S. Environmental Protection Agency (Washington, D.C.: Environmental Protection Agency, 1973), p. 1-1.

15 / From THE SANE SOCIETY by Erich Fromm. Copyright © 1955 by Erich Fromm. p. 19 Reprinted by permission of Holt, Rinehart and Winston, Publishers. (New York)

16 / Dr. J. Stamler, "Nutrition and the Present Epidemic," *World Health, The Magazine of the World Health Organization,* August-September 1970, p. 26.

17 / J. Lenegre, "The Modern Epidemic," *World Health, The Magazine of the World Health Organization,* August-September 1970, p. 5.

18 / Carlos C. Campbell, "Inside and Outside of the Stockholm Conference," *City Magazine,* Fall 1972, p. 10.

19 / Ibid.

20 / Ibid., p. 12.

21 / Carlos C. Campbell, "Insights on the City of Man From Isles of the Gods," *City Magazine,* Winter 1971, p. 18.

22 / Ibid., p. 19.

23 / Ibid.

24 / Ibid.

25 / Ibid.

26 / Ibid.

27 / Ibid.

28 / Ibid.

29 / Maurice Beresford, *New Towns of the Middle Ages* (New York: Praeger, 1967), Ch. 11.

30 / Ervin Galantay, "New Old Towns," *Progressive Architecture,* Copyright, Reinhold Publishing Co., December 1967, pp. 87-89.

31 / William I. Goodman and Eric C. Freund, eds., "Antecedents of Local Planning", in *Principles and Practice of Urban Planning* (Washington, D.C.: International City Managers' Association, 1968), pp. 7-15.

32 / Ebenezer Howard, *Garden Cities of Tomorrow* (Cambridge: MIT Press, 1965), p. 26.

33 / William K. Reilly, ed., *The Use of Land: A Citizens' Policy Guide to Urban Growth* (New York: Thomas Y. Crowell Company, 1973), p. 263.

34 / Ibid., p. 264.

35 / Thomas W. Lippman, Developer Withdraws from Fort Lincoln Project, *Washington Post,* 22 February 1975, Sec. E, p. 3.

36 / Vance Packard, *A Nation of Strangers* (New York: David McKay Company, 1972), p. ix.

37 / From THE SANE SOCIETY by Erich Fromm. Copyright © 1955 by Erich Fromm. p. 15 Reprinted by permission of Holt, Rinehart and Winston, Publishers. (New York)

38 / Ralph Keyes, *We the Lonely People: Searching for Community* (New York: Harper and Row, 1973), p. 9.

39 / Eleanore Carruth, "The Big Move to New Towns," *Fortune,* September 1971, p. 95.

40 / Felicia Clark with Toddlee, "A Broad Concept of 'Community' is What's New About New Towns," *Architectural Record*, December 1973, p. 130.

41 / Wolf Von Eckardt, *A Place to Live* (New York: Delacorte Press, 1967), p. 361.

42 / *Reston Today, Reston Fact Sheet, Spring 1975*, Gulf-Reston, Inc., 1975, p. 1.

43 / Robert E. Simon, Jr., "The Challenge of New Communities," *Challenge Magazine* (U.S. Department of Housing and Urban Development, August 1972), p. 11.

44 / *The Economic Impact of Reston on Fairfax County Government*, Booze, Allen & Hamilton, Inc. (Reston, VA, Gulf-Reston, Inc., 1973).

45 / *A Place Called Reston . . . 1975 Reston Directory* (Reston, VA: New Town Publications, 1975), p. 23.

46 / Constantinos A. Doxiadis, *Architectural Crimes*, Delos Symposium (Delos Nine), Document B No. 28, July 12, 1971, p. 5.

47 / Frank Lloyd Wright, *The Future of Architecture* (New York: Mentor, 1963), p. 176.

48 / William Michelson, "Social Insights to Guide the Design of Housing for Low Income Families" (Report delivered at the National Policy Forum, National Association of Housing and Redevelopment Officials, Washington, D.C., February 1967).

49 / Stanislav V. Kasl, "Effects of Housing on Mental and Physical Health", Man-Environment Systems (Orangeburg, N.Y.: 1974), vol. 4, pp. 207-226.

50 / "Reston: A Dream Has Been Saved", *Washington Post*, 14 September 1973, Sec. A., p. 26.

51 / *The Promise and Purpose of Columbia: The First Five Years* (Columbia, MD: Howard Research and Development Corporation, November 1972), p. 13.

52 / James W. Rouse, Speech before Conference on Community Governance, Columbia, MD, March 25, 1972, p. 11.

53 / Jean F. Moon, "Grassroots Seems to Have Finally Put it All Together." (Columbia [MD] Flier, November 29, 1972), p. 8.

54 / *The Columbia Association Annual Report, 1972* (Columbia, MD: The Columbia Park and Recreation Association, Inc.), p. 2.

55 / Roger Ralph and Gordon Ivay, Columbia Association Youth Survey, Columbia Association Office of Planning and Evaluation (Columbia, MD: 1973), pp. 3-4.

56 / Ibid., p. 17.

57 / Ibid., p. 27.

58 / Ibid.

59 / *Medical Services, New Residents Handbook, The Columbia Association* (Columbia, MD: The Columbia Park and Recreation Asso-

ciation), p. 49.

60 / James W. Rouse, Speech before Conference on Community Governance, Columbia, MD, March 25, 1972, p. 10.

61 / "Soul City: A Vital Experiment", *Washington Post,* 6 July 1972, Sec. A., p. 16.

62 / "Blacks: Soul City", *Newsweek,* August 14, 1972, p. 24. Copyright 1972 by Newsweek, Inc. All rights reserved. Reprinted by permission.

63 / Arnold Toynbee, ed., *Cities of Destiny* (New York: McGraw-Hill, 1967), p. 13.

64 / *Jonathan General Development Plan, 1972* (Jonathan, MN: New Community Services, Inc., 1972), p. 12.

65 / *Community Information Systems, People in Communication with Imagination* (Chaska, MN: Community Information Systems, 1973), p. 1.

66 / *Appleseeds* (Jonathan, MN), January 19-February 1, 1973, p. 4.

67 / Ibid., p. 5.

68 / Ibid.

69 / Ibid., p. 2.

70 / *Appleseeds* (Jonathan, MN), February 9-22, 1973, p. 4.

71 / *Appleseeds* (Jonathan, MN), June 2-16, 1972, p. 3.

72 / *Los Angeles Times,* 1 October 1972, Sec K, p. 5.

73 / *Irvine World News* (Irvine, CA), February 1, 1973, pp. 18-19.

74 / *The Register* (Santa Ana, CA), February 21, 1973.

75 / Ibid.

76 / George Leidel, "Seeds of Intolerance Find Fertility in Irvine", *Daily Pilot* (Costa Mesa, CA), February 4, 1973.

77 / Ibid.

78 / *Irvine Community Association Manual* (Irvine, CA: The Irvine Company, 1973), p. 1.

79 / *Annual Report of the New York State Urban Development Corporation, 1972* (New York: Urban Development Corporation, 1973), p. 5.

80 / Hugh Carey, Governor of the State of New York, Statement before the New York State Legislature, January 8, 1975.

81 / Edward J. Logue, President and Chief Executive Officer of UDC, before the New York State Senate Committee on Housing and Urban Development, January 16, 1975, p. 20.

82 / Ibid., p. 22.

83 / *New York Times,* 9 March 1975, p. 8, © 1975 by the New York Times Company. Reprinted by permission.

84 / Ray Watson, Testimony before the Housing Subcommittee, Committee on Banking and Currency, U.S. House of Representatives, Washington, D.C., September 16, 1971.

85 / William Magness, Speech at the Dedication Ceremonies for Reston International Center, Reston, Virginia, September 29, 1973.

86 / Section 702 (c), Urban Growth and New Community Development Act of 1970, Title VII, Housing and Urban Development Act of 1970, Public Law 91-609, December 31, 1970.

87 / Oversight Hearings on HUD New Communities Program, 93rd Congress, First Session, 1973, p. 1.

88 / Ibid., p. 8.

89 / Ibid., p. 43.

90 / Ibid., p. 151.

91 / Ibid., p. 213.

92 / *Getting the New Communities Program Started: Progress and Problems* (Washington, D.C.: U.S. General Accounting Office, 1974), p. 30.

93 / Ibid.

94 / Ibid.

95 / Thomas W. Lippman, "HUD Retreats From New Town Idea", *Washington Post,* 14 January 1975, Sec. A. p. 13.

96 / Section 710 (d), Urban Growth and New Community Development Act of 1970, Title VII, Housing and Urban Development Act of 1970, Public Law 91-609, December 31, 1970.

97 / Samuel C. Jackson, "New Communities," *Challenge Magazine* (U.S. Department of Housing and Urban Development, August 1972), p. 6.

98 / Victor Ferkiss, *The Future of Technological Civilization* (New York: George Braziller, 1974), pp. 165-166.

INDEX

/ A /

Advantages of New Towns, 20
Africa, 13
AFRICARE, 63
Albany, 5
Alcoholism, 10, 26
American Institute of Architects, 9
Annapolis, Maryland, 19
Anti-human construction, 12
Anti-urban bias of 19th century, 19
Architectural design, 20-21, 33-36
Architectural Forum, 9
Aristotle, reference to, 68-69
Arts, 172-75
Ashley, Thomas Ludlow, 195-203
Asia, 13
Audubon, New York, 23, 208
Authority, levels of, 12

/ B /

Bacon, Edmund, 3, 11
Bauer, Catherine, 18
Behavioral implications of high-rise
    living, 80-81
Biblical references to city condi-
    tions, 6
Black:
    entrepreneurship, 23, 138
    inner-city, 7
    neighborhoods, 5
    opportunity (Cedar-Riverside,
        Minnesota), 170-71
    population, 148
    residences, 5

Black (*Continued*)
    Reston, in, 42-46
    statistics, 5-6
    unemployment rates, 5
Black Arts Festival, 60-63
Boredom, 26
British New Towns, 235-37
Buffalo, New York, 5
Building Systems International, 24

/ C /

Carruth, Eleanore, 26
Cedar-Riverside, Minnesota, 23, 24,
        161-75, 231, 245, 246
Census Bureau data re populations,
        17
Central city survival, 162, 261-62
Challenges of New Towns, 111-15
Chicago, Illinois, 5
Chicano neighborhoods, 5
Cities, as civilization indicator, 3
Cities, population of, 17, 18
Citizen participation, 12, 17, 20, 58-
        59, 69, 72, 73, 150
Civic organizations, 17
Civil Disorders, National Advisory
        Commission on, 7
Civil Rights Act of 1968, 223
Civil rights legislation, 8
Clark, Kenneth B., 6
Classification of New Towns, United
        States, 23-25
Clearlake, Texas, 23
Cluster association, 71-72
Columbia Association, 90, 95,
        105-107, 110

Columbia, Maryland, 20, 22, 23, 69, 89-115
Commercial centers, 17
Common areas, 72
Commoner, Barry, 11
Common Ground Foundation, 47, 51-55, 73
Community associations, 189-90
Community Information System, 153
Community services, 265
Competition, economic, of cities, 17
Comprehensive approach to development, 9
Conet, Robert, 6
Congress, intervention of, 7
Conklin, William, 33
Cox, Harvey, 11
Crises of cities, 3-4
Cultural opportunities, 59-63, 190-91

/ D /

Day care, 110-11
Death rates, maternal, 5
Decision-making, participation in, 17, 25, 73
Decline in town planning, 19
Decline of cities, 3-4
Delos Symposium, 11
Demolition for urban renewal, 8
Demonstration Cities and Metropolitan Development Act of 1966, 7
Demonstration Cities Bill, 8
Density, 12, 79-80, 81
Department of Housing and Urban Development (HUD), 8, 22, 24, 180, 245, 246, 258
Department of Transportation, 247
Design, architectural, 20-21, 33-36
Despair, 6
Detroit, Michigan, 8
Developer, role of, 46, 72, 221

Development knowledge, lack of, 18
Development, need for comprehensive approach, 9
Development, per federal legislation, 7
Disadvantages in cities, 3-4
Discrimination, 6
Disease, 6
District of Columbia Redevelopment Land Agency, 24, 25
Divorce, 67-68
Domestic Affairs Council, 247
Doxiadis, Constantinos A., 4, 11, 79, 174
Drugs, 66-67, 104, 107

/ E /

Economic activities, 17
Economic competition of cities, 19
Economic development, 10
Economic Development Administration, 248
Economic integration, 263
Economy shift, U.S., 3
Educational services, 17, 63-65, 109-11
Education, elementary, 63-65
Elementary education, 63-65
Employment, 168
Engineering feats, 21
Environmental protection, 10
Environmental Protection Agency (EPA), 10
EPA (Environmental Protection Agency), 10
Equal housing opportunities, 5, 8
Equity participation, 24
Erie Canal, 5
Erikson, Erik, 11

/ F /

Fairfax City Housing Authority, 75

Fair housing, 46
Federal development practices, 5
Federal government programs, 7-9
Federal Home Loan Bank Board, 7
Federal Housing Administration, 7
Federal National Mortgage Association, 7
Fellowship House, 81-83
Fellowship Reston Senior Citizens Club, 82
Festivals, 165-66
Financial success of New Towns, 33
Flower Mound, Texas, 23, 245
Footpaths, 21, 33
Ford Foundation, 195
Fort Lincoln, Washington, D.C., 23, 24, 25
Free enterprise system, counter-effect of, 19
Free standing classification, 23, 24
Fromm, Erich, 10, 26
Fuller, R. Buckminster, 11
Future, 265-66
Future Shock, 4

/ G /

Ganada, New York, 23, 245, 246
Garden Cities of Tomorrow, 19
Garden City, 11, 18, 19, 20
Geddes, Sir Patrick, 18
Ghetto, 6, 8
Ghettoization, 5
Goals, 32-33
Goodman, Charles, 33
Governance, 21, 68-73, 136
Government (federal) role, 243-53
Governors State University, 138-39
Grassroots, 104-105
Great Lakes, 5
Greenbelt, Maryland, 19, 243
Greendale, Wisconsin, 19, 243
Greenhills, Ohio, 19

Gross national product, 3
Growth, 73, 83-85
   policy, 259-61
   urban, 4
Gunther, John, 25

/ H /

Halprin, Lawrence, 11
Harbison, South Carolina, 230-31, 245
Health services, 17
Heart attacks, 10
Heterogeneity, 32
Hickory School, 139
High rise buildings, 12, 77-81, 168
Highways, 5, 7-8, 17
History of New Towns:
   America, 19
   Europe, 18-19
Homicides, 10, 65-66
Housing, 73-83, 150-52, 184-88, 223, 263-65
Housing Act of 1937, 7
Housing Act of 1949, 7, 243
Housing Act of 1968, 195
Housing and Urban Development, Department of (HUD), 8, 22, 24, 180, 245, 246, 258
Housing balance, income-wise, 46
Housing complex, public, 9
Housing, deterioration of, 5
Housing, equal opportunity, 8
Housing, failure of federal efforts, 9
Housing, federal legislation, 7, 195, 243
Housing in New Towns, 17
Housing mix, 169
Housing prices, 32
Housing programs, 5, 8
Housing, public, 7, 9
Housing styles, 32
Howard, Ebenezer, 18, 19

Howard University Mississippi Project, 63
Hunters Woods Council, 71

/ I /

Ignorance, 6
Income level mix, 5, 7, 17, 26
Individual's rights, priority of, 32
Industrial parks, 17
Industrial Revolution vs. social conditions, 10
Infant mortality rates, 6, 10
Ingerbritsen, Karl, 50, 51
Initiative, citizen, 46-49
Inner-city residents, 7
Integration, racial, 21-22, 26, 27, 223, 263
Interaction, citizen, 22, 36, 52, 97-103, 150
Interracial marriage, 46
Interstate highway system, 7-8
Interstate Land Sales Full Disclosure Act, 22
In-town classification, 23, 24
Irvine, California, 23, 179-91, 227

/ J /

Johnson, Fred, 230-31
Johnson, Lyndon Baines, 6-7
Jonathan, Minnesota, 23, 143-57, 243, 245, 246

/ K /

Kain, John F., 5
Kasl, Stanislav V., 80
Keys, Ralph, 26

/ L /

Laguna Niguel, California, 23

Lake Anne (Reston, Virginia), 33, 36
Lake Anne Nursery School and Kindergarten (LANK), 47-49, 222
Lake Kittamaqundi (Columbia, Maryland), 93
Land sales regulation, 22
Land speculation, 19
LANK. *See* Lake Anne Nursery School and Kindergarten
Large scale developments, 20
LeCorbusier, 18, 78-79, 174
Legislation, civil rights, 8
Legislation, failure of, 8
Legislation for New Towns, 195
Leisure time activities, 32
Life expectancies, 6, 10
Location of New Towns, U.S., 23-25
Los Angeles, 6
Low-income housing programs, 8

/ M /

McKissick, Floyd B., 119
McKnight, Henry T., The Honorable, 153-54, 165
Magness, William H., 228-30
Manilow, Lewis, 134, 225-27
"Marseille Block", 79
Maumelle, Arkansas, 245
Mead, Margaret, 11, 26
Medical programs, 108-109
Metropolis, population of, 17, 18
Metropolitan areas, 5
Michelson, William, 80
Middle-class syndrome, 26
Minnesota Renaissance Fair, 150
Mission Viejo, California, 23
Mississippi River, 5
Model cities programs, 8
Mortality rates, infant, 6, 10
Mortgage insurance, 7
Mortgage market, 7
Multi-family residences, 20

Mumford, Lewis, 18
Municipal services, 5

/ N /

National Advisory Commission on Civil Disorders, 7
report of, 8
National Association of Home Builders, 196
National Association of Housing and Redevelopment Officials, 80
National Association of Real Estate Boards, 196
National Endowment for the Arts, 172-73
National growth policy, 8
Nation of Strangers, A. 26
Natural growth, removal limit, 21
Needs, human, 12
in Reston, Virginia, 84
"Negative power", 73
Negroes. *See also* Black:
in Reston, Virginia, 42-46
inner-city, 7
involvement, Park Forest South, Illinois, 138
opportunity, Cedar-Riverside, Minnesota, 170-71
population, 148
residences, 5
statistics, 5-6
unemployment rates, 5
Neighborhood, 17, 18, 165-67
basic residential unit, as, 12, 21
deterioration of, 5
New Communities Act of 1968, 244
New Haven, Connecticut, 8
New Town concept, 17-27
New-Towns-in-Town, 161-75
New Towns program, 8
Newark, New Jersey, 8

Newfields, Ohio, 245
New York, 5
New York State Urban Development Corporation, 207
Noise, 12
North Carolina (Soul City), 119-29

/ O /

Office of Management and Budget, 258
Office of New Community Development, 247
Open spaces, for common use, 21
"Operation Breakthrough", 8
Osborn, Fredric, 18
Overdevelopment, problems of, 11

/ P /

Packard, Vance, 25-26
Palme, Olaf, 11
Park Forest South, Illinois, 19, 23, 133-40, 225, 243, 245
Participation of citizens, 12, 17, 20, 58-59, 69, 72, 73, 150
Participation, parental, 58-59
Performing arts, 59-63, 167
Philadelphia, Pennsylvania, 5, 19
Physical activities of New Towns, 17
Place to Live, A, 26
Plan for a Contemporary City, 78
Planned unit developments (PUDs), 20
Planning, 7, 18, 188-89
Politics, 68
Population:
Cedar-Riverside, Minnesota, 170
Columbia, Maryland, 95
control, 10
projections, 20, 21
Soul City, North Carolina, 119

Population (*Continued*)
  United States:
    past, 3, 4, 5
    present, 3, 4, 5
Poverty, 6
Pricing, housing, 32
Privacy, 32
Pruitt-Igoe housing project, 9
Public housing, 5, 7, 9
PUDs. *See* Planned unit develop-
    ments
Puerto Rican neighborhoods, 5

/ Q /

Quality of life, 10, 19

/ R /

Racial integration, 5, 21-22, 26, 27,
    97-103, 263
Racial tensions, 99, 107
Radburn, New Jersey, 19
Radisson, New York, 23, 208, 245
Railway, transcontinental, 5
Rancho Bernardo, California, 23
Rancho California, California, 23
Rancho San Diego, California, 23
Rationale for New Towns, 25-27
Recreation, 17, 22, 33, 55-59, 82
Religious institutions, 17
Residential interaction in Reston, 36
Resource distribution and use, 10,
    11
Respect for individual, 22
Reston Community Association, 69,
    71, 72, 77
Reston Commuter Bus, 47, 49-51
Reston Home Owners Association,
    69, 71, 72, 73
Reston Players, 59-60
Reston, Virginia, 20, 21-22, 23, 26,
    31-85, 221, 223
Revenue-sharing program, 8

Riots, 6
Riverton, New York, 23, 245, 246
Roads, 17
Robert E. Simon Early Learning
    Center, 48
Rockefeller Brothers Fund, 22
Rockefeller, Nelson, 207
Roosevelt Island, New York, 23, 24,
    107-108, 245
Rossant, James, 33
Rouse, James, 20, 89, 224-25
Runaways, 104
Rural New Towns, 23, 24

/ S /

Salk, Jonas, 11
San Antonio Ranch, Texas, 23, 245
Sane Society, The, 10, 26
Satellite classification, 23
Sauer, Louis, 33
Savannah, Georgia, 19
Savings and loan associations, 7
Sculpture, 36
Segal, Florida, 164, 231-32
Sense of community, 151
Shenandoah, Georgia, 245
Shopping centers, 21
Simon, Robert E., 20, 31, 32, 37,
    46, 47, 60, 221, 222, 223
Single-family detached residences,
    20
Slums, 6, 7
Smith, Clothiel Woodward, 33
Social activities of New Towns, 17
Social conditions (generated by
    Industrial Revolution), 10
Social disorders, 65-68
Social interaction, 52
Social planning, 89, 169-70
Social practices, changes in, 8
Social services, 46-47, 69
Socio-economic integration, 27
Solutions to city ills, 6

Soul City, North Carolina, 23, 119-29, 245, 246
South America, 13
St. Charles, Maryland, 23, 245
St. Louis, Missouri, 9
Steamboats, 5
Stein, Clarence, 18
Structuring New Towns, 18
Styles in housing, 32
Subcommittee on Housing, 195
Suburban residents, 7
Suburbs, features of, 20
Suburbs, growth of, 4, 5
Suicides, 10, 26, 104
Support services, community, 9
Swedish New Towns, 237-40

/ T /

Teen-agers, 107-108
Telemedicine, 153
Toffler, Alvin, 4
Townhouses, 20
Towns, 17, 18
Traffic:
    automobile, 21
    pedestrian, 21
Transcontinental railway, 5
Tree removal, 21
Tuberculosis epidemic (of 19th century), 10
Turnpikes, 5

/ U /

Unemployment, 5, 6
United Nations Conference on the Human Environment (1972), 10, 12
Uprooting of city residents, 5, 8
Urban Development Corporation, 23

Urban growth, 4
Urban Growth and New Community Development Act, 83, 195, 244, 257
Urban Mass Transit Assistance Administration, 247
Urban Mass Transportation Act, 8
Urban planning, 259-61
Urban renewal, 7, 8, 243
Use of Land, The, 22
Utilities, 17

/ V /

Valencia, California, 23
Value systems, 63-64
Veterans Administration, 7
Villages, 17, 18, 21
Violence, 6
Volunteer efforts. *See* individual projects
Volunteer services, 71
Von Eckardt, Wolf, 26

/ W /

Ward, Barbara, 11
Washington, D.C., 19, 23, 24, 243
Watson, Ray, 227-28
Watts, Los Angeles, 6
We the Lonely People, 26
Westinghouse, 24
Westlake, California, 23
Williamsburg, Virginia, 19
Women's Center (Columbia, Maryland), 103-104
Woodlands, Texas, 23, 221, 245
World War II, post, shifts, 5, 7
Wright, Frank Lloyd, 80
Wright, Henry, 18